PASCAL RAYER

IT'S ME, MASTER SEGA

The Chronicles of Master Sega Vol. 1 and 2

From Heaven to Hell

This book is dedicated to Isao Okawa (19 May 1926 - 16 March 2001). Chairman of the board of directors of Sega for many years. Majority shareholder of Sega through CSK Holdings Corporation (which he was the boss but also the creator) He was certainly the greatest enthusiast of the Sonic Team that he will save several times on his personal fortune. One of the greatest, if not the greatest "Master Sega".

SUMMARY

Introduction Rémi Gonzalez

Mega Force Editor in chief

Chapter 1: The F1 duel of the Sega Masters

Chapter 2: From Pong to Sega

Chapter 3: Rue Barbette

Chapter 4: Sega Mistress

Chapter 5: Sega Europe: OPIO

Chapter6: Rue Sainte Croix de la Bretonnerie

Chapter 7: The Hotline's Pearls

Chapter 8: 1991 Review and Balajo

Chapter 9: The Sega Train 1992

Chapter 10: 1992 and Guadeloupe

Chapter 11: 1993 Year of Samba

Chapter 12: The ups and downs

Chapter 13: The Master's games.

Chapter 14: The Secrets of the Sega Masters

Chapter 15: The Sleeper Must Wake

Chapter 16: What is it then, Master Sega ?

Chapter 17: How I became Master Sega

Chapter 18: ADN Virgin Loisirs and Sega France

Chapter 19: Captain Nintendo

Chapter 20: The 46,000

Chapter 21: Bruno Charpentier

Chapter 22: Forgotten Wars.

Chapter 23: Kalinske From Heaven to Hell

Chapter 24: Out Run and Virtua Cop Lives

Chapter 25: Sega UK vs Sega France

Chapter 26: Piaggio vs Peugeot: Story of O

Chapter 27: Patrick Lavanant, the Black Cat

Chapter 28: The Berezina of Sega

Chapter 29: Parody and Nostalgia

INTRODUCTION

To begin this story, it is impossible not to give the floor to one or to one of you ! All these thousands, millions of children so passionate, sometimes more than we could be ourselves! This book is prefaced by Rémi Gonzalez, editor in chief of Mega Force Magazine. Passionate about Sega from a young age and as you may be ?

Rémi Gonzalez:

The SEGA era. A time blessed by the gods, for us, children more or less big, more or less pimple, who discovered the world of video games. The gods? Yes, I remember, that's what they were called. Our heroes, to whom we spoke, at the end of the telephone (telephone - for the most recent readers of this book), about whom we heard in our magazines, our televisions, in our mailboxes, with more or less tasty but always surprising ads, Irreverent, who made laugh, often, caught the eye, always.

Because that was it, Sega, an incredible marketing force that gave dream, made you want to acquire new games, and insert them in the cartridge port, not without blowing into it before, «just in case».

Sega, it was also and above all incredible experiences, the arcade at home, the cutting edge of technology, and games that we wanted to own, to play, again and again, discover new stories, new characters, new challenges, which also allowed us to furnish our recreation when we talked about our exploits with our friends!

Yes humm, you beat the boss at the end?" or "Did you see that if you do low left-right A+B you make a great combo?" were the kind of sentences, incomprehensible to adults, that we heard under the classroom.

Alex Kidd, whose music still resonates in our heads just talking about it, to Nights, whose name my parents hate so much I flooded them with «this game is insane, you have to buy it for me» for months, I was able to live iconic moments during these crazy years: see Sonic hit the jackpot on my Master System, enjoy Streets of Rage while playing with my cousin, cry in front of the combo "Mega Drive + Mega-CD + 32X" that I will never have (I caught up years later), discover, amazed, the 3D with Panzer Dragoon.

Being also present in this technological evolution (of which I didn't know much at the time, but which made games always better, year after year), living it from within, joystick in hand, was a dream, with the feeling of witnessing a spectacle that transcends ages and generations.

Rectangular controllers with 2 buttons, then rounded to 3 keys, then 6, soon with side triggers and joysticks, graphics 8bits, then 16, then 32, the sublime 2D of a Rayman or the sound «CD» offered by the peripheral to be attached to his Mega Drive are as many developments without equal as those that took place before our eyes of cherubim, in these 90 years, golden age of our favorite manufacturer.

 But then, to return to our subject, who were these gods? Impossible to know, but we were sure that we were talking to the best. To the cream of the players, to those who knew everything, on all the games of the brand at the hedgehog. No doubt we were fans of the controller, who lived and breathed only in front of a TV on, scarlet socket connected to the console of our heart.

 How did we know? Because they were helping us out of situations that were inextricably linked when we were stuck in a level, dungeon or boss. So they must have known all these games by heart! Having done and redone them, long, wide and across, having explored every corner, defeated all enemies, passed all obstacles, saved all princesses. The Ninja? They had it up in the air! Battletoads? In one run without losing lives! Dragon's Lair? Why is he on this list? It was so easy for them!

Real live video game bibles, these confidants of our weaknesses as gamer (we had to confess it to someone, and especially not to the friends!) were always there for us, when we needed them. With a simple phone call (an outdated expression today, called «boomer»), one could address to a deity of the Sega world.

We found their phone number in MEGA Force, the only magazine dedicated to Sega and Sega alone. Because yes, even the press was strongly committed to the brand! We could be part of a group too, the SEGA Club, and then we had the feeling that we belonged to something great, but that did not forget us on the roadside, not despite our smallness.

Sometimes events were organized (including the famous «SEGA Train» that traveled through France and offered contests, goodies and meetings with fans), and we could then come to discover these voices who welcomed us on the phone.

I did not have the chance to meet one of these Gods, it is so (although, once again, I made up for it much later), but I think I did not stop on my consoles to become a little like them, to persevere in my quest for children, who was the one to become a Sega game tester. "Is that a job, tester?" was I asked? I did not know at the time if I would ever be able to get into it; but it is still, and this is the last time I say in this preface, that I made up later.

Because Sega, that's all I just said, but it's mostly this: the joy transcending generations, the passion that is communicated from parent to child, grandchild, again and again. That's why I came back, much later so, when the time allowed me, to dream of a child. Today, I am editor of the magazine Sega at the time, resurrected by enthusiasts, partner of Sega and these Gods of our childhood: MEGA Force.

Because it was out of the question that SEGA, the manufacturer of consoles and arcade machines, be forgotten by a generation of players, we put today, us, small team of enthusiasts who give their time, working to not leave aside this whole part of our collective memory. Of course, the paper magazine is no longer, we have had to adapt to our time, but we are working hard to make this spirit so special that was able to breathe the Japanese giant, and to keep it alive for as long as possible.

Today is a special day: I am at your side, dear readers, in this preface as player, enthusiast, writer, tester, and with many other hats, because we are in the presence of one of these famous gods of our childhood, and he will tell you his story! Place... to the SEGA Masters!

Rémi Gonzalez, editor in chief of Mega Force Magazine.

CHAPTER 1

The Sega Masters F1 Duel

Gonfaron, circuit du Var. 22 November 2001.

It is on a truly exceptional day that this story will begin. The most exceptional experience I have ever had in my life, and this is because I was precisely "Master Sega" in activity at that time. In the right place, at the right time with this unlikely chance that only the Gods can grant you.

An absolutely splendid day, as so often in this corner of the world flooded with sun, almost all year, and if we only place from a meteorological point of view! Today, more than ever, time matters: really! Or more exactly it matters to me and totally. Like a sword of Damocles that could come suddenly to break me, to smash my dream, one of the greatest I can caress.

It could have been just another birthday! One more. Cruel and tedious rite, since we spent twenty years. An almost like any other day with however a figure, sugar (lots of sugar), chocolate (lots of chocolate) in addition, to carry. Sugar and chocolate will pass, will disappear most certainly, the figure will remain to him while waiting patiently for someone to come again to inflate it, from the following year.

I'm 29 this very day, so I'm in my 30th year and I'll be fine again. Well no!!! Not that one. Because it will remain the most beautiful, the most wonderful, the most incredible, the most memorable, the most unforgettable of my birthdays! And I could not have started my story otherwise as the electricity and emotion produced that day are still in each of the cells of my body!

With this incredible day, and some others that will follow later, I can die happy and welcome the elegant, the fringant Thanatos, the Greek God of Death, with the greatest smile. Approaching me, bright and graceful, he will then slowly blow "As a busy day gives us a good sleep!" And I will then follow by "A well-lived life gives us a peaceful death!". He will then conclude by "And life will start again, again and again, you certainly know it better than anyone else and almost as much as I do, you the "Sega Master"!

The sun will have me, we will have accompanied all day, sky intensely bluish, warm light, clear but not blinding, of the late season Var. The attacks of September 11 in New York are still in all heads. Risks of attacks, war in the Near East, our life will all draw and exhume in these deep pains a good part of its value! It is urgent to live, to continue existing as never before, even though shadows come close to us and worry us. Even if everything seems to be possible, wanting to collapse: Carpe diem, this day is perhaps a little more than another ? The last. But today it's the party! An incredible fiesta! Fabulous, grandiose, totally improbable, unexpected, not even in a dream! Even Sega had already given me so much.

The last two "Sega Masters" are on the track! Remus and Romulus? The Dioscures Castor and Pollux? Because yes, there was more than one Sega Master! There were even a good twenty, Masters Sega who will have succeeded each other including three young women! Which will not fail to surprise you to see some players petrify in need of solutions and tips for their games by dialing for the first time the line of Master Sega.

Romuald Merdrignac (one of the last Sega Masters but he was above all the first) and therefore me, Pascal Rayer, your columnist of the moment, after having crossed the years Master System, Mega Drive , Mega CD, 32X, Saturn and Dreamcast, we were going to compete on the Circuit du Var on real Formulas 1. Is not it a thing of sick people frankly!?! I still cling to believe it by looking at some photos memories.

After hundreds of various games in Super Monaco GP, Formula One or Sega Rally on Sega consoles, most often won by the first and then the second, we were going to measure ourselves against real monsters of power and technicality! On the black as bare, as hot as captivating asphalt of a circuit of just over two kilometres. We would clear the road closer to the ground than ever before. Ready to bite into the tar and pick up some gravel if necessary. Ready once again to shake the reason so that passion wins and explodes with a thousand lights and at least as many vibrations. This insatiable passion of Master Sega at the twilight of his glory: always wanting to be the strongest, the fastest. Super-Sonic speed of course! A Sega Master can sleep peacefully only if he has defeated. He will be able to accept defeat only if he has given everything, absolutely everything, until his last breath.

But this delicious moment also happened, without our knowing it (why and how would we be concerned about the rest?) as a kind of apotheosis or even swan song? Because, alas?!? Everything had an end and we were necessarily approaching it.

More than ten years already that Romuald and I were "The Masters"! Undisputed and uncontested, at least for the Sega games. Of course there were others! A good twenty so. Excellent players! Great "hotlineurs". All more warm and friendly, one of them than the other.

But to find ourselves there, both of us, chasing once again the fastest time, the record, on a real track, in the tub of a formula one, was not due to luck or chance. Personal point of view. And yet it was probably also a matter of chance and chance but who could really know and affirm it?!?

They say you have to take your chances! Force your destiny. That's probably what is wonderful about a destiny: to believe that luck was also part of it! It may seem contradictory but in all destinies, there is a part of chance and it is up to each one of us to seize it. Grasp and still grasp something that we do not see, that we do not measure and that finally can make you out of the banal and make you enter the annals!

She is sometimes right in front of us, and we must reach out to her with all our strength! Because a few seconds later this fantastic opportunity has definitely completely disappeared. Making the happiness of another probably.

If the Gods exist it is because there are people to believe in them! The more we believe in the Gods, the more powerful their powers are. In retrospect, I really believe that there are Gods of video games. And Romuald and I got all their attention, all their favors. For having served Sega faithfully for many years; we are rewarded tremendously! It is certainly there "this chance". To have believed, more than any other at that time, in our destiny, deliciously carried by a devouring passion. Inevitably giving us an almost divine strength: Sega was our religion and somewhere, perhaps, we appeared as these prophets for all those who crossed our path, as players of course. All those children, all those teenagers, with such a powerful infatuation that they pushed us ever higher. What I will not fail to tell you, to chronicle on different occasions later.

 The gods and children had given us power of attorney to take on all challenges, all challenges, all fights, from the smallest, to the most "Sega". We were you and you would be us!!!"

For now I must tell you about this incredible day or two of the greatest, most illustrious, in any case the two oldest Master Sega have faced! Again, most friendly, most warm, without any rivalry except that of a short moment. Just for the pleasure of having fun, to surpass oneself, perhaps transcend oneself.

And there "in all humility", just for fun, I will integrate well the credits of the series Amicalement vôtre with Danny Wilde and Brett Sinclair. Romuald has been for me for more than ten years as a second brother, both the best of friends but also an occasional rival, in the sense of opponent! One against the other at first sight! But above all with each other: a source of inspiration, energy to rise as high as possible in the night blue sky of the Sega universe.

Because being a Sega Master was also an opportunity to compete, to face the best players of the time. A Sega Master worthy of the name had to compete with the strongest. Romuald declared with a smile punctuated by a big laugh, in the issue 18 of the newspaper "Mega Force" of December 1992 that we were the best players of France, of the world! And even the best players in the Universe!

What is certain is that, apart from me, I will never meet a more fierce player than Romuald in this period. Otherwise maybe in the trade press with AHL, or JM Destroy? Romuald and I could take the lead for hours or even weeks on the most popular games such as Sonic or Landstalker! But also on really not possible games like "Last Battle" or "Indiana Jones" on Mega Drive, Ultima 4, The Ninja and R-Type on Master System. We played everything without exception, every game, even "failed" sometimes, even without commercial potential, was a new challenge to understand, a new challenge to take. And we would not tolerate any failure, no hole in the racket.

Like an endless quest, endless challenges: "Sega is stronger than you," you know... especially for a Sega Master! And this was the case.

Romuald, me and my parents who had been kind enough to accompany their offspring with their car, arrived very early at the stands of the Circuit du Var. We had never practiced Formula 1 before this day except in dreams and on consoles. But as you can probably guess: it doesn't count at all. Not at all. On the contrary, it could be a handicap as realism and simulation were still very limited at the time. He was even less likely to have slept in a "Formula 1" hotel between the motorway exit and Gonfaron.

To be lucky enough to get a few laps of the Formula 1 circuit, you must first take a mini training course on driving single-seaters with all the technical aspects that this entails, especially safety instructions. If you don't follow, you're just failing. Driving the F1 is the bonus of the day. And to prepare you as you test, we let you drive single-seater more powerful!

So we were prepared with Formule Renault. Mini formulas 1 that make about 200 HP but as their weight is very reduced (less than 500 kilos) they already offer exceptional sensations! Because at ground level, at equal speed with a standard car, we always have the impression of going faster. And then this car can still reach up to 250 kms per hour (but not on the var circuit because the straight lines were not long enough)

Although smaller, more picked up than a F1, when you settle inside you are already totally there! The pressure is immense and you can say that it's for your own good, but it remains an acceleration bomb that few people can't perfectly master in a few laps of time. And you understand it immediately as soon as you are released. What's great is that you instantly switch to F1 mode with this previously unknown environment. The sensations are just quite exceptional: it's like what you had tried to imagine but much better! We often remember his "first time" ! Well, I especially remember this one.

With a very important "physical" aspect on the accelerations and decelerations. The famous "G", gravity initial that can multiply the weight of your body by 2, 3, 4 or 6 in formula 1 (at the limit of the most experienced and especially the most resistant drivers) If I say it is because clearly for me there was no question of rolling "peep". And the "G's" I felt them for having looked for them! Because certainly more than speed, it is the "G's" that must be able to accept. You don't challenge your speed, but your own physical resistance to accelerate and decelerate. A multitude of times in a minimum of time!

The Formula Renault preparation allows the apprentice driver to test his physical resistance in the face of these new challenges. Fortunately for me even if I had not prepared specifically for the F1, I had a good "cardio" by practicing regularly running. Besides, after this F1 experience, I considerably increased my cardio practice by doing half marathons from time to time but regularly, until even two marathons at twelve months interval, keeping in a corner of my head that if one day "the gods" decided to let me get on a fighter plane, I would not faint, certainly not. This new improbable dream has often motivated me to overcome the fatigue of 10, 15 or 20kms of running.

My turn had come and like a two-year-old child riding in his first car with pedals, I was jubilating of excitement and pleasure! The adrenaline was peaking and I was about to drop it all. The acceleration is just mind blowing and it's a matter of quickly taking full measure. Not too much, not too little. I think I remember we were allowed five or six rounds. If it may seem short, you must still understand that the level of stress and pressure is such that time is necessarily extended. I still have in mind almost all the laps that I could do! With the Renault formula, then the F3 and especially with the F1. You must write in the depths of your memory all the track information. Those that cause problems, those that can take you away like a missile.

We were given so many safety instructions, and some things to avoid! Alcohol is forbidden during the course. Avoiding to double for example it is dangerous! Not serious? We should avoid to double but how is that possible on a track? We were also warned that in the long straight of the stands, there was a bump in the first third that could take off the car! And so possibly turn it like a pancake on a gust of wind! So you also had to avoid speeding too hard at this point! Personally I didn't believe it too much. Unless you master the F1 perfectly and attack like a fool especially on this bump, there was no danger. Not too much. Otherwise we wouldn't be allowed to fly. We "beginners".

Your heart beats for your greatest happiness and also a certain fear. Fear that must not leave you. Not a single moment. For death is at every turn. But it must be mastered. It is by dominating this fear, easier said than done, that you maintain a constant, sufficient and healthy level of consciousness and lucidity.

So the circuit: not very complicated, just what it takes to start. We turn clockwise. At two-thirds of the longest straight, you get out of the stands, accelerate, then turn a little left just before making a half-loop or almost before going back in an angle. A little further a chicane, steering left then right, then left and then it's THE MAGIC ACCELERATION! The first. A quarter circle then a first small straight line of 200m or we can start to send the gas, followed by a fairly gentle turn or we can continue gradually to really heat the beast. A final straight before the stands! This is where you can pass the 4, 5 and 6th... In any case on the Renault formula and F3. We can reach 180/200 kms in a few seconds. But now you find out that your body can be a pain: crushed on itself by the "G" effect in acceleration and deceleration. Nevertheless, and I didn't know it yet, on Formula Renault it's tenable. Exhausting, trying but tenable. Fortunately we were only doing 5/6 laps and it is when leaving the car that I understood that for a pilot not confimé, it was enough, even if one would have liked to do a little more in the heat of the action is charged to death in adrenaline. I was not on the edge of fatigue, far from it. However, in terms of sensation and emotions, I was already on the verge of breaking. I had not overtaken anyone, we were allowed to leave with intervals of ten, twenty or thirty seconds depending on whether you were able to quickly engage, or not. I think I remember that the clutch was pretty strong. It was just super mega giga too good! Tired, shaken, moved but with the irresistible urge to come up immediately. At least as quickly as possible.

Then comes the debriefing, everything went very well for everyone. Management puts more pressure on safety instructions. We will upgrade with F3, more powerful, faster. The last stage, still elimination, before the AGS Formula 1 and its 660 Horses! Yes yes yes yes yes... You have to hang on, it's 660 horses just that, it's scary! I love the figure and it's a shame that there is a third 6 missing.

We will also be presented with the Formula 1. Half red on the bottom, half gray on the top, much wider than the other cars, with tires also super wide. She is just beautiful but also monstrous! Exit slowly by hand, stands, they will start it and first of all, just make it purr! It's beautiful and wonderful at low speed, this extremely powerful but still quite gentle vibration. All the hairs of your body are erect. You are intensely swept by these vibrations as if multiple tigers or gigantic lions were starting to purr near you, in a stunning mix of fear and pleasure. Not a hair of your body will be called to stand before such melody.

But this sweet purr, very quickly passes into a more worrying feulement, before passing into an absolutely unbearable howl! Without a helmet on the ears, it is impossible to stay close to the beast. We understand that the noise is very loud when watching a TV broadcast, but we can't imagine what it really is next door. Even though the pilot's helmet significantly and considerably reduces noise, it is also a challenge to endure it for a long time.

However, this noise is an essential reference for piloting especially when you are novice. Because you do not have enough references on speed, acceleration, deceleration of these cars that erase all your known landmarks by being at ground level, without a cockpit and with a helmet on the head... Rather than losing some of your focus on the speed or turn meters; the engine speed is easy to follow! A little too much certainly...

Maximum pressure. We were getting closer and closer to our baptism of fire. And what a fire! There was something to do with it. Fear was definitely invited. Formula 1 is a monster that will have to be tamed. Being afraid is natural and even vital. The one who says he never has fear is either a fool or an unconscious man. Fear had certainly invaded me but I could rejoice in it. Make sure she does it now, not when I'm driving. It is the only way to seek and find maximum concentration, to perform the most appropriate gestures. All your attention must now be on the driving of this extraordinary, beautiful machine... but also deadly! In the literal and figurative sense.

Bad news! We learned that when driving in F1 we would be alone on the track! The explanation is extremely simple: maximum security. First of all because the single-seater car costs a fortune and it would be very unfortunate if two of them collide. And then because in the event of an accident, it is necessary to monopolize all human resources to intervene as quickly as effectively.

At this announcement, the direct duel with Romuald was over! My dream of passing too. But no! There is still F3. It was decided and locked, I would certainly never have the opportunity to double a single-seater on a speed circuit! I was going to pull out now that I knew about the terrain. I was going to attack. Driving in a single-seater car is not just to make fun of a nice car and make laps on a circuit, to make a poor chrono, and say later that we made it like we did the pedalo! No clearly no. You must attack again and again, you must hunt! Like all my many ancestors "Homo Sapiens", the famous "hunters gatherers", I will pick the day (Carpe Diem) and I will hunt the Eternity. And if Eternity was a day, then I will be super Sonic and keep accelerating.

I only had five to six laps to do it. And here we go! It will be obvious to everyone, the F3 is very clearly above the Renault formulas. It looks much more, is very similar to an F1: it's mainly the smaller tires that mark the difference, for me at this time, at least visually. Engaged on the track with a surprising increase in power, you then say not without fear that the jump between F3 and F1 should be even more important! But how is that possible? My excitement and motivation were at their peak. I was no longer flying a bomb, I was flying a missile! The accelerations are even more striking and you take expensive physically, immediately. But this moment of glory was going to pass very quickly and I had to enjoy it to the maximum! And double!

I must tell you that if "Phobos" the Greek god of fear was not very far from me, I did not think about it, I no longer thought about it (lack of time and maximum concentration), but Thanatos was gently placed on my shoulder and I thought about it every moment. However, without any real fear. And especially without him being able to distract me quite the contrary. Death is present everywhere, all the time, most often it goes to its occupations and visits you only after a busy life, during your last breath and to accompany you towards another life. But it can burst at any moment on a second or even a quarter of a second of inattention. Thanatos has long been my friend, he is his twin brother Hypnos, the god of sleep. My first book published in 2022: "Thanatose", is more or less dedicated to them. So Thanatos was with me, he was mostly there to remind me that in a turn, he could take me away. But it was not counting his brother Hypnos who in the first years of my life, had blown me almost to infinity a very unpleasant dream. I must have been between seven and ten years old, for several nights, over a period of weeks, I was having a terrible nightmare or I was on some kind of blurry track, and I would accelerate like crazy at a lightning speed. I saw the turn coming at a great speed but I kept accelerating without being able to do otherwise. Obviously at the turn I tried to turn right but I exploded violently in a kind of wall, I was going much too fast. And it was happening again and again. I was hypnotized by the speed and unable to react when needed. Psychically very trying, I woke up in the morning also physically rinsed. Perhaps this dream has absolutely nothing to do with it. But dreams always have a secret. Which can be revealed sooner or later.

Meanwhile I was again seized by this vision during my piloting! With the end of the circuit this acceleration curve followed by a straight line completely stopped by a turn at 90°. The more I gained confidence and accelerated, the closer I got to the sensations etched in marble following these recurring nightmares.

Especially since, as we tell you, we beat it even: to turn well in a tight corner on a F3 car, let alone F1, you have to get as fast as possible on the bend! And brake like crazy just before. It's the only way to tip the weight of the car on the front train. Because the front of the F1 weighs nothing without a big brake. You multiply then the stability and grip of the two front tires! The big brakes are essential. And the faster you get there, the more weight you have on the tires! Allowing extraordinary grip, necessary.

So it was programmed that I had to reproduce, with one detail, what was until then my worst nightmare, with a fatal outcome even if everything started again and again. It was confusing, disturbing, fascinating. But I also understood that I could transform here and now what was, what remained as a fear buried since the very beginning into something more radiant! Phobos, fear or even terror, was not far away and I was going to dominate it! I was going to dominate her all the more easily as I knew Thanatos, being on my side! " Defeat or die" it may seem very exaggerated but to concentrate in exceptional situations you must know how to transcend yourself. To Conquer without danger one triumphs without glory"!!! I was going to show Thanatos and Phobos again that, at least a few seconds, I could push them away, very far. There could always be an accident!?! But as with every second of our lives, a second of inattention.

I was taking full measure of the F3, or at least I thought so, I would accelerate again and again whenever the track allowed! And I was also able to measure the quality of braking at the end of these large accelerations. Physically we do not realize it immediately but we take expensive, very expensive. The "G's" are stacked on top of each other on you and you understand that not only is it better to have a "good cardio", but it is better to be well muscled, athletic even to support everything, as your whole body is pushed in one direction and then in another! We were like the Formula Renault entered one after another with a time interval that, I guess, was calculated so we didn't have to be on each other! To avoid double. But I went back to the F3 that preceded me!

I had tears in my eyes so much emotion was great. This was my dream. Driving in a car, alone, bof bof bof... But then I went back up, nibbling every meter! As we could do hundreds of times in video games! I was inexorably approaching as in a real competition. I had made the difference on my predecessor in 3/4 laps, it remained for me to choose the right moment. I wanted to double safely and cleanly. Without the organizers having anything to say about it. I hoped to double him in the acceleration curve but finally it will be just after the very big braking before the entry on the straight line of the stands! I think it's the braking that the experienced drivers can make a difference. You turn better and you start stronger. The driver in front of me must have felt a little too much pressure and probably let me pass. I was just passing him regularly and very cleanly.

IT WAS WONDERFUL! THE ABSOLUTE ECSTASY. I have rarely had to be happier than at that time. So it wasn't Romuald but just another pilot, unknown! The day could have ended like that. I was delighted. The shadow of death had weighed on me, but finally, Hypnos and Thanatos had shown me once again that they were and would remain the guardians of my life. Of my lives. Thank you, friends.

But the show was not over. I couldn't get over this crazy excitement. This great evening intoxication. The fear had completely disappeared and I felt touched by the grace. But it was necessary to return quickly with feet on earth. Quickly be scared again, at least a little. Because the F3, next to an F1, is a walk of health. But how can you imagine it especially after having the impression of driving a kind of missile!?!

New debriefing with telemetry. One of the pilots will probably fail for medical reasons, I do not know exactly but there was an alert. Our performance has been carefully scrutinized, analysed. I read it many years later, the company did not hesitate to put out those who would not drive well enough! That's what we are told! Like those who would drive "too well"!

And they don't tell you that. They don't want experienced pilots who will overshoot and test the mechanics. I think that's also why we only do 3 laps. Because it is probably from there that we can take a certain confidence.

The big moment finally arrived. We were going to pass one after another, each in turn, on the 660 horsepower Monster! By chance I was last. So I could observe and listen to the beast for about twenty turns. Each pilot would do three laps and not one more! We were six or seven!?! I really tried to collect all the information that my five senses allowed me to collect while collecting those of the F3 still hot. The Hearing is probably the most informative sense. Listen to the F1 engine regime throughout its journey. I also observed, as I could do, but from far, more often: all the movements: the accelerations decelerations, a priori connected with the noise.

I was very surprised to see that the pilots go slowly, really slowly! Finally. When we could finally let loose!?! So it might be more appropriate to go carefully. I was thinking first of all: the beast is scary! Very scary. Engine speed was not rising. On a scale of 1 to 10 with 10 of course, maximum speed at 12,000 rpm and engine noise unportable.

We had to go to 3 or 4, maybe sometimes 5 in the speed curve, so between 5 and 6000turns. But no more. The speed ratios were not too far away either. When Romuald passed there was a slight improvement. 5 certainly may be 6. I timed a few laps and it was not convincing. The absolute record of the lap is 53 seconds (64 for a motorcycle) for 2.3km, an average around 150km/h. The same day a confirmed driver was driving around with a prototype with the F1 engine and it was just over a minute! With a motor speed that would most likely seek the highest, the strongest of brief moments. The speed record on the track is a peak of 308 km/h!

The pilots before me were very careful. Too careful! I had to find out why! And I will know it soon enough! A new mark engraved with red iron in my head, flesh and heart. Finally my turn comes.

Very complicated start! It's way too powerful. I've seen them stall in first, so you have to start in second! There is not yet an embedded system to avoid stalling. With 660 CV and a "couple" of Tyrannosaurs herd it starts really well. Too good. You immediately feel that there is something "not normal" ! Supernatural!?! We barely accelerate and it already almost goes into a fury. I think it's immediately clear that we're not really on a fast or very fast car, but on an ground-to-ground missile or rocket. The force, the power , the energy that we feel no longer seems terrestrial but spatial.

The sensations are demonic, the accelerations lightning whatever the speed at which you drive. It is breathtaking because you are simply stuck to the bar regardless of your level of acceleration and even if you would only stroke the accelerator. You are literally crushed like a mushroom under the foot of a giant if you press too hard, too long.

It is indeed fear! The F1 is indeed an uncontrollable monster (at our level) and most will not dare more than caressing it for fear of seeing it fly perhaps in the sky. Add to that the incredible physical pressure that is exerted on you as soon as the acceleration grows. A superhuman physical and mental test that is difficult to endure if you are not prepared for.

But these three laps are the three most magical laps of my life. And yet I felt the rear tires skid when I was speeding a little too fast in the chicane. This being, it is amazing to see how much a F1 remains stuck on the road, if you drive "cool" it's the easiest car to maneuver! It sticks the road as perfectly magnetized.

But I decided to push the gears as far as possible. Whenever it was possible! To the noise therefore as the simplest and most reliable indicator, I made him sing, I even made him scream! My body then giving me the impression of petrifying, turning into stone and rather granite. Turning his head even slightly, moving his neck became like one of the twelve labors of Hercules. Not in the first round, where I was careful to measure the number of reactions. I would find that the braking of a F1 is very crazy! Even if you exceed 200 or 250kms, it stops, it can stop in a few meters! And once again your body takes a very expensive with the deceleration, and this while, just behind, it is probably acceleration! There is a form of masochism in driving a formula one.

And again I thought about my childhood nightmares. This fatal road trip. But once you've tested the quality of braking, you know that you can go really fast. What is misleading when you start in a formula 1 is that you do not know how far it can go! In acceleration and speed! It is so much above the other cars and everything we can have already known in cars, that even being at half of its power, and maybe even less, you probably think you are already on the cleat! I remembered that the pilots before me had not pushed the cadence. While there was space to do so (comparing with the race of the veteran driver). In the second round I decided to shoot each gear a little longer (like half a second! It's very long half a second in F1 at this stress level) and especially much louder. And what we discover does not put you on the ass (you are already! Two centimeters or just more of the gravel) but amazes you, you freeze the blood but you marvel.

You are not in a car, you are sitting on a missile that seems to know no limit in acceleration. That is to say, unless you change gear too much, much too quickly, we have the impression of being able to stay on a same speed until infinity (except for the first 2/3 gears). So that's why I only heard "quiet" lines! Because this line does not seem to be quiet at all when you are there!

A monstrous power, two "G's" to be taken in (and maybe sometimes a little more?) that bully you all the way, a very loud noise, a virgin brain of F1 (understand who has never been in such a situation and who does not know how to cope for lack of landmarks) It's a lot and often too much! To start really tapping into the heart of F1 power, you have to want to be scared, very afraid, and you have to want to hurt yourself, very very bad. You have to go beyond limits that you've certainly never flirted with! And it's very complicated because you already have to free yourself from your fear. In three rounds, it is impossible for a majority of trainees.

At my third, and like all others probably each at their level, I raised the bar even higher not without thinking of my friend Thanatos who remains close to me in case... I have no more fear, there is only excitement, pure adrenaline produced as never before! But you have to keep 100% of your mind control and I do not forget that the slightest mistake can be fatal for me.

For the last time I engage in the acceleration curve in which I push for what will be and surely remain my apotheosis! I will accelerate to the maximum and brake before the turn at the last moment! Can we stop in less than 10 meters? But 10 meters at this speed is how long!?! And that's where you should not lose focus the slightest micro second! Pushing "to death" you have the impression of folding space and time! At the beginning of a straight line, the end of the track is barely visible! Two or three seconds later she seems to want to jump on you, to climb on you! It is almost hypnotic as it is a bit unreal, that it even seems supernatural. For me at that moment there was no doubt that my nightmares of more than twenty years had finally found their meaning, their truth. Our unconscious, consistent dreams prepare us for all challenges, all dangers.

Once the race was over I was physically crushed but full psychically. Ahhh I did not tell you: I cried hot tears at the end. Of joy above all but also above all because the emotions, of all natures, were very strong. It was just too beautiful, too loud, too incredible, too exhilarating. Like in a dream but better.

This new challenge had been taken from the hands of Master (well I say that you have to reframe as a novice of course!) I don't think I could have done more because I would have done it!!! This is the satisfaction that will surely be shared by all the F1 trainees of the day! Everyone has necessarily exceeded! More or less certainly but each progress is important.

Romuald and I exchanged very little during the whole day. We stayed extremely focused throughout. Except for a few photo shoots. It was still very tense, we were being told safety instructions all day with a possible disqualification for the F1 in mind. Let me tell you that we could not be more focused than on that day!

So who was the "Master" that day? It doesn't matter. It was a discovery course and everyone could transcend themselves according to their means, a little, a lot, to madness... But to close this first chapter a little special on the years Master Sega, I can still tell you, you "teaser" that one day the group Cyberpress (Megaforce among others) will organize a big karting competition of high, very high volée with journalists (JM Destroy, Danbiss, Danboss, Manu and many others) and some masters of Sega. More than forty pilots, and this time there will be a winner.

It is a chronicle that I will probably tell in next volume of Chronicles of Master Sega.

CHAPTER 2
FROM PONG TO SEGA

We are in the very first days of 1991. The first Gulf War, the explosion of the USSR in 15 states, Yugoslavia in 4, Freddy Mercury and Serge Gainsbourg leave our world, "Dance with the wolves" win 7 Oscars, "Terminator 2" will be a hit all over the world. And it's also the madness of "Pin's"! But as far as I am concerned, it is the most important choice of my life because I will respond to this small announcement published in the specialized press:

"You are dynamic, you have a good speech, you live in the Paris region and you are passionate about Sega games. Virgin Loisirs is looking for telephone operators for the Hot Line of the Sega video game intelligence and assistant service. Good knowledge of the Sega brand and games in the Sega catalogue is desirable. Send your CV + photo and a handwritten letter to Virgin Loisirs..."

When I read it for the first time, I immediately popped! By rereading it several times I even exulted. I was then in a small maid's room in Dijon preparing for the first year of medicine. Not really reassured, can be even less motivated as the numerus clausus was not very high: 80 places only in second year for 450 young people often ready to do anything to be in the first car. Of the 80 entrants, 70 will be "repeat students". So it is almost a miracle to pass at first. The university system was not at all suitable for me, or rather I was not suited to the university system. The continuous checks of previous years allowed me at least to know where I was. The Faculty is the artistic blur XXL. Even if I had been rather successful in the bachotage the previous year at least for the Bac.

Between incessant war reports and almost live in Iraq and existential errands about my future, it was a real ray of light that suddenly gushed out of a specialized magazine and enveloped me with its magical aura. This job was perfect for me, no doubt possible. It will be and even far beyond my expectations. Hand sewn, custom made as it does not happen so often in a life. Like many of you, dear readers, most likely, most certainly, I played!!! I even played a lot. If the gods of video games exist, they made me appear at the most opportune moment! When they rang "ding dong" at the world's gates, they also hit "Ping Pong"!

I first came to this planet in 1972, seven days before Pong, which will become the world's first video game hit, was released on November 29 as an arcade machine. The very first console, the Magnavox Odyssey was launched in the United States during the year and will benefit from this first blockbuster of history simply named Ping Pong on their console. Magnavox will sue Atari/Nolan Bushnell and several other companies for patent theft and then collect more than $100 million in damages over several years, thereby settling, at least on paper, the origin, the authorship of the game that exploded the market. Both companies will see their business go very high. The whole video game industry was launched. I was therefore installed in the first box to fall, like Obelix, into the bottom of the pot and as soon as these machines would be widely distributed in Europe and thus in France.

In 1978, at the age of 5, I played with my 7-year-old brother, at the Créatronic Program 2000: The Rolls of the Moment and to play "Ping Pong" (or Table Tennis on some versions) which was then integrated into the console. Magnavox is the first company in the world to sell game consoles and will be a leader a long time before Atari appears on mainstream hardware. My favorite game was the "Jump of motorcycle" on which I will make hundreds or even thousands of attempts to jump ever further, always higher: a known refrain that will never leave me.

The games were really super ugly, the sound atmosphere very limited (fortunately), everything was to invent especially in terms of Gameplay but it was still SUPER EXTRA GENIAL! As much as buying a PS5 today!!! I swear! Because it was 46 years ago! Not serious almost half a century? Am I not so old?

I still remember as if it was yesterday when we plugged the Créatronic on the TV screen. And that we were able to "control" these small snowshoes to return a ball, so two, when we could then slalom between cars, and this faster and faster. So that at a certain point we could not really see the cars passing by and we relied on our knowledge of the arrival sequences of the cars. Very limited by playing it was possible to anticipate these sequences very repetitive, and so the cars, we could even close our eyes when the speed had reached its maximum. It was already mesmerizing for the players and probably already terrifying for others, from the outside.

Even the Mega Drive 12 years later will not be as exciting and emotional. At least not at the time of discovery. It is the all-powerful magic of the first times, even when this first time may seem, retrospectively, really close to pastels.

But the Passion could now grow and settle after being so surreptitiously inoculated (it must be pointed out that the life of these first sets was extremely limited and the number of cartridges remained very small). Game and watch as a reminder in the playgrounds for years, then the Colecovison and its extraordinary colors finally came out in 1983! Donkey Kong, Zaxxon, the Smurfs: I was upset! And definitely conquered! I will regularly go three kilometers back with my little feet, pretending to go buy bread, to go play on the console in demonstration in the Noveco store of Auxerre downtown where it was installed, Well in evidence, to be noticed by the greatest number, waiting more or less quietly for my turn. Zaxxon it was really terrible, it was like doing the Star Wars yourself with almost as much sensations as a "R360" many years later and without having your head in...

Star Wars that had seriously marked the minds in the cinema, me in particular, because it was my first film on big screen, late 1977, then barely 5 years old. An age when you still believed that what is on the screen is most likely real. The Empire counterattack had followed, then Return of the Jedi. The release of Coleco and Zaxxon allowed all the minots of the time to think of themselves as Luc Skywalker for at least a few moments.

Other machines will follow, including the Vectrex and its very simple graphics but in 3D rather effective. I absorbed evolution by evolution. I will actually make my weapons on Commodore 64 and CPC128 a few years later. Having known this period of video games often not very playable, or even totally unplayable, will be an asset for a Sega Master. Repeat and repeat again, tirelessly, tens or even hundreds of times. Never give up! Never be discouraged. Triumph!!!

I will also spend a lot of time in arcade rooms, especially at the "Spoutnik" in Auxerre! A place of perdition, depravity for the youth for some, a fantastic and mythical place for others (often with pimples and or first hairs on the chin). So I knew the Sega games perfectly! Well... Arcade games! Hang On,

Out Run, Space Harrier, Shinobi and many others that were great. First and second generation consoles + arcade games with very high difficulty and you are definitely broken to be able to play any game, and especially to finish it.

I bought the Mega Drive in early 1990 as an import in a Japanese version in one of the many boutiques on boulevard Voltaire in Paris! It was sold with "DJ Boy" game quite average but satisfying despite everything and that I will keep as a relic since it was my first. There are many games already on this great machine and I buy several, it is quickly a budget, a big budget, you know. Ghouls 'n Ghosts, Mystic Defender, Revenge of Shinobi is already a blast. It's still far from the arcade but the Mega Drive games really have a good look and especially the gameplay has become completely arcade. I won't tell you the story! The Mega Drive in 1990 (see 1989 in Japan) it's BOMB! At an affordable price compared to the Neo Geo. Detractors (Nintendo) will say that these are violent games! Yes arcade games are more action oriented, competitions, fights.

Anyway, my culture "Sega" is already well enriched although I know very little about the universe Master System. I respond to this announcement and present myself proudly and enthusiastically to Sega with two real handicaps. The first is that I am not a Parisian, nor close Parisien and even not Francilien! I am Bourguignon and I share my time between Auxerre and Dijon. Auxerrois for several years, I then continued my studies (second handicap) in the capital of mustard, in medical school, to hope to become a dentist or orthodontist. I did not know very well what I wanted to do with my life but as I was not too bad in high school, I committed myself to first and final scientists with dominant of Math and Biology. I was very strong in biology and life sciences (but not only!) Another universe that fascinates me. Medicine seemed to be the best way.

The meeting will be held at 8/10 Rue Barbette in the 3rd arrondissement of Paris and at the premises of Virgin Loisirs. A small, recent office building of only two floors.

Romuald Merdrignac: MAÎTRE SEGA lui-même!!! The only one at this moment: WHAOOOOOOUUUUU! And Jean Luc Satin who welcome us very kindly. Very warmly. I will know it later but these two pillars of the Sega Club (Romuald "the Master", and Jean Luc product manager consoles... Before becoming totally Mega Drive product manager when

Olivier Creusy will join Sega to promote the Master System) These two pillars are most likely the two most friendly, warm and welcoming faces of society. Nothing surprising when we turn to what is already and will be amplified as being "The consumer services" of society.

Jean Luc is extremely relaxed (I don't remember not seeing him relaxed... even if only once, in the months and years following) Romuald a little less, more concentrated. But the welcome by these two young men (around 25 years old) smiling and welcoming sets the tone and we are therefore in very favorable conditions to let our Gamer heart speak!

We are eight to apply for this position very quickly. Because time is running out! Sega consoles are becoming more and more popular! The Mega Drive has been released in France for a few weeks and it's the rush! The Master System is not left because much cheaper and closer to the catalog of "Nintendo", it sells like hotcakes in Europe and especially in France, surfing on the wave Mega Drive that makes a lot of talk about Sega. Romuald is starting to be overwhelmed by the calls of the members of the Club! He is all alone and he must know everything! Fortunately, for the moment, the Sega master line remains confidential and reserved for members of the Club. But this will change quickly even if it is not yet in the beginning of 1991.

To know this job perfectly, I imagine that for Romuald at that time, without help from anyone or anything, ie without colleagues, without solution guides, without internet, he had to experience a great moment of embarrassment and loneliness! Even if I do not doubt for a moment that the few times he did not have the answer, he rushed very quickly on the game to know more secrets! Because it's in the DNA of Master Sega: he must know everything about everything! And never leave a player on the edge of a path, too long. We'll just call back later. The kids, the teens were always lovely with us. They could understand that sometimes Master Sega had a flaw. But it didn't have to happen too often.

So we are eight postulants kindly invited to sit each one of us on a chair, side by side and very tight, while Romuald and Jean-Luc, they remain standing or leaning, sitting on a large table facing us! Jean Luc will give us a debriefing on the company and what he expects from Second Master Sega. Romuald providing him with some additional clarifications whenever necessary. They complement each other perfectly and we are therefore fully informed about the position! In particular its remuneration. 8000frs per month with a 13th month. To compare with a Smic at 5500fs at the time. We would be in equivalence to about 2500euros gross today. The salary seemed very correct to become "professional player"!

In retrospect, this appointment will resemble a little the school of the Fans in the background as in the form. With Romuald as Star of the video game. Jean-Luc as animator against eight opportunistic gamers who had to show in a few minutes what a pretty voice they were dressed. Because yes, if we did not sing, we were gathered to make our vocal production heard, our speech even our eloquence. We were asked to present ourselves but beyond the CV, which they already had in their hands, it was our ability to communicate that would be measured today. For a Sega Master, speaking clearly, distinctly with an adapted vocabulary is essential. I also imagine that a voice too hoarse, broken, a little scary could have been disabling.

So we were there and we went in one after another! I was the third or fourth person to speak. I can't say that I was super comfortable, I'm rarely in this kind of exercise even if it's ten times better today than yesterday. But I did the minimum service, or even more. As soon as it is necessary to speak of a passion, the heart and the mind are inflamed and exceed all reservations and even timidity. I must have checked all the right boxes but maybe I wasn't the only one! So there were eight of us who wanted this job. Seven Parisians and a provincial who is still studying medicine!?! I would know a few months later that if Jean Luc and Romuald did not hold me immediately, during this session of the fans' school, it was because they were uncomfortable with a Cornish choice: to extract me, to pull me out of my medical studies! Did they think!! Which I fully understand by remembering my parents' reaction when I told them that I would not continue my studies and that I would become "Master Sega"! " What? What do I hear? My son will not be a Dentist but a Hardcore Gamer Pro!!! Help!!!" , it is true that it is less prestigious and above all rather worrying. It must be remembered that at the time video games did not have a good reputation and especially they appeared as phenomena of modes can not more random economically speaking! Cf the rapid and violent crash of Atari in 1983 and other manufacturers of consoles.

They preferred to make sure and especially take someone who was immediately available: without psycho drama or states of hypothetical souls to manage.

This is therefore the opportunity for me to talk to you, a first time of Fabrice P. The second Sega Master in history. A colorful character that I will gladly tell you in more detail a little later as the memories are rich with him. We were about 20 Sega Masters. He was a good Master, a very good hotliner. Like most of us. He was on average age, 24 years old. Whereas Sandrine and I would be the youngest at 18 years old, and Jean-Luc the oldest with his 30 years! 18 years old minimum to start working of course! This is because when we met the Sega Fans, it was usually what we answered to them the number one question: "how do you become a Sega Master? Even the youngest wanted to be in!

Fabrice a good Maître Sega, from my point of view, but above all an important character in our history, not because he was the 2nd, the one who convinced Jean Luc and Romuald at my first contact, but because he had an amazing personality. Which will eventually give him big trouble.

As I came out of this first meeting with Sega and two of its most illustrious "employees", I was delighted as never before. I was caressing a little more this sudden dream of integrating an extraordinarily creative world, young, dynamic, exciting, exhilarating. Jean Luc and Romuald were not just ordinary employees, they were, have been, this extra soul that does not simply warm a heart already glowing, they stir it up and ignite it! These guys make you stronger than you already are! I returned to Auxerre, then to Dijon with even more hopes than ever. But I will not be contacted again. Not for this "second" position anyway! You know that it is Fabrice who will join Romuald in the first time. But everything will go very fast in a few months.

Faced with this failure (it is one), I try to relaunch my quest by responding to an announcement in the most mythical of magazines of the time: Tilt with, at its head, no less mythic Jean Michel Blottière. I send as requested my resume, a cover letter and a first essay: a video game test. JMB will then receive me at the Tilt editorial office for an interview. Warm, welcoming, very smiling, he is very enthusiastic about me! He loves my cover letter, my style, the energy and enthusiasm that perspurs but the test is not good! Not good at all. I must admit that I was not bold enough. Having no experience at all at this level although regularly reading Tilt or Generation 4, I had from memory made a kind of copied pasted of the most recent texts that had retained my attention. I plead the lack of originality and a fortiori a heartless plagiarism. The editor of Tilt will ask me to retry several games. New games. I took the opportunity of my trip to Paris to buy some import games for my Mega Drive, Boulevard Voltaire! That's when without knowing I bought a pirate cartridge! There were four games on it! Zoom, Klax... I saw only fire or a certain denial given the attractive price.

But the real good idea was to go back to Virgin Loisirs for a little courtesy visit to Romuald. I will not have stayed long but showing him that I did not give up the piece so easily will make my rib grow necessarily. Especially since he tells me that it will move, things will go fast at what is still Virgin Loisirs. He doesn't know yet when and how but it crackles everywhere. I also think I tell her about another huge passion in my life: role-playing! Dungeons and Dragons in particular, with friends, all of the super friends, a tray, dès, figurines. But also on computers and consoles! Without knowing, without guessing at the time, I had almost signed with Sega. We are parting but for how long?

I don't know if it's in May or June, Romuald contacted me by phone to ask me if I'm still interested in a job as Master Sega. I say yes, yes and yes. He told me that Virgin Loisirs will double the work and recruit many people, including Sega Masters. As soon as the start of September when the staff will be back from summer holidays. And if I still wanted it, I would be the 3rd. SOLD! I'm thrilled. It's the best day of my life (for the first 18 years!) Romuald is happy too, appointment is taken for July 31 and the signing of my contract.

I have no time to digest this incredible news. I tell my parents. My mother is knocked out! Maybe she hoped deep down that this project of "geek" did not succeed? She says nothing. On the other hand my father comes out with his big voice that must scare a masterful and theatrical: "If you leave the House for Sega, you will not put your feet here again"! It is very likely that, as always, he did not take the time to think for even two seconds. A superb enthusiastic reaction for his offspring, it is always nice! Finally they will accept it willingly, after having somewhat reassured them and they will also discover for themselves that what still seems an adventure, presents itself every day that passes, each week as an evolution and even a revolution. At that precise moment only the "Gamers" had seen coming the wave, the unique and historic breakout. For the general public, video games were toys with ugly images and annoying sounds. Apart from the children, we were still a little (much?) ashamed to say that we played video games. It was a form of subculture to the subculture itself. But the people, whatever they are (through time) need their "panem and circences", or bread and games as in Ancient Rome. The whole world will go to play even if it takes months, years.

While waiting for the 16bits wave to submerge all continents and while I still had not really digested this breaking news for me, I was going to leave the family cocoon, Auxerre, Dijon, my student life for the great, sublime, bright Paris! The "super provincial" who was in me until then did not believe! I had traveled France long, wide and across! From Arras to Carcassonne, from Pont l'Evêque to Saintes, from Crépy in Valois to Auxerre and then Dijon. France is a wonderful country and rich in all these regions but Paris had escaped me until then! (I will be captive there for more than 30 years! That will teach me!!! Finally if I exclude the two years of the Train Sega or I also traveled widely throughout France) But if there was only Paris in Paris!?! No problem you probably know, it's the Parisians!!!! And sometimes even "the cream of the cream! I will come back!

Wednesday, 31 July 1991.

HISTORICAL! Hysterical. I'm signing with Virgin Loisirs. For me, the pressure was going to rise seriously because I had to go and sign my engagement with Luc Bourcier, the marketing director. If Romuald was the Master, Luc Bourcier was our commander-in-chief! My "N+2". The general of an army of Guerrillas (wink) that he will not always assume, not completely. Probably a little bit outdated (who was not?) by so much passion, let alone some enthusiasts sometimes out of which we don't know where, from the Punk cuture? Which he has validated with the fabulous campaign of "Master Sega" and the biker straight out of Mad Max. But I'm going a little fast in the job because on this day of July, this army is just beginning to build. I add that, by preparing this book, collecting as many memories as possible, searching on the Internet and elsewhere, it is impossible to talk about those years without talking about Luc Bourcier because he is certainly, finally La mémoire, the only one, of all this time, with many secrets!?! From those years Virgin Loisirs/Sega France or all accelerated each year at crazy speeds (from 88 to 93 in any case). Hired at the very beginning by Jean Martial Lefranc (who will create Cryo with Philippe Ulrich a little later) and to take over the marketing, he is one of the first and above all one of the main artisans of the brand's success and its reputation in France.

I have few memories of this first meeting with him. Which must have been quite brief in the end. Luc Bourcier is tall!!! By the size! Taller than I am and yet I am 1,83m. Maybe it was also because he always held his head high, well raised! I often thought that it was good to have a head in the clouds! This perhaps saved him from having to say hello too often: "Oh sorry I didn't see you"! Like a brachiosaur walking quietly but determined and proudly among other smaller sauropods, children, and head bowed... For yes, it is necessary to know, the male brachiosaur, despite its colossal size, always walks proudly with his head high and raised. I had one in my garden for a while but I was very quickly ruined by the cost of its food.

In fact if I have few memories it is that they were caught up by a small incident which caused a great inconvenience, as far as I am concerned. I am sitting in front of him in his office with Romuald, also sitting on my right. My contract in his hands, Luc Bourcier presents it to me with the different closings, what I will be employed for, under which authorities, what he expected from me. Then comes the chapter of remuneration and he announces me to pay me the amount of 7500frs per month! I fall naked, am extremely embarrassed. I wait for him to finish his sentence and he asks him: "They always told me that this job cost 8000 francs!?!". What Luc Bourcier immediately replied that yes, but I'm young and inexperienced! I remember thinking: "The big joke! Without experience of Master Sega"? Perhaps he thinks I am a telephone operator or telemarketer?".

I spontaneously answer him that being young is an advantage not a disadvantage (and I did not yet measure how much my "youth" would serve me in all my tasks of Master Sega) and that to answer and help the children at Sega Hot Line I was certainly one of the most qualified. Going to the net, unstoppable fulgurant volley! Luc Bourcier in a smile may be a little yellow, then acquiesced to my claim. For me the incident was closed. It would be all the more easy as the whole environment otherwise filled me with happiness! And then in truth, even for zero I could have worked. But they will never know that or thirty years later!

This very slight incident, this clumsiness I suppose of a director who probably still has to manage tight marketing budgets "Virgin", will eventually play in my favor! It is in adversity that one can better measure the strength and talent of each other. I had turned from a snail to a snail of second an unfavorable situation against my "N+2". The chief of the army must have noticed that I was not a switchboard operator, but a real Sega Master. A warrior on whom to count a fortiori in the first line! Like the Promachos of antiquity in the Greek phalanges. A fortiori the goddess "Athena Promachos" leading his army or "Malioth" the spartiate in my second book "The City of Scorpions".

So I signed and was very officially committed to Sega for an indefinite period. I was happy to leave for Auxerre.

Contract signed, the top start had been given and although I'm still not Master Sega, I was going to receive a few days after the signing, a huge carton! Master Sega had cured me, he had sent me the entirety of the role-playing games and especially adventures of the Master System and the Mega Drive. On Mega Drive: several games Electronic Arts but especially Sword of Vermillion and Phantasy Star 2! Which were sold a blind in store. 600 frs of memory (more than one tenth of the SMIC) while standard MD games were around 400. Because these games had more memory than the others and you could save those parts on an included battery. This prohibitive price created a controversy. I loved games like this but it was too expensive for me! Papa Romuald Noël spoiled me by offering me all these games that he could not afford.

But he had given me mostly homework for the House! And I was not going to sulk my pleasure because in fact it is not, and it will never be work! At that time I ate everything with a voracious appetite. And that's when I finally discovered the Master System and I enjoyed it! Golden Axe Warrior, the Zelda from Sega! The "YS" game. The incredible Phantasy Star that is breathtaking both graphically and ludically. Golvelius, Miracle Warriors, Lord of the sword, Dragon crystal, and the totally impossible Ultima IV! Which gives to pull your hair and then your head.

A month before arriving at Sega, I was playing almost days and nights in a month of August summer Auxerrois always wonderfully lethargic! I will finish almost all of them (except Ultima 4) in three or four hundred hours of games. I was perhaps not yet "Master Sega" but "Master role-playing and adventure games"! A title that will be given to me later or rather "role play specialist". Title that some will mock or rather parody each other by attributing the titles to each other!

Fabrice who never missed an opportunity to laugh, gently, but sometimes also to break (it is said that he was the classmate who inspired a certain surfer to Jean Dujardin) had found new specialties to specialists. There was the specialist Sonic (normal), the specialist Master System, mega-cd, the specialist Kung Fu, the specialist Magnum 357, the braking specialist! But the top of the top is when you were named specialist "Out Run" or "Flicky". We will also have a specialist coffee machine! We could of course cumulate the specialties on everything and anything. The joke had then lasted long enough, except for him perhaps, for days and days. It was to tease you will understand because a Sega Master had to know absolutely all the games, or at least make believe. Prestige and we might become legends!

We were laughing with Fabrice. I was laughing well, Romuald laughed well, sometimes "yellow", but when he was in a good mood, he manifested his form of humor, very caustic, which will taste very little our 3 women of the service because Fabrice, who had many qualities, also had flaws, to start by being seriously misogynist. He didn't like people in general but it was even more true if you were a woman.

So that was for the preparations, from before Sega, or rather (and for a few more months) the before Virgin Loisirs! I officially joined them on September 3.

CHAPTER 3

RUE BARBETTE

SEGA ME VOILA! September 3, 1991. The first week.

It's on a beautiful sunny day that my story at Sega begins very officially, very concretely. We are still in summer and it is nice and warm, even in Paris. It's time for the back of school but this time I will not go to math or philo, even less anatomy or epidemiology. But I did my vacation homework perfectly. And these last ones are very little like the previous ones. I'm fed up with Phantasy Star and Mother Brain, I'm full of Golden Axe Warrior and Death Adder. I even tried to become an avatar (a prophet) in Richard Garriott's Ultima IV. "I'm proud of you" (I am proud of you...) thinks in my head again and again like the stick planted in the bronzes. I triumphed. I'm running as Master Sega Level One! Let's not be so modest: When you exercise several virtues of Ultima IV you are directly Master Sega Level Two! Those who know this game, will be sympathetic.

I go back to 8+10 rue Barbette from my 10+8 years old excited as a chip. I am probably also afraid, a little, much? But the excitement is too great. I present myself at the reception is it is Johnny "Romuald" Depp said Master Sega who comes again to look for me with his beautiful smile! Johnny Depp is not he not of course known for having been also Edouard in the hands of argents? Romuald had become Maître Sega after being "Tapestry-decorator". We go deep into the offices until we find Romuald's office which is in a corner of the building and not far from that of Luc Bourcier. One desk only, or two, must separate us. At the same time, the whole thing is anything but gigantic and we are in the Marketing and Communication wing. I see, I meet new faces and it's very moving. Little timid greetings. Especially by crossing a young blonde, in a suit, very attractive. I will learn later but quite soon (if you can say so) that she is called Alexandra, and she will definitely turn my head by inviting me personally, in all good honour, via Sega of course, to the World Karting Championships at Le Mans, a few days later! No but seriously, pinch me hard, very hard... Yes again please!

Fortunately we arrive very quickly in the Master's place and it would be a shame to let ourselves be distracted in this long and splendid day. A room of about twelve to fifteen square meters in length with a large window in the corner at the bottom left. Two large offices all equipped with TV, consoles, many boxes or game cartridges, posters, figurines, goodies Sega, mail from the Sega Club. The first Sega den/museum that inspired so many more 20 or 30 years later! No doubt, we are in the Nest of the Master and it is up to what one can imagine. When I arrive, Fabrice is sitting at his desk and quietly answers the phone! Once the call is over, we will greet each other cordially, we already met a few months ago. What is surprising to me is that, during the job interview, he was right next to me. And at no time did I think that he would be chosen! His "performance" had been the most sober, but apparently sufficient. I can finally put a face on the one who had cut me off from my feet. Who had temporarily broken my great dream! But I am not in any way revanchist because if the adventure had been postponed for me, it has the merit of existing! Finally! Yesterday is no more, tomorrow is not yet! There is only now!

Romuald quickly presents me the place, the equipment made available because it became at this moment my office, even shared, and where we would have to squeeze! Which did not seem to please Fabrice, unlike Romuald. I can start now! Not answering all calls but making a few. We will be three in an office of two one day then the next day four, the following week five and even six and we will then close until October: date of our move into a reserved space Rue Sainte Croix de la Bretonnerie! The current office will very quickly look more like an arcade than anything else! This first small invasion or simply intrusion of hotliners will be remarkable and noticed! Virgin Loisirs's workforce has risen sharply in recent months, but it is still a "small company" of 30/40 employees! So many new faces in such a short time, concentrated in the same place did not fail to unbalance the installed energy forces of the whole! Jean Luc Satin will then comment on this period of summer, suggesting that it was better not to be away too long in summer holidays under penalty of not recognizing many people when coming back! We were not the only ones who arrived...

More seriously, our arrival was still raising the pressure that increased with the end of year holidays. Yes, Christmas 1991 would be Japanese! Yes, it will be, for the most part, "SEGA" and even "Master Sega". I definitely played video games while being paid! But... it was like paying someone to eat food as fine as it tastes?!? Pay a sportsman to practice sport, a musician, an actor to play, a dancer to dance! But it was probably more like paying an alcoholic to drink! I say this knowing full well that drinking is a disease that can have very serious consequences. Playing will also kill many people, especially in Asia, who will most often forget to eat or drink. Extreme cases certainly and rare but important to highlight to engage, by the public authorities later, prevention campaigns against any addiction, especially when we will land the games On line with universe persistent 24h/24 but we are still very far from all this. And we will never forget to feed, hydrate, sleep and stay healthy. It was a message from the Ministry of Health" !!! it's done, my book can be published, we can continue!!!

Wouldn't they be completely crazy at Virgin Leisure? They pay young people to "play all day"! An expression I would hear hundreds of times when I talk to people about my work and activities, even with many nuances. So you're paid to play?" Firefighters extinguish fires, nurses make injections, soldiers make war, the Sega Masters play all day! Not only they paid us, but they will eventually give us all the games that came out so we can deepen our knowledge! An advantage that will be seriously abused after one of the Sega Masters started selling these games directly to the members of the Sega Club who called us! He certainly did not have the light on all floors that one. He betrayed us, he betrayed Sega, the Master Sega, he will be the first to be fired for serious misconduct. I will come back to this later in the "secret files" of the Sega Masters.

This first day was fantastic but I had gone to Paris without having a place! So and as we will affirm the Spaniards at home at that time in the media, it was their slogan: Viva una Aventuraaaaaa: Segaaaa! Slogan that hits significantly less than Sega It's stronger than you. Punch Line that was envied everywhere in Europe including England.

Romuald's good friend, Franck Licois who was also the boss of POS (advertising on sales places) had just released his apartment a few tens of meters from the offices! At 6 Rue Elzévir. It was a fantastic opportunity for both of us because if I took him, he would avoid paying a notice of one or two months! Sega gave me everything, absolutely everything and even the keys to my apartment! Small parenthesis in the genre "that the world is small", when leaving one day of the "6" I found myself face to face with Jean Pierre Soisson! The Mayor of Auxerre, from my small town to the countryside! He will also be Minister of State, President of the Burgundy Region. I never met him in Auxerre. He lived at 8 rue Elzévir to attend parliamentary sessions being elected, also, at that time, as a member of Parliament in addition to being Mayor. I will meet many other well-known personalities but it will not have much to do with Sega, with a few exceptions. I will not fail to tell it of course.

This incredible day was ending and already another one was coming! A night to recharge the batteries and recover from these emotions. And tomorrow I will meet the fourth Sega Master: Jean Luc Hadi!!!

On September 4th I woke up for the first time in my new apartment in Paris! So it was not a dream and I was going to check again by going to rue Barbette. I still had a hard time believing it, I will play almost all day and answer some calls from children in distress. The school year had begun and therefore the children returned home from 4:30 pm. But it was Wednesday today, so there would probably be a few more people to help. I meet Fabrice and Romuald who tell me that I would take half the calls. To give me a hand, of course, and it's mostly what I'm paid for! Yes because in fact being paid to play all day is a myth or even a legend! You have to play a lot and almost all the time but especially by helping all the shipwrecked Sega games. This is the only contractual point. Yes and no. It will happen that, a few years later, in an intermediate period post Mega Drive, megacd and 32X, we are paid mainly to play and evaluate the games! Because the phone will be fully automated! And will also become paid (the famous 3668) And because many shipwrecked people will start to not need us directly: the multiplication of bible-type publications (Marc Andersen will put in one pocket what he has taken in another) but also and especially with the arrival of Internet in all households.

I was installed and I probably had to play on the side of Fabrice's office! And that's when the third Master arrived! Big enough, brown, rather handsome guy, with glasses, a nice shirt, but certainly, at least, "thirties"! When he came into the room I didn't think he could be a new Sega Master! He just seemed too old for the job! Yet there was no age to be Master Sega and surely some of you will have even imagined him as an old Shaolin master, white hair (if any) and half blind. I thought for a few seconds that it was a new product manager of Sega marketing with which, at least visually, he was more "fit".

Romuald immediately comes to present him. It was Jean Luc Hadi, 30 years old (by memory), who came from the insurance world. He was above all a very good friend of Romuald and lived in the same town (but not in the same apartment) at Saint Cyr L'Ecole in the Yvelines (78). Fabrice and I would discover it day after day, week after week: Jean Luc was like a "big teddy bear", or rather like a Lamentin (you know, like the one at the zoo of Vincennes, that Sirene that we take for a deformed dolphin and call them sea bears). Very calm, very gentle, very affable, it will often serve as a stabilizer to a group of Sega Masters not really homogeneous in their characters. Jean Luc will become a good, very good friend. He will be a little our big brother to all and, above these thirty years, our great wise and respectable mediator when Romuald would not be there. We have made more acquaintance. Jean Luc was not a big player, he may not even be a player at all initially if not very occasionally. He will become one and fast! Necessarily. However, he was an excellent hotlineur by his increased listening skills, attention, empathy. While remaining as calm as possible under any circumstances! It is therefore a "big teddy bear", sailor or not, who will still happen to get angry sometimes, which will surprise his entourage. Jean Luc will become one of the key figures and characters of the Sega Masters, you'll find out.

We were now four Master Sega! Like the 4 Fantastic! The 3 Musketeers (adding D'Artagnan of course)! Like the 4 seasons!?! A nice set of "males" in need of adventures, escape, challenges. 4 Masters challenging themselves but only on screen. Because yes we could play endlessly but also challenge each other. I remember very well having challenged Romuald, as the opposite, to Flicky countless times! Not sure that playing this game really advanced our infinite knowledge of the Sega universe but we stole ourselves in the feathers of hours and hours for our greatest happiness! We were very momentarily in excess compared to the consumer services, the opportunity to exploit so many "two-on-one" games would not be presented as easily. These spontaneous challenges were finally part of our DNA, like a natural emulation, essential that will become mythical among young players! Sega is stronger than you: we could not not confront each other! It was not so much a question of who was stronger but one had to set the bar as high as possible. We had to be the champions of the record, the high score. Yes WE had to be the strongest.

And not a little bit. Ideal and incredibly happy marketing and communication proposal that will stick to society for a while. A Master shot from the Lintas Agency, the first to kindly accept to work for us when many other agencies had simply refused!

 SEGA C'EST PLUS FORT QUE TOI (stronger than you) and "Master Sega" are well born at Lintas. Written by Eric Niesseron and Alexandre Bertrand, then director of the creation of the agency. For you know, this slogan and its underlying character were precisely created to challenge, stimulate young males who began to have chin hair, with muscles that slowly swelled everywhere. And to honor this mythology of the Spartan agogy (period of education of young Spartans from antiquity to become the most formidable fighters of antiquity) Romuald and I fought each other savagely, tirelessly... On Mega Drive! The very powerful 16 bits and on the must-play game ... Flicky! Or adorable little chicks flying and chirping happily. It was still much less dangerous, less bloody than fighting with fists and swords. Bad language will tell that the Sega games were very violent but they did not suspect a single second that we were facing each other by Hedgehogs or Interposed Chicks. A well-kept secret for several decades and finally revealed!

More seriously, although all this is true, we defend, at least in terms of communications, a very masculine ideal, well virile, which will smell good sweat, swollen muscles, big slaps, the shots of becs but which will however be quickly beaten in breach by an incredible arrival, unthinkable (of-do I myself think it!!!!) but exceptional and formidably happy for the Masters Sega. Which you will discover in the next chapter!

If I was slightly surprised by the arrival of Jean-Luc Hadi in the Hotline with a profile far from the Geek of the time, I could reassure myself with "Robert Fabrice De Niro" and "Johnny Romuald Depp". Fabrice had false airs of the mythical Italian-American actor with whom he identified so much when for Romuald, it was more obvious (at least for the movie lovers). I was far, very far from imagining the thunderclap that would then fall on this embryo of future hotline XXL. We were the Sega Masters! We were men, real warriors, and some of us will be even... Tattooed!

Before the metaphorical thunder struck us—yes, I'm teasing a bit too much, aren't I?—in the following week, the second of this new chapter, there was another electrifying event (quite literally for the young "Gamer" I was!). The delightful Alexandra from Marketing would present me with a fantastic invitation on Friday, September 6. I had barely been there a week when I was offered the chance to attend the Karting World Championships, happening that year in France, specifically at Le Mans! Sega was the official sponsor, and I can't recall if my invitation was as a VIP or if it was an official engagement as a Sega Master, representing the brand at the various demo stands of Mega Drive and other Sega arcade machines. I probably would have told you that I was invited as a VIP, but as a Master Sega, they relied on me, my passion, and my expertise to manage whatever needed managing, assisting and guiding potential new Sega enthusiasts! Thus, a fantastic week was drawing to a close. Another was about to begin—and perhaps end— behind the wheel.

Chapter 4

Sega Mistress

It was my second week but the first Monday at Virgin Loisirs.

Everything moved swiftly, especially with Sonic. Sega was on a hiring spree. New heroes were arriving in droves on Mega Drive and Master System, to our collective delight: the Sega Masters. We would greet them, absorb their essence, or even become one with them, guiding them through all perils towards the pinnacle of glory and success. This triumph would then weave a vast web, ever-expanding around each Master Sega, and there was no time to dawdle. Romuald would one day say in press interviews, "Either go to work or run every day" (or words to that effect).

We were always the pioneers in getting our hands on it. The Christmas season might have been underway internally, but a major push in communications and marketing was about to hit the media: TV, radio, and cinema. The "Punk Iroquois vs. Maître Sega" battle was set to captivate everyone, and Virgin Loisirs was ready to go all out! It was crucial to excel at every level! Sega, long seen as an underdog, emerged as Nintendo's foremost challenger. Even more astonishingly, though we didn't know it yet, we would ascend to the leadership position within two or three years, a slim lead perhaps, but a lead nonetheless, especially in the 16-bit market segment!

Sega Japan was determined to get it right. The pace had to quicken. The company decided to acquire and reclaim its rights from all its European distributors. Virgin Loisirs was set to officially become "Sega France" come September!

During this pivotal week, which would see budgets skyrocket in the best way, a new recruit was about to cause a stir! It was like a bolt of lightning for me (there would be other, more intense moments, but this one was already unforgettable).

Without wanting to be disparaging, Sandrine was far from being the Greek Aphrodite who illuminated with her beauty the surrounding places (Insertion may seem unflattering but Aphrodite is one of the central characters of my "City of Scorpions" and it was therefore for me a bit easy occasion to promote it because

I am not yet published at Flammarion!). She had a little male side with those always cut short hair. But that did not prevent her from being extremely bright. It was even a real breath of pure air covered with a perfume, an essence of Spring! Almost always cheerful, often warm, full of life and fantasy. Sandrine illuminated our days with this incredible energy! Her youth, her freshness and also sometimes her naivety, even if sometimes she had to force the line a little! She was also frank, direct, sincere. She had many qualities! But from there to become Master Sega it is not a little abuse? Especially with all these macho guys who hang around video games? At least at that time... Because now it's much better, isn't it? Aahahaha.

It was a thunderbolt, an earthquake, a tsunami for us los muchachos parisinos not necessarily all "machossses"! ! The atmosphere was going to be seriously changed, and how? Could we shamelessly extend the competitions of the one who has the biggest console? The longest controller? The smallest memory card? 100% male or 100% female groups can quickly turn sour! Even acid. The mixture, even if reduced in this case, could be a guarantee of greater stability. The jolts generated by this surprising arrival would they go beyond the framework of the Sega Club?

I have to be honest, all feminist, but not at all militant, that I can be now, when I saw her arrive in the Hotline, I was really, really, really very surprised! Kind of gaping with breath taken! After our "Patriarch" Jean-Luc Hadi, we now had a daughter?!? No but it's not good the head Romulus? And why not a Punk while we're there? It would be so much more fitting! Imagine: you are watching the four mythical Punk ads, then played by a young Bodybuilder who will present and win the casting for having presented himself as a hedgehog!?! " Ian Harrison" he said ! It's a bit far-fetched, but we'll give him a great haircut at the Harrison.

The Harrison not yet Ford but Mustang at the Iroquois ridge comes to face Master Sega, who then has the voice of Patrick Borg (Son Goku in Dragon Ball Z) before having quickly that of Richard Darbois: the comedian who lends his voice to double all the films of Harrison, the actor, Le Ford, and notably for Indiana Jones. In both cases, a very manly voice.

And all amazed that you could be, all excited, shaken by the action, convincing special effects, all impressed and intrigued by the powerful voice of Patrick Son Goku Borg or Indiana Darbois Jones, it would then... Sandrine who would turn out to be a powerful and disturbing Master(sse) Sega? No, no, no, no, you're not going to screw us up, we'll have to identify our pre-pubescent teenagers?

Unforgivable sacrilege! Offense to the gods of video games! But after all, even among the Olympians, there were many goddesses! Athena was the Goddess of War (and Wisdom)? And how many Sega Maniacs are also fans of the Knights of the Zodiac? And Aphrodite who liked to fricotter with Arés the God of War, the spartans will make another goddess army! In honour of the Spartans, whom they even considered to be tougher and more merciless than they were. Many young people who are on the line of Master Sega will be paying for their expenses, at least for the first call with Sandrine! Then Aude...

Finally, a monumental mistake or Master's blow on the part of Romuald, Sandrine joined the team. Surprise effect past, she showed immediately you can not more sociable and especially very effective, she will quickly become a kind of mascot for the team by its presence, simplicity, smile and also because it is the only woman! Like Sonic, it transcended the species and even cracked the genus.

Nobody saw the Mega Drive coming! Nobody saw Sonic the Hedgehog coming against Mario and Luigi the moustachioed ones! Nobody had seen Sandrine coming. With a S... Like Sega! S as Sonic! She was a huge fan of this game as many players and even more (in proportion) players.

She is the only woman, she knows it, she will obviously enjoy it and will be like a fish in the water, a cock in the dough, a young woman in the middle of ten young men, and finally for the greatest pleasure of all. Almost at the gates of Paradise, if Fabrice, so nice, had not been in the team, he would never digest this arrival. I was so surprised when she came in that I didn't think to look at her face to see her reaction, and especially I did not know her relationship with women. I would give a few euros to have the photo of his head at this time!

One is the other will engage in arms regularly, a little later, in several weeks, with Fabrice of course as a provocateur. But if the boy is clearly misogynistic, he is also intelligent, yes we can be both, intelligence remains something very relative and even subjective. He will never, or very rarely, cross the red line. So Fabrice will hate Sandrine, who will give him back a little, but not too much. She obviously had other more important things to deal with.

However, and I will certainly come back to it, there was of course a small cultural shock that would therefore be crystallized and embodied by Fabrice. Such misogyny probably eclipsed everything that could be of machismo, more or less authentic, in other males. But at that point in history, Romuald, Jean-Luc and I had absolutely nothing to do with any kind of machismo. Romuald had just proved it (at least for himself).

While he would throw sexist or even obscenity-like punches at her, we will laugh about it discreetly, timidly, differently, shamefully? Personally I ended up taking it as a kind of spectacle. There was a theatrical side to Fabrice that bounced rather well on Sandrine because she had really good character, humor and also excellent resilience. At least in appearance. It became more of a kind of game where we don't know who really pulled the strings. Sandrine always stood up to her with a lot of humor without adding fuel to the fire. What talent you had, Sandrine! She knew all the lines of the films of the Team du Splendide by heart. Les bronzés, Le Père Noël, Papy is a resistance. Which will not make him more sympathetic in the eyes of Patrick Lavanant. The brother of Dominique Lavanant who will be CEO of Sega a few months (years?) later. But that's another story. All this to say that she often tried and managed to turn situations tense by humor, by her response.

Were the games, especially the Sega games, reserved for boys? A fortiori between boys? It was questionable at the time and is still sometimes discussed. Should all Sega Masters have chin hair and a chignon? The arrival of Sandrine and then a few months later, Aude and Bénédicte, attest to the fact that this universe would also become feminine. Not to the displeasure of some.

This second week at Virgin Loisirs/Sega France, and within the Hotline, should also be proud of the arrival of Lionel P. The 5th Master Sega. He was an elegant, smiling, well-mannered and therefore very polite young man. He was also intelligent, he had everything to be charming. But maybe he was more charming than charming, the difference, the nuance may seem very thin but his intelligence could sometimes lead him to manipulation. Natural and "normal" deviation?!? He used it very well and with good use most often. I got along very well with him and he was also an excellent hotlineur who also brought a lot of energy, good mood, fantasy. Which will more than compensate for the fact that he was not a very big player. "A big player" ? Would he certainly correct. His main defect was probably and certainly not to be in his place within the Sega Masters. Maybe he was a graduate, and the line of Master Sega just an opportunity to experiment in an environment in intergalactic explosion!?!

He will be one of the first to leave us, after all many months spent with us, and many laughs, laughter and all kinds of pleasant memories. Much later after his departure, Romuald will come to tell me that Lionel had applied to one of our partners, or former partners, probably one of the many third-party publishers of the Mega Drive era. He sent his CV by presenting himself for the period spent with us as "Director of communication"!!! We laughed! It seems that it is usual to inflate these CVs!?! The recruiters did not have to check enough but the universe of video games were not so great finally human resources.

This week ended with a fantastic extra! And what is simply incredible is that there would be another even more fantastic next weekend but let's stay in the right direction, in the direction of the arrow of time. The World Karting Championships in Le Mans were just around the corner. The young provincial I was never stopped pinching himself of what happened to him!

I remember especially this overheated atmosphere of competition where finally the players had not too much to do around the consoles because they had basically come to see the competition. And on this Sunday, September 15 it was the Final. To probably get the new one, the next Schumacher or Ayrton Senna, both of them passed through this formative stage before knowing the career in F1 that you certainly know. It is the school of champions! Nothing to do with the one who makes a great time on "Gran Turismo".

Even if it will eventually happen but are really, in the state, two very different challenges that are not close to meet except to be able to generate the "G" exerted on the pilots and all the physical consequences induced. And if it were only that. Anyway.

With my nice VIP Sega pass, I could travel everywhere, go take a look at the rather small track (it's karting not F1), rest in the VIP village to have a cocktail, a snack, meet the other staff members who met the media. And I could of course accompany the few onlookers who came to the demonstration corner of the Sega machines. The day was very short. Arrived on the circuit at 11 o'clock and left around 17 o'clock, but after integrating Sega into the heart of the Parisian headquarters, I had just made my first official outing/performance and this event added even more strength to the mountains of energies that I kept accumulating every day! Pinch me again please... Alexandra?

This magical trip from Le Mans ended one week, a news even happier than the first! Sandrine and Lionel had joined us. So there were six of us. Sega really became Sega with the takeover of Virgin Loisirs by Sega Japan, and we were very quickly feeling the difference: this latest news opening a totally magical and fairytale window. By which I would rush like all the other Sega next weekend! The Dream in big, the dream in Giant.

Chapter 5

Sega Europe : OPIO

The first two weeks at Virgin Loisirs/Sega had been more than expected. We were already six Sega Masters. Four new masters with Romuald and Fabrice and we were slowly but surely learning our craft by sharing calls on two phones only, but this number was enough for the moment because of the massive operation, the general public of Master Sega's line had not yet begun. It would start in October when our team will have expanded and we will be a little trained.

We could then compete and play like damned at the greatest hits of Sega. The games on Sonic were running and I could see how and why this little animal had quickly taken over the hearts of the players. The game is absolutely fantastic for all the reasons you know certainly very dear readers! Sonic is a bomb and we would also discover it every day, every week by the extraordinary creations sent by the fans of the Sega Club. Various letters for help, to receive games free of charge "by fidelity", to thank us, to encourage us, to tell us how much they loved Sega, how much they loved Sonic the Hedgehog! We also received many designs, each more successful than the other. It was very moving all this passion, all this love that pervaded these testimonies of pre-teens, children and even grandchildren sometimes. We will also receive amazing fanzines around the Sega universe. These small amateur magazines certainly but full of talents that sometimes had nothing to envy the publications marketed in the press because always stuffed with an amazing passion. Months and months later, after the release of several adventures of Sonic, we would literally stay on our asses by receiving and discovering many drawings, regularly, finally twenty? About 30? From a very young artist, who by memory was probably pre-pubescent, but had a talent, an absolutely fantastic pencil stroke! What she drew was close to the work of a professional and these illustrations could have been used for commercial purposes as they were precise, neat: simply beautiful! It was very beautiful but it was especially very hot!

The young artist, who was not yet definitely out of childhood, made illustrations of Sonic, Tails, Amy, Knuckles particularly "hot". Or especially the breaks of Sonic and Amy Rose could be particularly suggestive! Obviously if you go on the internet now and type something like "Sonic Amy Sex" you will come across thousands and thousands of illustrations and even porn videos. But I must say that at the time, when the internet was just babbling, it was a shock for me to discover this intense passion with this very sexual coloring coming from a child or pre-teen of ten to twelve years old probably. Romuald will invite him (on the initiative of Bénédicte) to come and see us at the line of Maître Sega and we will then be even more for our expenses! Because the little lady, although very young, had a certain aplomb. She could have felt a bit embarrassed? Just a little... Embarrassed? By this "very slight diversion"!?! What not. She assumed completely. At the same time it was much more naughty and sexy than porn (not a single drawing of the genitals, just poses, very suggestive attitudes). I don't know who kept these drawings but I would have liked to keep at least one. I don't know what happened to this girl full of talent and if she reads me?!? Contact me !!!

This connection with the Sega fans was a source of happiness! It is especially Romuald who will benefit because if we were all Master Sega, he kept all the activities of the "Club", except direct assistance to players, including the monthly letter of the Club that he wrote entirely, passionately and with great humor. But he communicated well on everything that could be shared, joyful, filled with love and passion.

The Sega Club under the leadership of Romuald and Jean Luc Satin had created very strong links between the first maniacs Sega and the Brand. Master Line Sega + monthly mail + club card + small gifts for the most loyal players + a whole number of small privileges. But the Mega Drive wave was going to take it all away. The Sega Club continued for months (even years) but the "privileges" of the early days were gradually losing their intensity, their exclusivity. The Sega Master line would be open to all (and what a success but we also spent, a little but not too much, in "industrial" mode), the specialized press exploded, carried by "Consoles+", the first 100% console magazine, then quickly with "Megaforce" exclusively Sega, led by the illustrious AHL at the editorial level, finally you understand we were entering a new era. Sega had become much more than a club of enthusiasts. We could claim and even become the world center of video game enthusiasts!

Finally... We would fight hard for this place with Nintendo! Many will have to choose their side!?! Or not.

Virgin Loisirs became very officially "Sega France" and we were all very satisfied, very proud and full of wonderful additional hopes! Everyone but one person! Philippe Ulrich at our side seemed very embarrassed by this acquisition. He would be obliged to leave the premises before the end of the month! Sega France had of course taken over all the activities relating to its own business, its brand but did not take over the activities relating to Virgin. The French designer had found his place to develop his creations, and so DUNE, within the subsidiary distribution of games of the Virgin group, it will be necessary that the company of Richard Branson face him a small place in another subsidiary! (Virgin Games, probably?). This exceptional situation contrasted with everything else. The excitement was palpable in Marketing. In fact it was boiling.

I don't know when, how or by whom! We learned! But the latest news that came this week was even more intense than all the previous ones! You should not pinch me this time but rather slap me! It came from Sega Europe!!! Sega Europe say? Yes, this new entity sounded like the Great Napoleonic Army! Germany, Spain, Austria, the United Kingdom and France together (but under British authority) formed a pan-European entity. We had become legally and therefore officially Sega France but visually we still remained Virgin Loisirs a few days time to update the software. Sega Europe has sprung into our hearts and minds concretely faster than Sega France and so that we don't forget, we were all invited to the first seminar, to the first European conference of Sega Europe! A big party, a celebration, a great mass and it would be over three days at Club Med in Opio! Close to Nice. This Club Med is one of the world's holiday company showcases. Golf 9 holes, heated outdoor pool, indoor pool, sauna, aerobics, 15 tennis courts, fitness rooms, restaurants, disco, we should be fine!

At this announcement, in the hotline, we all had to look a little bit wrong!?! Club Med d'Opio!?! But it's good right?!? Very good! I think we didn't have to take the whole measure immediately. Because we didn't know this Club Med. Because an announcement is always a little dry and it must be detailed to start taking body, to enter your reality! And here, I really thought that if it was definitely not a joke, after all I was in the VIP at Le Mans last weekend, there was probably a mistake. Marketing was invited but not the "hotlineurs"? Not the Sega Masters! But no, the news was going to be confirmed in the minutes, the hours that were going to pass! Documents finally coming into our hands:

"We are all invited to attend the European Seminar from 21 to 23 September which will take place at Club Med d'Opio. You will find attached a table summarizing the reservations made for your transport to Nice. At the airport of Nice, a representative of L'American Express will meet you and take care of your transfer to Club Med. Upon arrival at the Club, you will be given your room key and a voucher worth CHF 300 for your personal expenses. Breakfasts, lunches and dinners are covered (drinks included). Any additional costs incurred during the stay must be paid by each participant on the day of departure. You can enjoy the club benefits (list of activities). A cocktail will be served on Saturday evening at 19:45 by the pool, followed by dinner at the restaurant Les Olympiades or tables will be reserved for you. For the "party-goers", the disco will open at 11 p.m. On Sunday morning the conference will start at 9:45 sharp and end at 12:45. Lunch will be served between 13h and 14h. From 14h to 15h you will be free. 15H departure of the Olympiad. Each participant will be given a t-shirt with the colours of their team. Non-participants must be present to encourage them! These Olympiads will end at 4:30 pm. At 7:30 pm, a cocktail will be offered followed by a gala dinner (correct dress required). A show of about 5 minutes per country will be presented after dinner. And meet from 11:30 pm at the disco for a crazy night..."

That's the initial flyer and how this seminar was presented to us. Exactly. Alexandra will give us the final detailed program and our plane tickets a little later!!! There was no doubt about it! Christian Brécheteau, the DG or Luc Bourcier will not come to me just before, "No you little finally do not come, you are just a Master Sega who plays all day and we will even pay you for this, but there is still not push too far in the nettles! You agree? We've been too nice to you?"

" My flight ticket indicates the flight IT6645, departure 12h55 from Porte F to Paris Orly on September 21 with the company Air Inter.

WHAAAAAAAaaaaaaoooooooooooooooooooouuuuuuuuuuuuuuuuh!

It will also be my first flight! (I'm only 18!) With an arrival on one of the most beautiful bays in the Mediterranean. The landing at the seashore will be absolutely wonderful.

We will arrive on Saturday in the middle of the afternoon at the Club. Handing over keys, luggage tags, notebooks, tickets to drink, club credit card. Time to settle in the room, to go around the owner and we will already be in early evening. The Club Med Opio is very beautiful, it is especially well inserted in the Provencal countryside or Nice hinterland and I had not seen anything so beautiful at this age. So I was in heaven. I would discover places much more dazzling (they are numerous all over the world) but at that moment it was just absolute happiness. Thank you Sega. Thank you Sonic. Thank you Romuald.

This seminar was a unique opportunity for all Sega representatives across Europe to meet, discover each other, around the company and the brand but not only. The weekend had its seminar/meeting part with tons of presentations, figures on the state of the sector, the forces in front of us, the objectives to be achieved. All speakers would speak in English, a language that I read much more easily than I understood it when listening to it at the time (it has improved significantly since) With the heat of the moment these meetings were slightly soporific and not only for non-membersEnglish speakers. But also a relaxing party or even fun! PHEW! Especially after the first dinner. On 22h we had a show! A show, then, where each country presented itself in its own way. I do not really remember the content, more or less hilarious except to know the ephemeral artists but they will not fit into history a priori. Nevertheless I remember the Spanish (or the Austrians?) I am not sure of anything anymore.

I believe that they are the ones who have reproduced this cabaret show with reduced actors: reduced to Dwarves! Or you see only heads, hands and feet but of several different people. Clenched one on top of the other (everything else being cleverly draped) before starting a very folk dance with movements not at all synchronized. Voluntarily of course. Applauding the meters, they had won by a wide margin! Bravo the Spanish! Or the Austrians! Bravo all the others anyway, bravo the Europeans, you had to dare this kind of show in front of these colleagues office, much less perfect strangers! A little tour at the disco after, but there was not much people so finally the evening ended relatively early and so much better; we would be in shape for a very full day the next day.

Sunday morning is the breakfast ecstasy! There is the little thing that made the success of Club Med is largely sat its reputation! Tons of things to eat. Salty, sweet, you can find everything absolutely everything, fresh and in quantity! I gained more than two kilos on the scale, going up to Paris. I had fallen for pastries, addicted to sugar that I am, alas!?! Since always! Once full, new meeting: THE weekend conference. Over three hours with a coffee break in the middle. I have no memory of it but its length. Lunch on 13/14h and the next appointment will be the famous Olympiads officially renamed "Fun Games". Sega employees will then compete on many games of type race bag (I think Romuald and Jean Luc Satin have done very strong, we all will have given it to heart's content!) balance game or nothing should be overturned.

All these burlesque games will be played but we are a little too many for everyone to participate? Nevertheless, we will encourage our colleagues to work as planned for a real moment of relaxation and competition.

New start of the evening, cocktail at Bar Paladio then dinner at "La fontaine", we will enjoy, my taste buds still remember these fresh and grilled fish that I was able to enjoy like many others. We, the Sega Masters, guests of the last minute or almost, take advantage of this event for integration purposes! I was already perfectly Sega, blue from blue, before returning to Virgin Loisirs. And I will be all the time, my whole life for different reasons but not so much for having worked there for years, even if obviously it does not take anything away from nothing, you can see it for yourself. I probably thought that life is crazy! Sometimes. You have dreams, very different from each other, sometimes unattainable (which you believe of course) and all of a sudden the latter catches you, no longer leaves you and gives you even more than you would ever hope!

Three weeks had just passed. Already. Master Sega, Romuald became my friend, he will even be a little more than a friend: a brother, a twin? I was paid, very temporarily indeed, to play! Especially at all the novelties and a little before everyone. Right next to us, one of the greatest French creators who was preparing the adaptation of Dune (Licence qui fera ou aura encore fait l'actualité near the release of the book you read with Part 2 of the film version directed by Denis Villeneuve). Virgin Loisirs really became Sega France. I discovered other extraordinary Sega Masters, of which I have not finished talking. They sent me to the World Karting Championships in Le Mans and now to the Club Med in Opio!?! What will be next week? What? Radio? TV? A seminar in Japan? Why not the Olympics? (Sega was official sponsor of Barcelona 92) And why not a trip to all the cities of France? In a train with the colors of Sega? And why not also Formula One while we're at it? After sponsoring, to make the teeth on karting, Sega will quickly spend the second by sponsoring the Renault F1 team with Alain Prost as Driver! And football is also that right? Football for video games? And vice versa...

What I did not know, or rather what I did not imagine, is that "Master Sega" was, it became the concrete link between marketing and the very numerous consumers. And the number of opportunities to represent the brand was going to explode. But the Passion Sega, in the hearts of many players, could not incarnate in the press officers or director of communication. Who were probably very good in their professional relationships, but not with the players.

We Sega Masters, we had the passion, the precious Sesame to illuminate even more children's eyes! Some more than others. Of course, you also had to be able to receive it, share it, transmit it. And sometimes even teach it at its best! That's how I made my hole. I was an adult since I was 18! I was even quite tall (I'm still but I should start shrinking) but when I see the photos from that time: yes I was almost a teenager! Or not too far. I was a "big kid"!

End of third week. There was still one left to continue purring with pleasure glued on each other without any real pressure. But as early as October, the great battle against Nintendo was about to begin. Punk was going to be talked about again and we really had to show that at Sega, we were the strongest.

CHAPTER 6

RUE SAINTE CROIX DE LA BRETONNERIE

The capacity of the premises of the headquarters of rue Barbette reaching saturation, we will leave them to move to 14 rue Sainte Croix de la Bretonnerie, one of the most lively arteries in the Marais. For a "brand new" hotline, its real start in an open configuration to all, with a dozen Master Sega inside in open-space.

Le Marais is a central and historic district of Paris. It is very lively both during the day by these many museums and other historical monuments and in the evening for these many bars and cafe theaters, such as the Café de la Gare and the Point-virgule. The Marais is also very well known for hosting, gathering a very important gay community. Having been approached several times, and without asking anything, I was tall, young and rather handsome, I dare not imagine what it would have been if they had known that I was a "Master Sega". This character feeding many fantasies whatever your orientations, your sexual preferences. However if I have been approached several times in the street, rather in the evening, it is most likely less than any pretty woman in the same time interval or whatever she is. The Marais district is a quiet area where people are respectful of each other. I loved this neighborhood it was full of surprises, amazing and wonderful things.

We had just settled in and we were watching a clown show right in front of the windows. Indeed we were very exactly in front of the "Point-Virgule" and at that time the artist Gustave Parking finished his show on the street! We were then in the front seats, outside working hours, many Master Sega were still there after 7pm or even 8pm and 21h. Slot where the first session of the evening of the Parisian Clown show ended.

Years later, I will meet a lyric singer who, like many in this art, was only "semi-professional" (the famous intermittent, some are more so than others!) She introduced me to a gay couple because one of them was an opera singer and he had become her friend through performances and shows. To make themselves happy and round off their end of the month, they would sing from the opera, Place des Vosges under one of the many arcades, on Sunday afternoons when it was sunny. To the delight of tourists who sometimes showed very generous. Because they sang very well. I will accompany them several times, charmed by the voice of this young woman, but not only the voice!

Regardless of my activity as a Sega Master, and even though it took me months and years to adapt, to feel really good in Paris, I was happy and still happy about all this multitude of magical encounters both by Sega and at the same time more simply by being "Parisian". The Marais was full of surprises of all kinds.

But let's get back to what you really care about!

We were six rue Barbette (maybe seven or eight?) and we would complete the team very quickly once installed in our new premises rue Sainte-Croix.

But this installation in front of the Point-and-Coma would be only a parenthesis for us. We would stay there only a few months to spend, however, the huge Christmas season, the first, which was looming. Because if we, Master Sega, let go of the pressure for a moment regarding the demographic curve and its management, the problem would quickly arise in Rue Barbette and Sega would still have to find new premises to accommodate these new employees.

Now in a suitable space and optimized for a dozen Master Sega, with a desk corner for each of us, separated from each other by thick partitions, special Hotline, that is to absorb the noises of neighbors, We could finally start our mission!

At six Masters Sega of the street Barbette, five others would come quickly to join us in this open space. Ludovic, Franck, Jean-Philippe, Olivier and Marc. By memory we were eleven. As we were also going to work on Saturday, we had to put two teams together. Who would alternatively take turns answering calls on this very important day of the week when children are not at school. Romuald our chief could not be there with us the six working days and worked of the week, he had to choose among the Masters Sega, two subordinates who would take the orders of the Hotline on Saturdays. This promotion would be accompanied by a slightly higher salary. Although it was a promotion with bonus dizzying and stumbling to the key, I did not claim this position. There were advantages but there were disadvantages. Which were not really noticeable at the time.

Romuald and Luc Bourcier, the N+1 and N+2 will discuss their choice. They will finally retain Jean-Luc and Marc. The two oldest Sega Masters. The most "respectable" therefore and probably those who will have more authority. I tell you frankly and sincerely it was the right choice. Romuald had complete confidence in Jean-Luc, he was a good old friend. And Mark had authority.

I did not imagine that this choice was, once again, the choice of the Gods. My destiny as a player! Great and passionate. And it was only a short time before it was different. Although Luc Bourcier had tried, awkwardly, to demote me on my arrival on my contract through my remuneration, my stubbornness had to seriously mark him so well that he had proposed me as "sous-chef" with Romuald. But Romuald had tipped and replied that I was the youngest, certainly too young to place my authority on people with a few years more on the clock. At least that's what he will tell me to explain his choice. Romuald is intelligent and I think he felt well. Did he imagine all the advantages? All the disadvantages? For the nominees? As for the rejected! Because I was not the only one who wasn't chosen! Lionel could have been just as well. And Fabrice the second Master historically, several months the right hand of Romuald, must certainly have eaten his brake to this non-promotion.

This choice of "Hotline manager on Saturday" had therefore passed me a few centimeters from the nose! I had a chance of Sick but I didn't know! And why friends? Well because I would very likely become, if I were not already, one of the best Sega Masters (to prove day after day, week after week, month after month, year after year...) because I was free from all obligations! No responsibility, no management to follow and to be followed, I was in pure Player, free electron. And I will become the first choice Sega Ambassador on many occasions. Trains Sega of course but also shows, public and private demonstrations, radio, TV and sometimes some very high class events, that's what I will tell you in these chronicles.

I believe in fate and I love this mischief. He sometimes gives you small blows of sticks or you might feel frustrated, hurt, humiliated, but it may also be because, eventually, he has much better, later, to offer you.

JFK, President of the United States, will one day, before being assassinated later, on November 22, this famous phrase: "And you, my fellow Americans, don't ask yourself what your country can do for you, but ask yourself what you can do for your country ..."

At Sega I never had any doubts, hesitations or moods. I was in my place. I often wondered if in marketing, communication, sales, some were in their place, retrospectively to change what else? But I was exactly in my place because when the Passion is so ardent and bright, you are always in your place! I gave without counting to Sega, and many of you through the consumer services and it was a continuous joy, an absolute happiness. And we learn it more or less quickly with time, the more we give, the more we receive. I will be one of the greatest Sega Masters for different reasons but also because you were already there to "communicate" with me! And because even 30 years later, some of you are still here to share this fantastic energy.

With eleven Sega Masters, we were thus on our way to a first and colossal season of "consumer services"! Installed each, each in our individual nests/Box made hands we were quickly put to work. The free number of the Master Sega Hotline would now be communicated everywhere and all the time! On the boxes, on the notices, in the advertisements. We were each preparing for the big landing. But we were still more than two months from Christmas. So everything will go quickly but still crescendo. We would start to get a lot of calls always after school ends, classes end and of course on Wednesdays and Saturdays. We had a good morning in the week to play quietly but also and above all to get into battle order to organize our strategies of assimilation of knowledge of the games. We were of course going to distribute them fairly because they were growing in number and will not cease to be so for several years.

Of course I continued to prefer adventure and role-playing games. Electronic Arts were out a lot and after finishing King's Bounty, Faery Tale, Might and Magic II, in addition to all the games of the genre marked Sega,

I could tackle a new challenge that will resist me, this time, several weeks: Rings of Power.

I really had a hard time, much more than Ultima 4 on Master System, because this one I will finish without any outside help. Rings of Power will test my patience, put to the test my will as my resistance. I will be marked in my mind with red iron. I had to both progress through the game, discover, unravel the plots, write a solution while the game was entirely in English and with an interface, approximate gameplay, and all at the same time answer the phone and troubleshoot all the Sega shipwrecked. It's sometimes very difficult to concentrate on both and I had to stop playing quite often.

Most action and platformer games can be played while answering the phone. But not Rings of Power, and like all games you have to understand what is being told in a language that is not yours. I had to juggle good weeks and keep all my cool to stay professional and welcoming on the phone, which remained THE priority. But this first experience of course make the job come back and burn it permanently. Because that was the Sega master: being able to help out many people on the phone while producing solutions on a complex and non-linear game, which others could use. Some of us will go to the specialized press in particular to write game solutions. Marc Andersen himself will propose to join the team of Megaforce, at Boulevard McDonald at the time, from the first issues. The Salary would be substantially better there but he did not know, he did not imagine how much I had the heart Sega. I will spend a little evening at Megapress with the then AHL, JM Destroy, Danbiss, Danboss and others to take the temperature. To be honest, I preferred the Sega one. We ended up being a kind of family.

So we were eleven ready to fight for all kinds of challenges, monsters and labyrinths. After having more or less presented the first six Sega Masters, a few words about the next five that will join us very soon rue Sainte Croix de la Bretonnerie. There was Franck and Olivier. I speak in duo, not that they formed a pair, but alas, I know very little about them. They were among the youngest of us. They will remain very discreet and even a little bit effaced! Not that they were certainly, very viscerally but (and I speak of it all the better as I could have been in their place) it was much less easy to impose themselves in a group which already began to have certain habits with strong, Sometimes very strong personalities. As in all social groups, everyone takes his place and the last arrivals have only crumbs (As in the wolf packs with the Alpha and Omega). It is then to take all the measure of the forces and energies in presence so as not to wrinkle anyone, and little by little make his nest with much patience. Although very discreet, they nevertheless had the profile of the Sega Masters. Passionate and fierce players, they will also be very good hotliners. They will never be blamed, even for their discretion, because after all, isn't the hard-working player a sort of lone wolf lurking in the shadow of a cave? We had some very social Sega Masters (like Romuald, Sandrine, Lionel...) and others much less. We probably still were like all the passionate Sega players: it was a force, a Mega force!

Marc also joined us in this Masters' return. Not really the biggest player, nor even the best hotlineur, without being bad of course, it is especially his involvement within the Hotline that will be noticed. Among the three or four older, he will quickly become a leader due to lack of competitors. Nobody in the Hotline, except him, wanted to be "Leader"! Maybe not even Romuald at his post. A true Sega Master does not feel the need to be a leader among "humans", he just wants to be the best to join, on the Sonic Mount, the other Gods of video games!

Fabrice not really a diplomat, Sandrine and I too young, Lionel a little too often casual, no it is Marc who will play the Gendarmes in the next months, the next years. Someone had to do it.

His great size and involvement will make him a perfect sous-chef of Master Romuald. I remember Marc as the man who would have beaten Henri Leconte several times!?! At the training course. He would talk to us about it for months or even years. If he had the passion of video games, she was very discreet. This is probably what will make the biggest difference between him and everyone else.

There was also Philippe of terrible memory. Our first "Dark Master" (but not the last). So without wanting to burden him more than he deserves, the relations with him were not very warm, barely cordial. Was it just because of her Hard Rock look? Metal? Heavy Metal or whatever? He was the closest of us to the form, to the television campaign of Master Sega, and yet he was out. He will take pretty much everything with a lot of lightness, too. Philippe had inspired me nothing but mistrust, he often seemed nervous when it was necessary to explain even for things without really importance. I will not share anything with this young man except this form of reciprocal reluctance towards each other, increasing over time.

A bit nervous and a heavy smoker, he was with Romuald (nobody is perfect), Sandrine and Ludovic among the four big clunkers who would create each day a thick cloud of smoke within the Hotline which, unfortunately, was not really well equipped in terms of ventilation. For weeks, months we would live almost in family, in this place arranged just for us, certainly in family but often the head fogged and with eyes that sting! Fortunately, the Evin Law was not far away and smokers will have to isolate themselves so as not to bother their colleagues or neighbors.

If my memories are also "smoky" with Philippe it is not so much by this toxic consumption and its misty character but by two major events that will unfortunately give bad reputation to the whole Hotline which did not need this as the aprioris could be numerous. Two events, two shocks even, which will probably make say and even write to Luc Bourcier, many years later that "At Sega France we were still closer to the court of miracles than to the Palo Alto Start Up" (you know, in California). If the wording is tinted with humor it remains no less condescending; but not surprising for someone condemned to look so high. I am more aware when he also talks about an army of Guerrillas ready to set fire to toy stores! Obviously the metaphor, because I assure you that it will never be anything but a metaphor, is much happier. And as much in the Sega Masters as in many of their "disciples" players, Sega was and is more like a religion than an army of mercenaries. All excess included.

The first of these two shocks, on which I will return in detail later, was probably only "cultural". On the other hand, the second will be worth to Philippe to be purely and simply dismissed, thrown out definitively.

And finally to conclude this review of the year 1991 and these Sega Masters, I also present you Ludovic. Ludo the malice! I loved Ludovic as many Sega Masters did. It was a bit of the male version of Sandrine. Always in a good mood or almost, always wanting to play, have fun, laugh, so it was a cheerful character who took very seriously his role of Master Sega. He was also very jokish and it was therefore quite complicated to know whether he told us the truth, or not, whatever the conversation, the subject. However, if he liked to joke, he was a bad liar and we could guess pretty quickly when it happened.

Dynamic, playful and full of energy, making him an excellent hotliner. But he loved to party! I also remember that he played card games in the evenings. He often came to work at the Hotline slightly exhausted by too short nights.

His "Box" was right next to mine and so I could easily hear him on the other end of the line. He was really good at his job, and his profile was perfect for those who contacted us. However, it happened that this exchange was short! Suddenly I can't hear it anymore!?! At all. Will he probably finish his call and go to the bathroom? Because if I no longer heard it, my phone did not stop ringing, he, while his remained silent. Calls are distributed evenly between the stations and then to the next station, each in turn. It was easy for me to know whether or not Ludovic was on the phone knowing that he was just before me in the transmission chain. I had already caught him "once or twice" asleep at his post. As it had happened "once or twice", I also end up noticing one day that his phone was still plugged in!?!?! Which immediately piqued my curiosity and I unplugged the headset that connected it to the telephone handset to plug in mine. And then, of course, I had to prospect for a weak and shy "Allo", not thinking for a second that... But yes and what a surprise, what a memorable memory now: A man answered me "Yes allo?"!

What a joke!!! What an enormous joke I thought!!! I then woke up Ludovic so that he could finish his work. I don't know if I will report this tiny, tiny incident to Romuald, but falling asleep on the phone, in conversation, Ludovic had done it! How many times?!? The "funniest" is that his interlocutor had not hung up! It happened "once or twice" and nobody will blame him, especially not me if I had to take those calls if he didn't take them. Ludovic the joker still had this childlike, naive, innocent and enthusiastic side. We would forgive him, all of us, all those little mistakes, these messes and these badly disguised lies. Because he was a great amuse-bouche. He was probably, outside of the certified, administrative age, the "youngest" of us.

We roamed day after day, made our weapons as we could, all very solidary to each other because we had to become real, unavoidable Masters Sega. The passion already burned us a lot, but the contact with so many children and enthusiasts sometimes even greater than us, we instilled a colossal pleasure and energy. Calls could seem repetitive at times, "you have to do up, down, left, right then ABC and start at the same time" but they always came in the day to have a small voice too cute, laughter, smiles, wink, a farce kind of "I'd like to talk to Mario please". As surprising as it may seem, it was better not to be too nice with the children on the phone because otherwise we risk immediately making us friends with whom we would end up having a conversation. And who will be tempted to remind us, remind us again. Too often.

I had a 7-year-old Pierre who, for at least one moment, called me several times a week! Imagine the number of calls he had to make to get me before I came across him, since we were a dozen on the phone. After a certain time, we quickly clarify to the most faithful of them, that we could no longer "discuss". Which they would certainly understand, so some of them will call in off-peak hours whenever possible. The Hotline is not always, every day, an easy activity because you also have to be able to manage dissatisfaction. If we were taken care of by the children, it was quite different by the adults. Some parents would yell on the phone to tell us that it was outrageous to produce a game in English even when its practice was not essential for progress.

Admissible and questionable claims but above all on another tone. What seemed very funny in this training part is to have to wait for some complain that a game was too hard, while others, and sometimes on the same day, could complain about the opposite on the same game. Finally, the difficulty was probably perfectly solved. I will come back to these many anecdotes of the Hotline.

We finished at 6 p.m. But we often stayed late and sometimes even much later. A small hard core was formed with Romuald, Jean-Luc and Me and we left most often after 19h or 20h or even 21 hours! Jean-Luc and Romuald were very good friends and they had a little moment of relaxation, relaxation and debriefing. To relieve the pressure of the day and possibly prepare for the next day. I was the only one of the Hotline to live a few meters from our mysterious lair so I was never in a hurry to go home. Nobody expected me, Jean-Luc and Romuald will become my two best friends very easily and with time excellent friends. And I can tell you now that, on reflection, my adventure Master Sega is also and above all a fantastic friendship with Romuald. We have gone through all the years, or almost, "Sega consoles" and even a little more, together 14/15 years! A real Odyssey. Many memories I wish to tell you.

It was the time of the "fines"! Eau de vie de vin? Fine Champagne? Not just alcohol like rum, Djinn or tequila. It was not so rare that we would take a bottle of alcohol to three especially on Friday, even if more often to four, five or six because the "hard core" had regularly more flesh and matter. Other Sega Masters would gladly join these improvised aperitifs according to their availability. And all, even very young, we could drink our youth more than by the only drunkenness! Because make no mistake, it was not a meeting of the alcoholics anonymous! We were just extraordinarily happy to live on our passion! Together. As a family, as a tribe, we drank three or six, this elixir of youth: The line of Master Sega.

Chapter 7
The Hotline's Pearls

We could write a complete book about the pearls of the Hotline, but not sure that you will not get tired of it quickly. We were at our peak on fourteen or fifteen lines at the same time. Able to properly process more than 300 calls per day by Master Sega, that is significantly more than 4000 calls per day.

Let's start with our charming language and speech approximations that can generate misunderstandings, misunderstandings, and therefore also laughter or smiles! The Sega Hotline was obviously an opportunity to test our knowledge of the Sega universe and therefore Sega games. But it was also an opportunity to test your language skills in English as well as "French English"! Because if we had to know the entire catalogue, we sometimes also had to know the Sega games of "John Michael Approximately" (a singer who knows only half his text) That is to say the games whose titles were not really well pronounced.

The French are not known for their knowledge and practice of foreign languages (even if it has evolved well and favorably in 30 years) we had therefore amazing pronunciations. We should have written them all down at the time, but it was so common and even trivial that sometimes we don't even pay any attention to them. So we had for example the game "Chipsnobi" in which the Shurikens were probably replaced by chips!?! Very salty! It was especially funny in live when the person tried to pronounce the title correctly and they couldn't. Of course, we forgave them all because we were far from being perfectly bilingual. Very far.

I present you a list of Sega games not found, do not look for them except in another dimension! Can you identify the original games? We had, easy to recognize, Landtalkeur, Cac Shot, Eurtworm Gym. Harder: Mitaine Magic, Spasse arrière, Hot Rune, Last Blatte, Moteur Base. And the hardest: Motte Air Motte! But the most famous, the most frequent, being without a doubt "Angon and Super-Angon". Small hint for this last game: nothing to do with the famous French singer of Indonesian origin if not maybe the swing. We also had "Ninja tea" which will be associated with "Chipsnobi" for a small snack in the afternoon.

Nothing really transcendent in the genre, at least to write it, because all the magic and hilarity of these words lies in their sound. Recording them would not have been enough, they should have been recorded in audio.

There are also games that were never pronounced the title as : "Teenage Mutant Hero Turtles: The HyperStone Heist" which will be simplified by "Tortues Ninjas", or "Where in the World Is Carmen Sandiego?"

And then there were the "too cute" calls! Really too cute. My phone rings and I answer: "Hello, it's me, Master Sega. What can I do for you?" I wait a few seconds and nothing, no answer but I hear the breath of a person. As I know that sometimes children are a little shy at the first call, I take it with a lower, slower voice! "Allooooooooooo? I am Master Sega and if you want I can help you with your game." Still no response after many seconds, but I can still hear a breath. So I repeat again: "Master Sega speaking, do you want me to help you? The third time was the right one, I hear the phone's handset falling and crashing to the ground! Then a cry, the scream of a little girl who starts to run...

"MOM, DAD, I HAVE MASTER SEGA ON THE PHONE'! I am already laughing but I stay focused and wait a few seconds, not being quite sure that this call will take. Twenty or thirty seconds pass and I hear someone take the phone handset! It's the little girl. Then I said as low and soft as possible, "Hello, how old are you? What's your name?" Finally, a response from a cute little voice: "My name is Chloé and I am 3 years old" !!!! Then "It's you Maître Sega?" It is clearly the most magical call of all my life as Master Sega. Bluffing and very moving. How did a 3 year old girl dial the number for Master Sega's line? Surely an adventurous and daring "HPI"!

We also had the calls of La cité des 4000 (A La Courneuve in 93). Many young people in this city have started calling us to tease us, especially on Wednesdays. We will never know how many they were, if they were all together in the same room, calling us each their turn or each of their side by putting a point of honor to identify themselves through their city! They were not bad but provocative. Sega "it's not right", Nintendo is better. Sonic it does not go fast, he has a small... Zip. Mario is big, he has big biscuits. Street of Rage is rotten, Final Fight is too crazy. Most of the time, it remained a child's play even if the first calls were a little more spicy. Looking back, I think it was a small group of kids who were bored. The Sega Masters offered them an opportunity to have some fun. We had dozens and dozens of calls from "The City of 4000" for several weeks, several months, they presented themselves as this. Every time one of us had one online, he would signal to the other Sega Masters: "I have the city of 4000 online"! And there were several because we would have at least two at the same time sometimes. To try to disturb us but we were totally zen because they were only children and if they did not all like Sega yet, it was likely that one day this will become the case. If they originally wanted to disturb us, we did not play their game, and the more they called us, the more we were sympathetic with them. We probably converted them otherwise to the Sega games, to the Sega hotline. Obviously after a few months, they could not, they could no longer tease us.

A monomaniac also called us regularly. He played almost only one game and what a game: Pit Fighter! A hyper violent game in "motion capture", which, from memory, had preceded "Mortal Kombat" in the ultra gore genre. He called us to perform the "combos", special attacks of all kinds! He called for tips, tricks, codes. We were quickly going around it but he did not get tired of calling us! And as I have had it myself many times and we were a good dozen...

A rough game of brut that considerably limited the exchanges with us! It is probably necessary for all tastes as for the whole sewer (Says the Master Sega who had enjoyed years before on "Barbarian" on Commodore 64!). This game was very controversial because really violent and accessible on consoles for children! It had some success but without measure with the license Mortal Kombat, to which it certainly opened the doors. Family associations will not hesitate to take the game consoles, especially Sega, to court, which they consider too violent and therefore dangerous. The same processes that other "media" experienced in their time: books, cinema, television. I will not rewrite the history but yes we had monomaniacs and unfortunately sometimes on games not really the most virtuous! Fabrice, many months later, will not fail to propose to appoint among us a "Pit Fighter specialist".

Let's go back to a little more sweetness. We had many fans of Sonic the Hedgehog and it was sure to pique the curiosity of children! And why is it blue? And why is it alone? (Sega will add many friends!) Are these beautiful red shoes that make him run at this speed supersonic? Yes the Sonic enthusiast sometimes handles the French language in the old style with elegance! Where is he going on vacation? Does he work with you? I assumed the children approaching Sonic's life outside of these playful adventures as so passionate about this incredible little creature! I would invent little stories while concluding most often, by a warning especially before leaving on vacation: "That your parents are very careful when driving on the road, not to crush it! Sonic had already lost many cousins in this way... For some of them, there is no doubt that Sonic existed somewhere. But where?

Sonic's success was unmatched and the questions about him could go well beyond the scope of the game. Although the request for help and codes on the different versions of the game, was by far, by far the first, the most important requests. The fans told us about it and asked us on the phone and some of them sent us beautiful drawings! Sometimes naughty. Moreover in the research on the subject I came across "forbidden" videos of Sonic and Amy. Imagination can feed many fantasies, especially about innocent and asexual creatures!!! A priori.

We did not provide the SAV. The technical part of consoles, failures, repairs. Not directly, in any case, we could just direct or reorient people. But it was not uncommon for us to receive calls about this. We could even "fix" their failures! When they were more imaginary than real. I've had many calls from people who couldn't get their machines to work. And for good reason, some people had not connected the console to the mains! Others had not inserted a cartridge in the slot of the console, or they had just put the cartridge on it! Some had plugged in the power, inserted the cartridge, but had not put the console on "ON" (the famous "On" of "Angon"!). I often wondered if it was a joke or a test call!?! I'll never know.

The most embarrassing calls were those that were not translated into French! There will be a lot of effort on the Mega Drive side, especially on all games with high potential, but a large number of Master System games and some Mega Drive adventure and role-playing games would remain in English due to lack of budget for translation. It was not always easy to explain it to parents who could sometimes pay substantial sums for a cartridge! On rare occasions, some parents will ask to speak with "superiors" to express their dissatisfaction. What we most often answered that we, the Sega Masters, were there to help them too. It was even one of our reasons for being and existing.

"Quackshot" with Donald: we will have many calls because a game unfortunately remained in English, presented as a platformer but with a small part "adventure" non-linear! A certain impatience of the players, who only read the notice very rarely, will force them to call Sega to know how to leave the first level! This concern will be even among the great classics of the Hotline. You had to actually pop up the menu and select "Call the airplane". " Quackshot" is a little jewel of the Mega Drive that will sell tremendously well without having benefited from a legitimate translation!?!

Sega and Nintendo it was, you know, an intense war on technology, games, communication, marketing and that passed, for many, through the most passionate players, the more attached to one brand or another! We had the pro-Segas who smashed Nintendo machines (it's for children, for babies) and vice versa the pro-Nintendo came from time to time give us little claws. A rivalry that, although it has considerably faded over time, and also with the arrival of Sony and Microsoft, still exists in some players and reminds us how this war was very exciting in places! The most brilliant attacks are mostly from video game creators who would steal their weapons as if their lives depended on it. To Mario, Sega would respond Sonic. To Zelda, Landstalker. A Final Fight, Street of Rage. Although the Super Nintendo is a little more powerful than the Mega Drive, Sega even allowed itself the luxury of beating it unquestionably on some licenses, everyone will remember "Aladdin" on Mega Drive with prodigiously fluid animation.

Because if the SNIN offered a superb 3D mode with games like F-Zero or Starfox, the battle was mainly on 2D games whether they are platforms, sports, fighting and/ or action. Obviously opinions differed significantly whether you have the blue heart or the red heart.

All this to say that we had heated conversations with both the "pro-Saga" and the "pro-Nintendo". I loved this video-playful war, not in what it could project of aggression, violence, often fake, even if the words could sometimes turn to pain (heads) but in what there was ardent passion often drawn by bad faith (on both sides of the rest...) "Sonic he is very bad, Sega games are very violent, Mega Drive games they are less beautiful...". " Mario is ugly,

Nintendo games are for babies, SNIN games are certainly beautiful but they are slow, it often slows down on the screen...".

Of course the most clever, the most passionate, and the more wealthy will have gotten out of this fight by buying the consoles of both brands. Swearing only by the quality of the games. But it was frankly less funny. We loved this confrontation so much, which will be found to have been a formidable emulation for creators and artists on both sides.

What put a little balm in our heart in this often absurd but magnificent battle, is that some of our players who played on Sega but also on Nintendo "confessed" us (were they all objective?) The Sega Hotline was much better than the Nintendo Hotline. For digging a little deeper into the subject in different ways, at Sega we had much less pressure to shape and aim our work! We had to help each player in need, but we could also give them time to share our passion. I recently saw the official figures of the Nintendo Hotline at the time, especially during very tense periods like before Christmas. They announced almost 1000 calls per day and hotliner (their record) When at Sega we would handle between 300 and 350 maximum of the maximum. A day is eight hours of work and therefore 480 minutes. We therefore devoted a little more than one minute per call (in busy periods anyway) which is more than enough to give a code, extremely short to assist a shipwreck in an adventure game! At Nintendo we did all this in less than 30 seconds!?! Claire, hotline at Nintendo for three and a half years, then "Yoda" at "Nintendo Player" (the official Nintendo mag) will say in Player One: "At the end I could not see a phone without immediately destroying the odious object".

You will draw the conclusions you want, and everyone can find a truth in it. As far as I'm concerned, I think that in the figures of Nintendo there is (or rather there was) a good part of propaganda. It's a form of amazing instinct in business: systematically inflate the numbers, at least when it suits you. At Nintendo, it was necessary to make a figure apparently.

Chapter 8
1991 Review and Balajo

The year 1991 was exceptional! For me of course, because I had joined the Hotline of the Master and I was living a kind of daydream, but also exceptional for all employees of Sega France. The whole company was now rubbing their hands. Nearly a million Sega consoles had been sold in 1991 in France. A record but also, and even more so, a rapid acceleration of sales that did not falter. Approximately 600,000 Master System, 200,000 Mega Drive and 100,000 Game Gear. But these figures could have been even more substantial as the structure of society had been flexed, without breaking down, under the weight of this acceleration which was stronger than expected and for which it was not yet perfectly calibrated.

Many difficulties had appeared in the logistic and IT: delays and errors on order preparation, unacceptable delivery times, missing deliveries, billing errors, inability to fully process telephone calls.

The teams were going quickly, and once again, doubled! The logistical capacities would certainly triple, and especially very quickly. The wind of success was blowing so strong that it was difficult to anticipate enough and correctly: putting the bar at the right level was a real challenge.

"Virgin Loisirs" had become Sega France in joy and good mood, with a wonderful seminar in Opio, an immediate and widespread significant increase in wages (I then went to 8500frs per month a few weeks after my arrival) But also in pain! Everything should be corrected in 1992: a new record year, a year as hysterical as historic we will (re) see together soon.

Let us go back to 1991. Advertising campaign signed Lintas exceptional, ascending notoriety, lightning and even stratospheric amount to 98% in some surveys (that is to say, there were only 2% of the people interviewed who had never heard of Sega. Probably in the Creuse!?!) The brand will be in the Top 5 of favorite brands behind Coca Cola.

Sega and Nintendo will be the first volume advertisers on TV at the end of the year for several weeks! Putting themselves on the same level as all car manufacturers. From memory it was almost impossible not to see a Nintendo or Sega ad in the weeks before the holidays if you watched the ads for a few minutes. Christmas 91 was announced "Japanese" and it will be more than one could have imagined. If Mario and these machines were still well ahead of Sonic and these consoles, especially thanks to the Game Boy, the plumber began to feel the hair of those moustaches rise up and tickle his nose, because its market share was falling fast, very fast. 1991 was exceptional. 1992 will be homeric!

We would celebrate, all Sega together, this very beautiful year 91 completed, on January 27, 92 (and even for some on January 28 also) at the Hilton Hotel, in the 15th arrondissement of Paris, in the "Salon Orsay" more precisely. This room can accommodate up to 400 people on 430 m 2, plus a 200 m2 fireplace with refreshments and all sorts of things to snack on and eat (later in the day). A magnificent temporary Showroom that would both make the balance of the company in a first time with all kinds of projections on a giant screen, numbers, many figures, advertisements, communication plans, objectives, past, We were all sitting comfortably so that we didn't miss anything.

All the teams of Sega France were therefore gathered exceptionally for this great mass and we could even meet the "nomadic employees" that can only be seen very occasionally at the Parisian headquarters. The sales staff from all over France, each and practically everyone, by and for a region. With however two or three sales on Paris and the Paris region! This will be one of the very few opportunities for me to meet and talk with them.

They will be the stars of this seminar because warmly congratulated and generously rewarded! By a very rich and probably very "corporate" applause, coupled with more concrete gifts for having reached and even exceeded their goals! Management would thank them one by one in front of all the other employees: BRAVO BRAVO!!!

The best performers will win a trip abroad and various rewards. This ceremonial seemed to me more than deserved in view of the Christmas performances. These sales were my new heroes! Time for an evening! They were out there fighting tirelessly to bring out Sega, the consoles and all these exciting games that are overwhelming a growing number of homes.

These awards marked the end of the "Presentations, Various and Varied Information" part! Now for refreshments and entertainment! We could then slowly slide from our chairs to canapés! But this time, to taste! Refreshments were not lacking and the Champagne could flow generously. Stars in my eyes and bubbles in my head, I didn't miss the opportunity to approach some Sega salesman. Far from being a drama, I was not recovering from the lack of passion of some men and women in marketing. So I thought I'd make up with the sales people. FINALLY! Some of them played and sometimes they even loved it! Not as much as the Sega Masters, but they appreciated what they were selling. It was a very nice moment and we were very happy about what we were doing and probably what we would do. Except that... I was far from imagining that these sales would be so loose! (Thank you the Ruinart! Thank you the widow Clicquot or I do not know what other bubbles dosed... You will have them well pushed!)

So I do not know if it was false modesty but the two or three salesmen, including "the Parisian", with whom I will talk, will confess to me that in reality they probably had no merit! Because the "products" sold themselves, like buns. Finally they did not boost the offer personally because the demand was enough and even grew a little faster than anticipated! We had a lot to do with a tsunami on the demand side.

Even more surprising, but this time it may not have much to do with Sega, the sales people told me that they were going even soft, TRES soft. And that, at the very least, they were even using all four of their brakes to avoid overshooting their targets. The ideal is to make 105/110% of the goals and no more! Why? Because by doing a little more, but not too much, you have done your job, you are warmly thanked and you receive a bonus (and even a big bonus in more kind of travel all expenses paid if you are the best among the best). On the other hand if you make 120 or 130% you are also thanked but not more! The turnover, the objectives you have achieved this year will be used as a reference year next year. And so we will have to do more to get these bonuses! Here is a strange system, apparently generalized in the business, which pushes to do enough, certainly, but especially never too much!? Frankly I fell on my ass. As if the market console and video games in thermal-nuclear explosion could be so finely and wisely calibrated!?! I would learn the same, but much later, that there was also a logistical problem, which I reported a little earlier, which probably also impacted the flow of sales for this Christmas. Until then I thought that we should beat the iron while it was hot, but not too apparently.

It was very nice, for the very young rookie I was, to discover some of the threads of this business. Even if sometimes I will fall naked. But all these little things more or less amazing are not unique to Sega. Far from it. Even in the biggest, best known and strongest global companies, you can find things that are as amazing or even more amazing. Because ultimately, we are only "men"! Except maybe to become a myth, a legend like "Master Sega"?!

But we would not only discuss Sega in this long evening that was coming! It was time for everyone to enjoy themselves and the environment was generous. The champagne was pouring, the canapés were lying down and piled up at the bottom of our throat, everyone was more or less letting go, and as very often, according to his level of responsibility! Authority and credibility, of course.

It was not very late and the management offered to all who wanted to continue and finish the evening at the Balajo. The legendary dancing bar near Bastille in the 11th arrondissement. Most of the Sega Masters will move there without making old bones! Because we were on Thursday night and the next day we had to go back to work. Especially since to have gone there early enough (21? 22h?) there was not a big atmosphere, because of the lack of people, but arrived numerous, we would change all this quite quickly.

While most of the Sega employees won't be there for long, there were a few who wanted to enjoy this party night. I did not have to take public transport to return because the Marais touches the Bastille district and so I could also stay a little longer without worrying too much about the return. My colleague Maître Sega and friend Jean-Luc, being in the suburbs and quite far from Paris, had asked me the day before if he could come to sleep at my place, which I replied favourably, indicating that I had a sofa convertible into a double bed and an extra mattress. In the effervescence of the evening, in a semi-darkness and while our alcohol rate had seriously risen, all so that our minds fade away and our bodies come closer on wild rhythms, I had seen nothing of probable or improbable connections related to our "genetic programming of semi-reproduction".

Jean Luc was a handsome guy, with a natural charm, relaxed and smiling like George Clooney. In the evening he had probably more or less alpaguated a young woman from Sega France. The Balajo is a dancing bar, not a nightclub, so closing at 1am? Maybe 2am at most. The dancing evening ended at the very moment when we had become many to be very cheerful, very festive and probably already too drunk (in this order or another of course...). As we knew each other (Jean-Luc, the young woman and I) that it was getting late and that the young woman did not necessarily live next door either, Jean-Luc had this sudden and very opportune idea to offer him to come and sleep at my place! Because there were three places! The young woman hesitated for a few seconds: and like her, would you have felt some kind of trap? Before you accept! Our ability to discern, as you know, is seriously impaired under such conditions. Situation of the most impromptu certainly but friendly (it is beautiful naivety still) even fraternal, confusing and confusing situation but how could I have refused when it was an opportunity to insert myself more in this society that had already given me much!

Finally, in solidarity, I accepted without a second of doubt the trap in which I had fallen! We walked back from the Balajo to 6 Rue Elzévir. A little fresh air did us great good. We were still in levitation, in full flight, intoxicated with bubbles and irresistible music that continued to carry us, so light, although the trajectories seem a little less obvious.

When I arrived in my small apartment, a studio with exposed beams according to the consecrated formula, especially in the "Marais", I proposed to the young woman to sleep on the mattress that I was arranging, Jean-Luc and I would both sleep on the sofa. We laid down quietly, ready to receive and embrace Morpheus; who would come again to free me from a most ridiculous situation. The calm, the silence, absent for hours and hours, had irresistibly settled. I couldn't believe my eyes but for weeks or months, everything had become a little crazier and I probably had to start by getting used to it.

As I was inexorably sinking, through Hypnos the god of sleep, into the kingdom of his son Morpheus and upon a mountain of soft cushions, I was suddenly torn away and recalled by a rumbling but familiar voice.

What had happened in Jean-Luc's head? Had an old demon taken possession of it? He had not fallen asleep, quite the contrary, because he enjoined Catherine (we will call him so to preserve his reputation even if there is surely prescription) to come and find us in bed!?!

Did he forget that we were already there two? There was no room for three? Maybe it was cold and we could squeeze? Still between two worlds, I did not understand the situation as it was, but everything would become clear in a few words. Jean-Luc will then say something about "Listen Catherine, you have heated me, you turned me on all evening so now you come..."

Enormous confusion as far as I was concerned! I had not seen anything, I was totally foreign to this matter, and especially they did not see me!? Or so little. Ready to dress up and leave them alone: explain! But I will go or at the same time now that everything is closed?

Catherine's beginnings and attempt to defuse a situation that could really go into the dummy... In the literal sense. She was really and sincerely embarrassed but for whom? For what?

"Heh... yes yes but good; we drank, had fun, that's all" !

Jean-Luc does not seem convinced and lists everything she has done, everything she has told him. Finally, she had turned it on, but was it really with all her reason? Or another one, well drunk, discovering uncontained intentions, almost animal and letting themselves be overcome by these words?

Because we had walked for a moment, because we had taken the air, because she had probably come back more to earth, Catherine had regained her lucidity and a certain modesty. She then continues, not to deny her attitude during the evening, but to relativize it under the influence of the lightness and intoxication of this exhilarating moment. She seemed really embarrassed and felt also, most certainly a little trapped! A great confusion was setting in for her, as for me!

What was Jean-Luc actually proposing? A three-way plan? Or should I sneak away quietly so they can settle their differences somehow. I was totally dumbfounded! Jean-Luc saw that she was retreating completely or even permanently, so he took it a step further and attacked again.

"Good Catherine, you have to take it. You can't turn someone on so much in one evening and then tell him after that it was just for fun! Too much is too much, I don't like it. You're making fun of me... You're making fun of me REALLY!"

He plays the guilt card very clearly, but sincerely. Which seems legitimate except to take into account our blood alcohol level. Whatever it is, it works! He makes her feel guilty but it does not take anything away from the confusing and uncomfortable situation of the moment, because they are not alone! I'm here and right here! " Yay! Here I am, friends! It's my home..." I thought". Only... Apparently Jean-Luc had not calculated me at all except to be, perhaps, an amateur of "threesome"!?!

Catherine seems lost, she even starts to cry under the pressure and tension. She got herself in a complicated situation or probably a little voice keeps telling her that it's great! That she has been looking for it... And another who tells her that all this is grotesque, that we must stop everything because it's nonsense. What will we say? What will we think of it?

Endless minutes of negotiations will follow, a real battle of strength on which Jean-Luc will not let go. He will "work" her without malice, just insisting on the responsibility of our actions and words. She had to take them!

So much so that Catherine finally frees herself from this tension and then proposes something completely unexpected but salutary! Neither of them had calculated me. They were trying to settle their case and I was still, at that moment, a witness! Always a little stuttering and embarrassed by the situation without being petrified, she says that she can not, she has never done it like this. It's too much for her, and she is scared! And I understood her so well that I would have liked not to be there myself. After maybe twenty, thirty minutes of procrastination and psychodrama, Catherine finally lets go! And she offers nothing more and nothing less than... From...

"Start" with me!?! " Ok Jean-Luc you won, but I start with Pascal!"

You will probably think, rightly or wrongly, that I am playing the victim. I assure you that at no time did I have a say! And now this employee and colleague of Sega was proposing a sexual relationship without, at any time, I could think about it, much less want it!?!

I confess to you that I imagined a few seconds a parody of "threesome" and it totally horrified me! A threesome, ladies and gentlemen, I probably won't say no, but as, a little, all men, I imagine, it would be preferably with two charming young women! Not with a hairy man from everywhere... All George Clooney he could, or seemed to be! Frankly, I was not and still am not. Catherine had just saved me from a situation that repulsed me even if Jean-Luc was, and certainly remains, handsome man: very little for me! I was very surprised by the turn of events but it came as a liberation. This Catherine offered herself to me, to myself alone without my having asked her, and she made Jean-Luc disappear for a few moments. Even if he had stayed right next to it. I pass you the trivial details about this totally improbable relationship but it happened what happened and without too much effort!

We would only talk about it to very few people and our lives would then resume as if nothing had happened. For me it was a deviation, an alteration of reality, a parallel timeline that had slipped on my natural line under the effects of alcohol. No denial, I know that everything had happened but I was mostly a spectator, privileged perhaps but a viewer as in a dream, a little more realistic.

I also assumed that it was a patent or a rite of passage from the life of a young provincial to that of an adult Parisian, all the more so living in the Marais (Although we all know that there are also many things of the kind and even in the most remote villages of France!) Being Master Sega reserved me many surprises and "new games" I did not imagine.

Chapter 9
The Sega Train 1992

In this fratricidal war between the two Japanese giants, Sega would win several important battles! In Japan, the USA, Europe, France: sometimes at the same time and sometimes at different times, on different consoles. We would have great battles and we would even have our own Austerlitz! That we could still celebrate years, decades later.

There were the slogans, the communication that hit wonderfully in 1991 at the most opportune moment: "Sega is stronger than you" ! Suddenly and miraculously, a very mysterious "Master Sega" comes out of his torpor, projected into the spotlight, and into that of millions of televisions. A hot advertising campaign that will inspire envy and jealousy from other Sega subsidiaries around the world! With the exception of perhaps just as great American slogan: Sega Does what Nintendon't. To be compared also with the "Viva una aventura: Sega" of Spain or "To be this good takes AGES, To be this good takes SEGA" in the United Kingdom.

The French communication agency Lintas had found a magic lamp and apparently will not lend it to these European neighbors. Because of this lamp was a Genius, until then totally unknown except for some subscribers of the Sega Club often passionate about "Master System". A Genius who could almost grant all the most cherished wishes of the players! Dreams indeed! But mostly challenges and sometimes nightmares. Almost everyone rushed to face this Genius with a cavernous voice (Patrick Borg at first, then Richard Darbois the comedian who will lend his voice to Harrison Ford/Indiana Jones in these films, in the versions dubbed in French). Sega had landed a huge "Mega Direct" right in the face of Nintendo that had been quite dozing for years, purring on its high golden mountain, dotted with peaceful games and good-natured!

This direct right-wing violation that severely struck the holder of the title would be followed by a surprising because unexpected left-wing direct even if some bad languages may speak of plagiarism. I want to talk about the Sega Train! A Trafalgar hit, a Master shot, a Genius shot, which, if he did not knock out Nintendo, would seriously damage it! Some "Nintendo players" will take the hit on the spot, at "the enemy", a little disappointed. And may be ready to switch from one side to another.

Yes of course, in front of the Sega Train, there was the Nintendo truck. A "Super Tour 92" inspired by the "USA Nintendo Tour" which eventually Sega will also be inspired. But so much better and especially so "Sega" (Faster, further, stronger... The firm of Sonic will also be the official sponsor of the Barcelona Olympics). The Super Tour 92 to promote the launch of the Super Nintendo, it is Alain Milly, probably the best technician of SOS Nintendo at that time and the "King of Classeurs", as well as four or five other animators who will visit dozens of cities with many Game Boy and Super Nintendo demo booths. They will even go on the beach tour during the summer, a ten-month adventure where Alain and his colleagues do just about everything on site. Installations, cleaning and disinfection (Only installations! Not colleagues!!!) demonstrations, competitions and security! A beautiful and great odyssey but also trying and smelling as Alain Milly will report years later. This adventure will not be repeated the following year but this opposition between Sega/Train and Nintendo/camion will mark 1992 as the year of the mother of battles between the two Japanese, protruding their torsos ostensibly dressed of Mega Drive/Sonic for one and of Super Nintendo/Mario for the other. Sega you all know will not win the war, but he will have put his opponent to ground and the regular at least that year on the front 16bits.

Sega France had therefore taken to its advantage this formula of nomadism and direct encounter with these passionate players. The Truck is already taken, Sonic and his gang will take the train! A train all in the colors of the Japanese firm, a convoy in the colors of Sonic. "Sega is stronger" and the Train, it's much stronger than a truck, and it's especially much faster. Sega had managed in a short time, almost in a hurry, to cut the grass under the foot of Nintendo, counterattacking and surpassing its rival. At least on the form: the battle of the Image with the general public, which, mostly, would not move for one event, neither for the other, was largely won. The Sega Train would remain forever stronger than the "van" Nintendo. The Sega

Slogan will then be more symbolic and more, day after day, week after week, month after month, year after year: Mythical!

This convoy fell as a gift from heaven by tens of thousands of children and adolescents, will cross the 23 largest French cities to meet the general public. Event supported by an important national advertising campaign relayed by NRJ and Canal +. Sega will welcome at the station from 10am to 9pm all visitors wishing to discover the world of the brand, with French and foreign novelties and on the Mega CD. They will also be able to test the Master System, Mega Drive and Game Gear consoles. More than 200,000 visitors were expected, and will come!

For the passionate fans, Sega reserves a whole car at the biggest score contest ever made on the master system and the Mega Drive with two Sega Hits: Monaco Grand Prix and Sonic. Every day more than 40 competitions will take place with thousands of gifts to win (pins, T-shirts, caps, cups...)

Each city crossed would invite its four winners to defend the title of champion of France in Paris during the French final which will take place in May. The winner of this French final, (who will be "Fabrice", a very Maître Sega name, a young Parisian of 17 years old) would then go to Barcelona in July 92, at the time of the Olympic Games, to challenge the other European countries and win may-be the European Champion title.

The train was made up of several cars. Four of them in the colours of Sega. In the front, just behind the locomotive, you had both cars. A queue would form all day to access the different sessions of these contests. More or less experienced players will compete on Sonic or Monaco Gp. The next two were demonstration cars. The Sega universe, in showcases, consoles including the Mega-CD, the Game Gear and its TV Tuner that worked perfectly and often aroused admiration (the tuner will never officially be released in France), and some free practice games in another car with new releases as "McDonald Global Gladiator», «Fatal Fury», «Tiny Toons Adventures» or even the fabulous... "Flashback"! Moonwalker, Sonic, Stret of Rage, Mickey Mouse and Donald Duck on Game Gear will complete this free practice. In order to keep the traffic of passionate players flowing, the power was cut every ten minutes. Two or three arcade machines were also present in this discovery space whose the much appreciated "Rad Mobile", a car racing game, or a small Sonic was hanging and swinging under your nose when you drove! There was also the fighting game Arabian Fight.

A second queue would form all day and we let people, players and their parents in more or less depending on the external pressure but they had plenty of time to discover everything without being able to play all the games presented. The visit was relatively short but it was enough to amaze the children for a moment. Time to discover a game that had not yet been released on console, or time to try out Rad Mobile or Arabian Fight.

And then for the connoisseurs, the initiates, for the faithful of the Sega Club, there was also "Master Sega" in this demonstration car; in flesh and bones and who would welcome them! Club members will not have to queue in a car or another when they present their Club card: an advantage, a privilege that they will not forget even 30 years later. Some "faithful among the faithful" in procession, who would meet their "high priest" of the video game!

It was at that moment that I understood that we, the Sega Masters, were, at least for many of them, worshipped, even revered for a smaller number. The little 7-year-old Pierre who often called us on the line of Master Sega, had come to see me with his Mom and Dad. He who was so talkative on the phone, could not get a sound out of his mouth when he saw me! He did not dare to lift his head to look at me, he was very, too intimidated. Probably crushed by too many emotions, all at once, for such a young boy. But so happy, obviously. It was a very emotional moment, I could have been in his place if I had been his age and lived it the same way. I will never forget this seven-year-old Pierre, who alone symbolized everything that I loved to be and do in this wonderful custom suit that I had been given to try on, wear and never leave. Him and the little 3 year old "Chloé": you are dressed for several centuries! I was most likely a kind of hero for him! An older brother?

Between the Gods of Video Games (Creators like Philippe Ulrich or Eric Chahi for France at the time, but especially the Miyamoto or Yu Suzuki in Japan), the Giants that could be confused with the managers because they never run out of air (producers like Sega, Nintendo, Capcom, Konami), the Cyclopes, making the lightning of Zeus but a little too often blinded by the sun (marketing and communication) and the simple mortals (the players are becoming more and more numerous and passionate), between those who lived hidden, withdrawn from the world of humans, on top of the highest mountains, and those who lived down in the green valleys, there were "Demigods".

For those from above, they were nothing more than bastards (Of Zeus all the same! Most often), unfortunate hybridizations, unwanted, pariahs who lived below. But it was precisely for those below that the situation was quite different, a point of view that is bound to be. They were supermen, almost gods who would still have to fight again and again to try to rise up to the level of Papa Zeus. We, "Masters Sega" were demigods for children and young teenagers because we could tutoyer, from time to time, the real Gods of video games and especially... We could challenge them, face them! More simply have fun with them! Again and again. Because we knew where, when and how to find them! We had all the keys. Game Over? No never! This is the whole of Master Sega's Mythology and some of us will carry it for eternity as the Titan Atlas will carry on his shoulders the celestial vault. To the questions "What happened to the Sega Masters?" "Do they still play"? "At what level"? "Master Sega one day, Master Sega always"? You will have to be patient, very patient...

Half-gods probably (to each his culture, his lexicon, his poetry, his imagination, his lyricism), the Sega Masters were also, and have perhaps remained, a link between two worlds, two unconciliable universes. It was one of my first shocks when I discovered Sega's marketing. Alumni of HEC, MBAs, Sup de co and all other major business schools had invested in all strategic levels of communication and marketing. I had nothing against them at first but I was very surprised that none of them are "gamer"! Even a little? Just I will take it from Luc Bourcier, director of marketing, that he had played Tetris! Maybe as much as I had smoked cannabis!?! Curiosity is not a bad flaw! Or did he play other games, like a duet during lunch break with Olivier Creuzy? Or Florence Cornillon? But perhaps they were too ashamed to admit it!?! We will never know the truth about it.

It will be necessary to wait for the Saturn to see appear the "first players of consoles of great schools"! With Cédric Maréchal who will make a very good career (still today) in the video game industry. Cédric was almost as passionate as a Sega Master! And it made me very happy and my heart would warm to see this kind of profile land. Among enthusiasts, from Sega, he even let me write several summaries (pitch) of Sega games, on Saturn, adventure games and role-playing games that were found at the back of the game boxes. The literal translations were frankly not good! From Japanese to English, from English to French, they were often hollow, without souls. Knowing the games to have them even most often finished before they come out in official version, I could breathe energy into them, the strength that these games deserved. Even if we have to admit it, these pitches were rarely read! A big thank you Cédric, a small gift but a great pride!

But before Cedric, and if we exclude Jean-Luc Satin who, without being a player, was sufficiently playful and with a lot of naturalness as talent, had caught the air of time (probably thanks to his proximity to Romuald), I felt good, and I will obviously not be the only one, There was a cultural gap between hotline and marketing. However, it was not necessarily much bigger than the one that separated at the time, players and non-players! Don't count on me to vilify people in marketing and communication. They were doing their work with the training that was supposed to be the best, and certainly the best. To sell games, soap or phones! It is precisely because things were as they were then that I could and could take this place, My place. As a trait of union between two worlds not really compatible! One closer to "The Miracle Farm" and the other closer to "a Start up da Palo Alto". We all have one leg a little longer than the other.

But let's return to the Sega Train. These gods, who were and always will remain with me: as long as I believed in them! Of the five weeks of the first Sega train, I will make two and I will be the only one to make two. The first and last one thus covering all of Western France. Romuald, and most likely Luc Bourcier, had given me their full confidence. I was really very honored, very proud but especially mega-super content! Sandrine will be one week, I don't remember who will do the other two!?! Romuald will be but in 93 it seems to me.

We will start in Paris Montparnasse, the capital, and the Sega train will logically stop there two days on 11 and 12 April. Then the 13th will be Rennes, the 14th in Caen, the 15th in Rouen. I was part of a team of professional facilitators, young people aged 20 to 30, a mixed team, some knew each other, others not but the mayonnaise would take quickly because everything would contribute to its success even if Paris had to wipe the plaster with a record affluence that will give cold sweats to security. It was the commotion, limit bousculade at the very beginning but this first weekend the busiest close to chaos would allow to organize definitively well in the regional metropolises.

The train was therefore made up of four cars in the colours of Sega but others were reserved for the animators and some technicians from the SNCF who would accompany us to move the train from one city to another. They were old "hotel" cars but luxurious (at least in their time) like Pullman cars, very known with the mythical Orient-Express. The compartments, the rooms were entirely wooded. It was beautiful although a little out of sync with the world of video games. It would be both an unforgettable trip in space but also time with this retro frame. We didn't sleep particularly well in these cars of another age, it was cracking everywhere, all the time, but it was unusual to wake up in a decoration dating from the roaring twenties. I had the extreme privilege of having a room/compartment just for me! This train would have been used many times for film shoots. A plaque was engraved in the most beautiful car of the train: that of the restaurant for breakfasts. This car was used as a set for Jean Paul Belmondo in one of these films ("L'Heritier" in French"). All in wood of course, we had a 180° panoramic view because this car was the last one on the train. It was sensational, it emanated from this magical place so many energies, vibrations. And we would have breakfast every morning together for a light brunch that was served to us. I don't remember for lunch, but in the evening we all went together, all the animators, to a restaurant near the Train Station of the moment.

The only drawback for these cars of another age is that we could not move them quickly. They were not planned to exceed the 100 kms/hour, I even believe that to preserve them the SNCF would move them only at 60kms/h. So to move from one city to another, we would move at night certainly but a fortiori when there was no traffic. The movements often took place in the middle of the night from 2 or 3 o'clock in the morning and before the SNCF traffic resumed. The train was not very quiet and especially we were often not bad swung from one rail to another. Small minor inconveniences that would not spoil this wonderful adventure! I will go to bed in Paris for the first time and wake up in Rennes. I will go to bed in Rennes and wake up in Caen, etc. It was just magic and I won't forget those moments later when I would travel by myself in Europe via night trains.

We did the animations between 10am and 9pm. We wore a very nice grey sweatshirt with the colors of Sega and especially the colors of Sonic, who had his logo created especially for the occasion. The animators all had a K-way Euro challenge 92 (which I wouldn't have!?!) I had no other task than to represent the brand and welcome the enthusiasts in the discovery cars of the Sega consoles. I will be asked about the Mega-CD, its release, these games, its capabilities. It was a lot of dreaming, at least at that time. It was an important technological leap with games in filmed and interactive sequences like Night Trap or Tomcat Halley, very spectacular. Not to mention the sound quality that was close to perfection. The Mega-CD was a magnificent showcase for the Mega Drive and would certainly maintain sales of the latter at a very good level compared to the Super Nintendo.

I continued to do my job as Master Sega but this time in Live and flesh and blood among the players! It was like a kind of apotheosis after only a few months at Sega. I was at the heart of the most important event in the Sega sphere. I was among the most passionate players, I Sega Master passionate between enthusiasts! I was a bit like the Pope in St. Peter's Square, or Taylor Swift in concert. It is a bit exaggerated certainly but all the children knew and feared "Master Sega" ! However they did not know his face.

They will ask me very few autographs, they will only take very few pictures of me, with me (smartphones did not exist) on the other hand the less shy children will ask me very often or systematically how we could become Master Sega! My very presence, my existence, before them, lit hundreds of stars in their eyes and it was a great happiness to be able to trigger even more fervour and passion. Yes it is possible, this is not a dream! You can satisfy your passion like no other and in addition be paid for it! They would have liked to be me, at least... Being in my place of course! The dream of a whole generation. I can never thank enough all those who made these wonderful moments possible. The dream continued and intensified!

Apart from the passages of the Sega executives in Paris Montparnasse, I will then be on tour, the most important person of the Sega Train for all children and teenagers presenting! Even if their attention was focused on a need to discover, play and sometimes even win! I didn't really realize it at the time, because I just wanted to do my job properly and my shyness, my youth, made me still very modest. It is this timidity and youth that will make me live so intensely this unique and exciting adventure! The "big timid" are known to be also the greatest adventurers so everything can seem more difficult or even impossible for them. But in this particular context I was in my element. I will never be more.

Although very largely occupied by the animation in the train, I could make micro-visits of cities crossed! Especially during the lunch break. I had the pleasure of discovering the surroundings of the Rennes train station, and I have a very good memory of it. As I will have a good memory or even an excellent one later on of Limoges, Angers and especially Nantes. I will discover in the latter the Tramway, very close to historical monuments, wonderful public transport that would still take many years before reinvesting Paris. This being the surroundings of the Stations are not necessarily the most touristic and therefore the most attractive places in a city. The last city-stage I will cross, Orleans, will not excite me so much. My first week from Paris to Rouen was ending and I will return to Paris three weeks before joining the train, by plane, in Bordeaux. I will then do Limoges, Nantes, Angers, Le Mans (where I had already passed for the world championships of Karting) before concluding by Orleans.

If meeting, talking, exchanging, sharing were pleasures constantly renewed with children, adolescents and sometimes adults, many hours each day, my little solitary pleasure was to buy me my Consoles + and devour it in my cabin, almost in secret!!! Outside working hours, the team was still mostly whole, gathered for dinner outside, or in the breakfast car, which also acted as rest rooms while drinking tea or coffee, Which was a great limitation on privacy. My Consoles + had become my best friend, my confidant, the one who brought me back to my life before! Not that everything that happened around me displeased me, quite the contrary, but it was a lot of emotions, adrenaline and I needed, very naturally I suppose, to purge myself! To clear my head! And for that nothing better than these little moments of pleasure to oneself, nothing but oneself! No phone, no internet: The Adventure certainly! With a magazine in the role of "doudou"!

In the May issue of the magazine (which I will read between Bordeaux and Orleans) there would even be a report on the Sega train and this debut in Montparnasse! I was in the magazine, in its news!!! And also outside browsing it, to discover it!?! Disturbing, disconcerting, as if I were on both sides of the mirror!!! But it was also very joyful.

Chapter 10

1992 and Guadeloupe

If 1991 had been exceptional, 1992 would be just as exceptional and perhaps even more so. The management of Sega had even offered some kind of bonuses of returns at the end of the year, to the Masters Sega, for the most assiduous, the most friendly, the most efficient on the phone and also outside the phone: discover, test a maximum of games, make solutions... A very nice carrot of several thousand francs to get that accompanied another carrot even more exciting. As of the beginning of September, we were offered all the Sega games that we published and distributed. Dozens and even hundreds of games (finally) that will be offered to us free but with, implicitly, the duty to play during and after work. Each game was sold 200, 300 or even 400 frs per unit! I let you calculate the advantage in huge nature that we had. In my case, and from the beginning (we had some games but not all) it was mostly huge savings, since I didn't have to pay anything more to satisfy my passion. I remember a Friday in November when we went home with about thirty games at once! You had to have large bags to bring them all at once.

From 14 to 18 years old, I was in the arcades (Ghouls'n Ghost, Rastan Saga, Black Tiger and many others). All my pocket money and summer jobs' wages were spent there. At 17, unable to break into arcade machines I decided to start breaking into Mega Drive games. There would be no more money left but I built a fortune in game cartridges! Fortunately for me, I will eventually enter Sega! And I will finally discover that you can buy something other than video games. I will then buy, and like Romuald, tons of Laserdics, but never as much as he.

At that time, Sega was still distributing almost all the Mega Drive games. Third party publishers will be emancipated one after the other and it will be a very big loss for me and every Sega Master player and collector. American publishers like Acclaim, EA and Activision at first, then unfortunately, a hundred times alas, but later, the Japanese as Konami or Capcom. Fortunately 92 as 93 were rich, very rich in outputs and we have certainly all invested in a new library! I still have a good package, a real treasure for collectors, even if from the "retro-gamers" of the first hour, visionaries!?! They took some of the best copies from me.

They will offer me, like others at the Hotline later on, to get away and join the editorial team of a specialized magazine, like Megaforce with which we were very close. Significant increase in salary at the key, I will decline the offer for different reasons but especially because they could not offer me this extraordinary advantage in kind and tax free! Being paid was and remained almost incidental for me, even though, of course, it had to be possible to pay these bills.

More than ever in 1992: we were passionate, we had nothing to pay, all the Sega games were given to us, we discovered them before anyone else, exclusively. We accumulated almost unlimited games and knowledge. The codes, the tricks, the solutions, we infusions, Sega masters overpowered day after day we became!

New Sega masters joined us during the year: Richard Homsy, Damien Lebigre and Jean-Philippe R as well as Dominique Roux. The first one will not stay with us for very long, he will quickly join "Consoles +" and sign these articles under the pseudonym "Spy". I have a very good memory of Richard. He was passionate, intelligent, good sense of humor, sociable, all to be an excellent Master Sega, which he will have been, but he would prefer a more journalist work in which he will fully flourish many years.

Damien and Jean-Philippe were two well educated young men, well behaved and with unquestionable eloquence. They arrived together, they knew each other and will form a duo almost inseparable! They were perfect for the job because simply passionate, curious, very sociable... They will not make old bones either and will leave more or less at the same time carried by other winds.

Dominique Roux was a real alien! Not really a very great player he was on the other hand really very friendly, calm, peaceful, attentive, kind what! But I often wondered, talking to him, if he was completely with us or if part of him was elsewhere!?! Connected to a parallel world! His spirit did not always seem to be with us in the present moment! A little bit perched? In the Lunar star or further still? Mystery!!! He and Jean-Luc will eventually go to Cryo, join Jean-Martial Lefranc and Philippe Ulrich.

In September 1991 we had the Club Med at Opio to celebrate Sega France and Sega Europe, early 92 we had the Hilton and the Balajo and well to celebrate the success of the year 92 we would go this time in Guadeloupe! Three days of seminars! All Sega employees are invited to go roast the pill under the sun of the West Indies with unlimited fruit cocktails! Dream, dream again, only dream! 92 so rich in emotions with the Train Sega, interviews on TV, radio, sometimes events like the salons, Super Game Show of course, private parties for La Fnac, TF1, the BHV, Printemps, Piaggio... Sega was the news and we occasionally, but always opportunely, went out of their cave some Masters Sega to meet this growing public, to bring passion, more passion even further, always higher. And I often had, with Romuald, the best pieces.

The Passion, the key word, we can never say it enough! And that is how we would hear the call of these fruits: Maracuja as it is called in Guadeloupe. Papaya, Dragon Fruit, Cinnamon apple, mango, watermelon, carambola, pineapple, guava and many other exotic fruits would all try to make a small place in the bottom of our glasses.

So I don't know if you all know, well, the Antilles? Guadeloupe, Martinique, Sainte Martin, Saint Barthélémy... Well, maybe I'm wrong? Maybe it's just a cliché of a "guided" tourist but it seemed to me much easier to find rum than water!?! I actually wondered for a moment if we could have water? In hotels, in clubs, mineral water must be more expensive than a glass of rum?!? And when you ask for a fruit cocktail, we certainly put some fruit juice but it's only an alibi to make you drink rum! A dose of fruit, two doses of rum! The hand of the natives always seemed heavy enough?

I am "addicted" to sugar but compared to the "Outremers", I am really a small player! Everything is much sweeter. In the West Indies as well as in Reunion. They can't eat our metropolis yoghurt or drink our fruit juices: they're not sweet enough! And for good reason, living in tropical countries offer fruits of an unmatched freshness all year round and formidably sweet. But the local industry must certainly still add sugar. In fact, it is a certainty.

So they serve cocktails with a little fruit and lots of rum! If you do not pay attention to the dosages, you are cooked in two or three glasses, especially if you are on a market with the sun at the zenith. Finally, all this to say that in Guadeloupe you have tons of tasty and fruity fruits and they make delicious cocktails. But if you let the locals dose you every time, I believe that you can die in less than 24 hours and if you traditionally drank little.

We were going to spend three/four days of dreams (three nights) in the Caribbean in a beautiful hotel where everything would be taken care of and we would only have to discreetly raise our hand to be served... Rum! At will, with a little fruit in it anyway.

Sega teams will leave, half, half, in two different planes as is the custom, for safety reasons. It was my first international flight and I was actually excited as a chip but I was certainly not the only one.

As we were not leaving for very long, I had not really cared about the local weather conditions! Had I just thought about taking a pair of sunglasses. No sunscreen or cap, bob, headgear and I will pay very expensive on site but especially when I return. The plane trip went very well, take off and landing without any problems but it is always very fun, as far as I am concerned, to observe the heads of colleagues in these moments that may seem to some "critics"! Because most aircraft accidents happen during the take-off and landing phase. A widespread neurosis that does not rely on much as the chances are low! Extremely low! The only time I would have a little apprehension when getting on a plane will be a few days after the attacks of September 11 in 2001 leaving for the island of Reunion. Fortunately, that day, for this long crossing, they had the excellent idea of proposing, to broadcast "Amélie Poulain" which I saw for the first time, in the small screens inserted in front of each seat. I remember thinking at the end of the film that if I did "jump" like all the other passengers, it would be with one last nice vibration. It does not prevent that take-off, let alone land always give very strong sensations, intense emotions that will remain engraved in a corner of your memory.

Arriving at the airport of Pointe à Pitre, we were immediately seized by the heat but also and especially by the humidity. Who is not accustomed, will feel, neither more nor less than suffocation. It's a little better outside with the air and wind circulation but the tropical climate grieves you in the throat to the proper as figuratively. You end up not thinking about it and getting used to it. Once all landed, luggage collected, we will be transferred by bus to our hotel in a cheerful atmosphere led by some sweet agitators including Jean Luc Satin and Franck Licois ("bout en train" manager of the PLV and who had done me a good service when I arrived in Paris) and to a lesser extent Romuald, Lionel, Sandrine. We were still far from the atmosphere of the Bronzés but we would soon serve "fruit juice cocktails"!

The first day will be quickly closed, we arrive in the evening at the Hotel with a first small tropical rain. Nothing that is harmful or bad omen on the contrary, because the stay will be very and fully sunny. A little too much! This stay would pass quickly, very quickly, too quickly. We finally had only two full days on site. The other two days are severely cut by air transport and transfers, all arrival or departure preparations.

Two days of seminar, relaxation, idleness and entertainment that should, in theory, bring us closer to each other, loosen a little conventions, professional uses, freeing us from some a priori. Maybe!?! Telemarketers, Salesmen, Masters Sega, Marketing, Management and Administrations all bathed, flooded with Sun, joy, good mood and rum arranged. There's no doubt that something will happen. The question is what? If the Grande Soufrière, the volcano of Guadeloupe was peacefully asleep, we should still be able to spring something big, huge because Sega is like that: always stronger!

And I must tell you that something exceptional has happened. Nobody could have imagined. We all had a great second day. An excursion was scheduled, the hotel was perfectly equipped with all the comforts you can expect from a very high standard establishment. We were housed in a multitude of small buildings separated from each other, in beautiful rooms with balconies and sea views! And of course, the centrepiece of the facilities: a very beautiful and large swimming pool to certain and deserved success because when you bathe in it, you then had on one side for only horizon the sea, the ocean, as if the pool was thrown into it.

Breakfast, lunch and dinner were imperial. Unlike the seminar in Opio, we will not be overwhelmed by the company meetings during the day. And to be honest, I don't really remember them anymore except that being this time "franco-French" they will have been much more digested because freed of endless redundancies between countries.

Everything was fine, everything was going well and we were about to have a gala evening, proper dress required, or we would have a wonderful dinner served with thousand flavors and as many island sweets at a dancing disco until no time, in the Hotel itself!

I never had what you might call a "big dive"! Nevertheless, immersed in this exotic setting, with extraordinarily friendly and smiling staff but with the hand often leste, with the band of Sega Masters always nice, as other employees of Sega just as much to the tune, I drank and chained more than reason of many fruit cocktails, a priori. You could ask for more juice, there would still be half rum. Anyway you will understand, I think that soon there should be no more blood in my alcohol. Hummm... There must have been a lot of alcohol in my blood. But I wasn't the only one. There was no contest but I think a lot of the Sega Masters started to become round like shovel tails!

At the end of dinner, we were invited to go and warm up the dance floor. The juices would help us considerably in this task. Not that everyone had lost their shyness, at least their reserve, but they were well taken. And this space dances quickly fulfill all its promises. Obviously, we start slowly in order to attract the greatest number and accelerate once the majority has taken it easy. The temperature was rising slowly but surely with the fruits of passion, rum, joy, freedom, stimulating and very catchy sounds of the local DJ, essential conductor of a successful evening.

The number of dancers was constantly growing and we could find almost everyone!?! We were fine, really fine. I cannot say it for everyone, but we were getting closer to "the great escape", the total escape of body and mind, when he even began to climb up, a little bit of madness, once the majority was completely uninhibited. Without necessarily talking about drunkenness, we had shifted noticeably into unfaked joy, collective rejoicing and it was very pleasing to almost everyone, these moments of unifying relaxation, to make us forget a few moments, weeks, months of hard work...

The photo, the shot could have been perfect but it was without counting that at Sega, it is always stronger than you! Stronger than John Travolta in Saturday Night Fever is it possible? Stronger than Jean Claude Dusse in the Bronzés? Stronger than Punk in Master Sega's commercials? Well mix me these three and you will have a little idea of the incredible performance that was going to be given by one of the Sega Masters.

Philippe, our Hard Rocker with long curly hair had certainly not snowed the fruity and very sweet drinks that we were served at will. Like others, he felt comfortable on the dance floor. But the mood was one notch, then two. He started to get into a trip that only he had the secret. He no longer cared about those around him. Was he in a form of musical trance as the Shamans and other medicine men could do it around the world, to invoke spirits or even gods?!? He seemed completely possessed. He therefore began to dance and dance again, or rather to perform singular movements peculiar to the spiritual leaders of the first peoples. Maybe it had something to do with hard rock? Metal? Heavy metal? Music arts that I don't know very well. From the outside, it seemed totally free, intuitive, animal or even bestial. He was completely in his trip and nothing else, no one existed anymore. Sometimes performing movements as wide as sudden, he began to make space around him. He first took the place of several dancers, then half the track before emptying it almost completely. Everyone had moved away to watch him "dance", or rather to avoid taking blows, because he seemed more and more possessed by I don't know what demon of the dance!

I am neither an expert in dance nor an expert of the first peoples but there was really something from another time, another space. It was totally surreal and this demonstration was more and more amazing! He jumped in all directions, ran, hopped, maybe also prepared for the world championships of athletics? Or gymnastics? He made us the "Air guitar", and certainly simulated all kinds of instruments but which ones? I was unable to guess because it went in all directions.

We were all, little by little, totally hypnotized and dumbfounded! Philippe literally seemed to explode and I wondered if someone had not served him something else than sugar!?! As his performance lasted, he would strip! He was in a full trance, these clothes were flying, flying all over the room! Gratifying us almost entirely of his nudity, would he end up in the simplest device, the costume of Adam? The DJ continued without blinking to string up the tubes, yet everyone had stopped... Except for Philippe who seemed to have more energy than the hundred people around him.

Imagine him with his long mullet cut, and curly, and his body well hairy. A devil? A monkey? A gymnast? Jean Claude Travolta? John Dusse? An all-powerful Shaman of an Amazonian or Malaysian jungle? Malaise, we were dangerously close to it for sure. We Sega Masters, we knew Philippe because he was one of us! Well, we thought we knew him until today! As to whether he was one of us, it seemed much less obvious to me now, in this life, in this temporality.

This performance as spontaneous as unexpected, of a man excited, endiablé, giving himself in spectacle and finishing it almost naked had literally electrocuted the present assembly. No applause, no encouragement, we were very much in silence for very long minutes and we had wisely moved away on the edges of the track. Maybe fifteen, maybe twenty minutes? Waiting patiently for him to finish, that he releases the track for more wise paces!

At no time he blinked, he had to stop by himself, completely covered in sweat. I had no juice, having given everything as if he was passing a final exam to I don't know who or what, like for the Shamans, he had to reach a kind of enlightenment by falling from fatigue, completely empty. But this crazy trance had finally stopped. The public will return to the track, but very slowly. As it was already late, many will go to bed with this incredible show in their head. Philippe was one of the "Maître Sega" and I believe that with this performance, we all had to be warmly dressed for winter and for a while. It is often said that the devil is in the details, but here it is a Sega Master endiablé who blacked them with paint.

To be honest, I was as shocked as amused! What about the others? We were in "a gala evening", just bourgeois and without forcing the line, Philippe had teleported us into another dimension, another age. Finally, even if I said to myself that everyone would think what he wants (when we see what we see, when we hear what we hear, we are right to think what we think), his greatest fault was to deprive the vast majority of a moment of communion.

These moments are as fragile as they are rare. Philippe had shown, above all, a monstrous selfishness. It was not so much in the form as in the substance that he had fished. I hope that he has at least enjoyed this moment for himself and that he can laugh and make people laugh by sharing his memory in his own way.

From another point of view, and if we take away all affect, personal emotion, ethics or morality, it will have been the most consistent with the slogan that made Sega France what it will be in a large part of its representation, in the collective unconscious for many years! That is to say an ascending teenager "dirty kid", or an adult who wants to remain a teenager, uneducated who obeys nothing nobody, disrespectful, irreverent, a rebel, a lone wolf in need of challenges, landmarks, who will really and only do what he wants! While looking for, perhaps, someone who can stop him, who will be stronger than he: a master, his master! The Punk of the Sega pub? As with the creature of Frankenstein, Sega, its direction, its marketing had not so much generated a monstrosity as an uncontrollable and uncontrolled creature. It was very difficult to set limits, whether they were good or bad! Some "uncontrollable creatures" had entered the Hotline of Master Sega, it was perhaps not so aberrant that finally when we approach so often provocation.

The next morning we will leave to visit one of the islands of "Saintes", charming small islands in the south of Guadeloupe not to expel the "evil" that had penetrated us but just for a good dose of farniente. We were not really cool and we found ourselves in the boat, in the open Caribbean. The more cautious will take pills against sea sickness. Not being very "medicine", I declined several offers. And as if Master Sega needed to take pills! The Saintes were not very far away from the boat and even by boat the trip took only half an hour. I wasn't boasting, I knew that I should stay on the bridge and look at the horizon so I wouldn't be sick! However, most of those who had not taken pills started to feel bad at all! Several of them will throw their lunch overboard because without being especially strong, the sea was still agitated enough to beat us well. Sega Masters who had not taken a pill fell one after the other. Emptying over the edge and rushing into the toilet at the bottom of the boat that was carrying us!

I was struggling with all my strength. I was less and less good but I held! Until a pressing urge forced me to go down into the ship's hold. Fatal error! I was losing my bearings and finding myself more shaken than ever. But it is when I arrived in the toilet and especially when I saw myself in the mirror that I received the coup de grâce! My face was yellow, white, green, I looked really bad. When I saw myself, everything in my stomach came back up. I emptied myself as if I had never been emptied. And it was great for me. I felt so much better afterwards.

I got back up and we finished this little trip to arrive in a beautiful small port! With at its entrance a house in the shape of a fishing boat; probably a trawler. We will spend a few hours on a beautiful beach with fine sand. A nice sailboat a few tens of meters was anchored offering us beautiful photos. On our arrival we could witness a fabulous spectacle: a school of flying fish, tiny fish, green, blue, silver passed just a few meters from the edge of the beach.

It was a magical moment, a beautiful bay secluded and quiet without too many people before we arrived. Too bad for those who were here before us, much more alone! They saw themselves "invaded" by a horde of tourists wearing strange T-shirts covered with blue hedgehogs with red shoes!?!

We will go swimming in the turquoise and shallow waters before sunbathing a little. This enchanted parenthesis will pass much too quickly but it will have perfectly existed! We will return to the dock of the small village, waiting for our boat to come and pick us up.

We will also have the chance, the happiness to see in the distance, the Club Med One, huge sailboat/ cruise ship of the Club Méditerranée, able to accommodate 440 passengers. Where he was, it seemed small to me: just a big sailboat! But it was bad to know him because it is simply gigantic! It was a new vision of a dream that concluded this little trip in the best way.

We must, alas, hundred, thousand times, prepare already our return to Paris. Even with very little sleep, the hours had passed faster than anywhere else!?! Time seems to expand or contract according to whether one is in Heaven or Hell. Einstein would probably add that it does not exist anyway, that everything around us is just an illusion. Finally some illusions are still much more pleasant than others and you sometimes wear them even for eternity. Eternity of a day or eternity of always no matter.

It was only when I left Guadeloupe, especially when I arrived in Paris that I realized how much I had paid for my place in the Sun! I was half-burned ! Red as a peony, the whole skin of the face would eventually peel in the few days that came. Well done for me, I had not at all mistrusted, especially when I was looking for the sun, I never found it! In the tropics, the sun is often above your head, but it's not that he can't see you! Quite the contrary. I was not the only one to come home bright red but I must probably be in the top 5 and Biafine would become my best friend within 48 hours. We all came home with a light heart and a head full of beautiful memories. Even if "Philippe" had not necessarily helped us in our integration, we were happy and proud to belong to this company.

Chapter 11

1993 Year of Samba

From Guadeloupe to Brazil Tropical: 1993 a real year "Samba", a year "Ayrton Sega"! 1993 it is also the box office of the film "Les Visiteurs" by Jean-Marie Poiré. Oscar for best film for "Impitoyable". Golden Palm for "The Piano Lesson". OM C1 European Champion. Release of Depeche Mode's latest album: Songs of faith and devotion.

1993 would be for Sega still an exceptional year and dizzying in sensations and emotions, especially for all those who had, at least a little, the Brazilian heart! We started the year with a trip and seminar in the Caribbean, in the French Antilles and more precisely in the pearl of Guadeloupe. We could not have started the year better.

The success of the Sega Train in '92 was so fantastic, in every way, that it was put back on track the following year for a new and even more exciting edition, with a European final still in focus. Because it is a European Challenge bringing together thousands of players across the old continent to find the Champion of Champions! The Nintendo Truck will stay in the garage: what a shame!

All visitors to this edition will have an ice cream bar offered before or after competing in Sonic 2 or Ayrton Senna Super Monaco GP in addition to the various goodies offered to contest participants. And then you say "a bar of ice cream"!?! Whaoouuh too the "ice cream" Sega! If I bring you the info is that for me there was a year Train Sega without ice, and a year train Sega with ice, the one where I gained 3 kilos in 5 days! We were not going to throw them away anyway!?!

It's still the year of Sonic, the hero of a whole generation: The second adventure of the fastest hedgehog in the universe will be the best-selling game in the world on Sega consoles when all the counters are permanently blocked! And it's also, and even more so, the year of speed, always speed, even more speed for the Mega Drive with Ayrton Senna Monaco GP. Train + Sonic + Formula 1: Senna is stronger than you!

The king of arcade and speed simulators has been brilliantly invited to the Queen of motor racing: Formula 1. Since the previous year, he has become the official sponsor of the world champion team with Alain Prost behind the wheel. The latter will win his 4th title of World Champion in 93, his last, in the colors of Sega! We will all remember his beautiful Sonic helmet and especially the small legs of the hedgehog drawn on the sides of the shell of the F1, which ultimately only reduce the size of the driver!

Moreover, I have some very confidential information to share with you! It will be reported to me by a journalist who was hanging out in the stands, near the Champion, words that I deliver exclusively! Alain Prost slowly advancing towards the hedgehog who was also recovering from many emotions for having followed the race in its entirety, he nibbled a delicious Donuts with caterpillar, spiders, earthworm and chocolate (it's almost as good as Gloubiboulga mustard in less). So Alain Prost whispering in his ear: "Sonic: I'm your father"!

In 1993, the Hotline will also welcome new Sega Masters: sometimes to follow up on the hasty departures of some! We will welcome the second Sega Mistress: the well-named Aude Rauzy! A pretty young woman very cute, as the future DG Bruno Charpentier will tell you about the women of the Hotline. She will thus break the monopoly of Sandrine who had almost transformed the Hotline into a personal male harem! You should know that it is by seeing Sandrine on television in the Jean Luc Delarue program, "La Grande Famille" on Canal+, a report about Sega's Masters, that Aude, then looking for a job, will apply immediately as "Sega's Mistress"! Is it possible that many young women did not apply because "Master Sega" "should have been" presumably a man!?! Fortunately, Lara Croft would soon be showing her face.

Aude was a very great "Sega Mistress" and she will be all the more so as she will become a few years later the High Priestess of the sculptural, sublime, divine Lara Croft and sacred temple "Tomb Raider". But this story will be told to you later!

Nevertheless, when the "live" calls are deleted, when the surcharged numbers have been imposed, alas, when you continue to call Master Sega but that he will no longer be really there, it will be the voices of our Aude Croft, of Romuald Depp and of your servant, Pre-recorded, which you will hear! For announcements, contests, tips and solutions! Our "Mario Martial", not yet among us in '93, was great the controller in hand, but we did not always understand what he said behind his big mustache!

If Aude was not the first, she will be the last of the Sega Mistresses and before joining the teams of Cyberpress for other adventures. In the meantime, we would also have Bénédicte "Stig" Legrand, whom I will talk to you about in the next part because she will join us in 1994.

Pascal H will complete the team this year and it is reluctantly that I will tell you about it. Sharing his first name, and his first name only very fortunately, he was embarrassing me. Really. The greatest poet ever met, he will be nicknamed "Baudelaire", speaking of "Hairy Pies" when he evokes, sometimes, women and he was also very proud to tell that he had gone to the Bois de Boulogne to be spoiled by Brazilian transvestites! (Oh yes I'm talking about the year Samba!! Course of miracles: + 2pts!). Adding, luxury of details, including that they knew how to do it better than "the others"! Did they probably want to talk about "quiches"... Sorry for the "Pies"!?! Fortunately nobody, outside, will ever know anything about these not very fitting ways with the image that one could make of a Master Sega especially when you are 8-10 years old. He will go quickly to Cyberpress where he can "taste" and appreciate the finesse and delicacy of his prodigious and incomparable spirit to a wider audience.

It was during this year "Samba" that I knew my quarter of an hour of glory with the program "A fishing hell" by Pascal Sanchez on FR3. Romuald asked everyone at the same time, on the hotline, if one of us would like to be filmed and interviewed. Nobody seemed very excited about this prospect unless it is a certain shyness that holds us back!?! Because it was my case, I knew that I would not be able to do much but after all it was so exciting to "go on TV" that I decided to take the challenge. For an entire afternoon the team would film the Hotline, each Sega master from behind playing and answering the phone at the same time! Aude then glued frantically many cups through Donald/ Quackshot!

I will be questioned in front of the camera for at least a good hour, maybe two! To finally appear a minute, one minute and thirty in the TV report! Yes it works like that, you are bombarded with very different questions from each other, you do not have time to think and it is quite good for sincerity and authenticity from a journalistic point of view. But in the end, with editing, you can't imagine for a second what will be retained and how you will appear to the Lambda viewer. It was obviously not a political interview, a controversial subject and yet when I saw the report, I was so proud to see myself in the box! But I was also very disappointed with this bitter taste that remains in the mouth for a while. Television with a striking magnifying effect, we see it, and especially everyone sees the defects in the background or in the form! What imperfections, but with this incredible magnifying glass, you, under the spotlight, see only that! Because it's not like in the movies where you reenact a scene until it's perfect. The montage will make me repeat several times the same expression "to the extent or..." to the point of letting you think that I would not be able to start a sentence otherwise. Which may have been the case with 4 or 5 technicians, a journalist and a bright projector in full face. But I may be the only one to notice it!?!

More fun and jubilant the last question in voice-over in the report: "So Pascal, what is it like to be a Sega Master?".

Answer from me, but the journalist during the interview did not ask me this question, at least not like that! " As long as (ahaaha!) we have all the games, and can play them all day..." I was climbing, I sealed my own caricature in front of millions of viewers! It was and it would always be vain to want to nuance.

As for Sega France as a whole, it is especially the F1 World Championship that will make the news "sensations" rue du Colonel Pierre Avia. Sega is therefore official sponsor of the Renault team with Alain Prost as leader aiming once again for the title, the fourth in its history may be!

This Championship will be one of the most exciting in the history of F1 because beyond an umpteenth duel (and unfortunately one of the last) between the two Titans: Prost and Senna, a certain Schumacher already came to grill them, sometimes politeness! And a certain Jean Alesi also pointed the tip of his nose. 7 wins for Prost. 5 for Senna but once again he won the Queen of races: the prestigious Monaco GP.

Sega will offer 15 VIP seats at the French Grand Prix in Magny-Cours, near Nevers, on 4 July. As we were still very numerous (around 140) there will be a draw! And among the Sega Masters, it is Aude, Romuald and Philippe who will have this famous privilege. Aude freshly landed at Sega and will even be the first to be drawn from the ballot box! It's Sega Magic! Like me two years ago, who had just arrived and who finds me 8 days later "VIP" at the World Karting Championships in Le Mans, Aude was paying a ride to the Gods of F1 just arrived at home! Nice welcome gift!

So Titanic F1 race to live in VIP box just above the finish line for the Sega Masters as well as a dozen other employees of the House. Champagne and petit fours to comfort the spirits and stomachs for this certainly extraordinary but also stressful moment! This fantastic and memorable ride demands almost as many bubbles in your glass as connections from your neurons! It's all over the place: Samba!

Official partners of Renault F1, the "Sega" will even go into the stands at the end of the race to approach the cars, congratulate and have an autograph signed by Alain Prost himself! Who had just triumphed once again, getting closer to the record of 5 titles by Fangio and pushing Senna away with the same length (with 4 and 3 titles if you follow!!!).

But all the intensity, the emotion of this exceptional moment frozen in time will reach its climax with the presence a few meters away from the absolute god of F1: the late Ayrton Senna. The moment is magical as the Brazilian champion is getting closer to his dramatic fate, because he will not finish the following season, on May 1, 1994 in Bologna during the San Marino Grand Prix, Ayrton Senna will definitely be part of the legend after a terrible accident, you may know, alas, from sad memory! But our three Sega Masters will have been able to see and approach the greatest F1 Master of all time! The champion of champions and absolute master on the incredible track of Monaco.

Ayrton Senna was with Sega: "I love you, neither me!" Half engaged with the video game manufacturer via "Ayrton Sega Monaco GP", Senna will not bear that it is Prost who is chosen as driver by the trio Williams/ Renault/ Sega which then offered the best car! The one that could allow him to win a 4th title in place of Prost! Ayrton Senna came to Sonic with great pleasure because the sales of Master System in Brazil were fabulous, unlike in Japan and the USA. The local Sega Distributor, "Tec Toy", led by Stefano Arnhold wanted to have his "Mickael Jackson/Moonwalker/Brazilian", understand a living god who would associate with the brand by a particular game to stimulate or even explode sales! The deal will be made easier because the president of the time of Sega was friends with one of the most powerful leaders of "Honda" who was then "motorist" of F1 in particular McLaren that drove Ayrton Senna.

Many young Brazilians had a Master System, and it won't take much more for Ayrton Senna to want to offer a game in his name, with his technical participation in the design of the game. All the young Brazilians could play in Monaco GP without breaking the bank because the Master System was very affordable. The Brazilian Champion will sign the deal with a derisory cachet however he will ask for royalties for each game sold. Three million copies will be sold in a few weeks when it is released!!! A new Master hit!

If Senna was in the small papers of Sega and Honda, he was not necessarily in those of the Williams team and the Renault engine manufacturer. Did Sega have a say as sponsor when Williams Renault had to choose between Senna and Prost?!? Certainly, but their influence was very limited.

Also, the Brazilian champion remaining on a pushy F1 at McLaren was green with rage but he will chew his brake quietly, not without a small joke that did not lack of spikes: Every F1 victory, he will stick a hedgehog crushed on the hull of his McLaren! He is the best driver and even with a car with "medium" performance, he will therefore stick 5 crushed hedgehogs including his victory at the European grand prix in the UK which was fully dressed by Sega! Under a heavy rain, the divine Ayrton Sega... Sorry... Ayrton Senna will climb all the drivers one by one to win the race "Sega/Sonic"! As soon as the conditions are more difficult, fast month circuit, more technical, rainy weather, he is the Boss. Undoubtedly. He was especially so because he had an opponent of his size, the only one who could compete with him: Alain Prost of course. The glory of one will rest forever on the glory of another! Achilles will become Achilles only by beating the formidable Hector at the foot of the ramparts of Troy.

Chapter 12

The ups and downs

We, the Sega Masters, had been able to measure our popularity on and through the Sega Train, as well as at different fairs. I will not tell you anything by pointing out that it was stronger in young people, very young and rather in boys than adults, especially women.

I was able to check it myself on various occasions with very contrasting results, notably at the event for the launch of the Mega-CD in France in September 1993. Sega had invited a large number of people, among these most important customers and partners, to the "Bains Douches" in the center of Paris. Totally privatized in the early evening, the box will be gradually reopened to the general public from midnight.

At the time "Les Bains Douches" were one of the most trendy, the most fashionable night clubs in Paris, or even the most trendy, David and Cathy Guetta will become the Masters a few years later, welcoming the top people of the show business.

Under the shadow and light, rising star "Sinclair", Sega, Virgin and Megaforce in its number 20 will offer a mini audio CD of the singer. The MegaCd naturally proposed an accession to the musical world and as much to make it known through strong symbols. Les Bains Douches for the VIP, the young singer full of talent Sinclair for the general public through an extract from his first album on a mini CD. An excerpt, a song that will be appreciated by the Sega fans, but the message was passed.

All Sega employees were invited to the official launch party, which took place during the workweek! Many will decline the invitation, others will just pass and the last will not make old bones! Jean-Luc and Catherine will not "sleep" at my place! But I remained vigilant! Arrived on site around 20/21heures, it is Cathy Guetta in person who will welcome us with open arms, with a huge smile! She will take care of everything, she will take care of us! She is no longer a waitress, she is responsible for the "Vip Room"! It is here and now that she builds her legend of the Queen of the Night! From

Paris to Ibiza and through Sega! We will not be surprised in the years that follow to see her fly to many successes with her DJ companion.

Once back in the Baths, she will propose to the young women of Sega, especially our two Mistress Sega, which Aude who will remind me most of the details of this anecdote, to dress them in atomic bombs with dressmaking dresses, and to become the princesses or rather the Queens of the evening! Cathy Guetta was very nice and enthusiastic, this evening was our evening and it had to be unforgettable! Fairy Cathy would make sure at any moment! But maybe she was too enthusiastic because the boss did not agree! The evening would be made up of the teams of "Sonic" we were not "Fuck me I'm Famous". And I was even going to check it out a little later.

But the "Soniquettes" will find other pleasures! Even dressed in Sonic T-Shirt and black pants! Especially by being able to go rub and prick no more nor less than the most beautiful guy on Earth and in the Universe! The star model Greg Hansen!!! In flesh and bones and 22 years old! Me, it didn't do much for me, but... Catherine? Catherine? Where are you?

We would have plenty of time to celebrate the Mega-CD, this new promising support that would turn and turn again, like the DJ decks and as our heads maybe at the end of the evening! Sega had given us all three drink coupons that we could exchange at the bar during the Sega event and especially after, when the box would be reopened to the public. A good aperitif between Sega colleagues and a good opportunity to discover this mythical place of the Parisian evenings bathed by the freshness and all powerful energy of the couple Guetta, at the very beginning of their prodigious ascent. We will tremousse slightly on home sounds and Philippe will not have, will not have the opportunity to make us a Saturday night fever coming from another age or another culture.

Midnight was fast approaching, the vast majority of Sega's employees had already left for home. Michel Bams, the head of communication at Sega, and incidentally the most handsome guy in the company, this probably explains it, had been there all night promoting our new baby to the CD stand among the many VIP guests. When I say "the most beautiful guy in the box" I mean the company! Even if he would probably not have to blush to be compared to Greg Hansen!

As master of ceremony, exchanges and communication, he was armed with a super power: the sulphating shot or champagne machine, loaded like a mule with drink tickets. Not seeing many familiar faces around him, after midnight, he came to me to give me all the tickets that he had left! I must have had the face of a young student who was stranded and lost at "L'Anfer" in Dijon (the most sought-after club in my time in the Burgundian Metropolis and this, very likely, thanks to the residence of another famous DJ on the rise: Laurent Garnier).

But for me tonight it would be more like heaven since I found my pockets full of tickets for Boisson! Could I play it tonight too, "Sinclair" or "Lord Brett Sinclair"? Maybe even see it in the Bob Sinclar style!?! In one case as in the other improbable "Magnifique".

Being still a "local" of the stage I did not have to worry about the return and transport, I did not live very far. I never had any courage to date in a club but I had enough to give me a little, with all these tickets, several dozen, and therefore what to bait some girls.

Three pretty young women, at first sight pretty, but you should always be a little wary in the semi-darkness, especially when you start to be drunk, three beautiful young women were tapestries, or sofa... They seemed really bored or pretending to be bored (each one his technique for bait!). Taking my courage with both hands, I go to meet them, greet them and offer to "buy" them a drink! What I would never do in normal times but "good to the adoptive parents", I did not like to waste and these many drink tickets burned the bottom of my pockets.

The young women look at each other and smile. They agree to drink with me. I am obviously delighted even if I feel that this is not me, but not at all. But I am not uncomfortable. It's just a new challenge in which I've been given lots of credits, enough to play and replay several games. I ask them what they want to drink and the Champagne wins all the votes! So I go to the bar and get four flutes and thousands of bubbles in it!

I give each of them their sparkling cup while being able to see that these ladies are certainly young... And a brown made up! Very complicated to give an age but they were most likely of age.

We drink, we have a sip or two and they seem to be willing to talk. We present ourselves by name, and quite quickly, they ask me what I do in life. I spontaneously answer that I am "Master Sega"! Patatras, what did I not say there!?! Their smiles fade, they look for each other. It will take them no more than 20 seconds to gather their things, get up from the couch and go far away, very far without saying a single word of politeness. Waterloo plain, a cold wind would cover my pain. I was of course extremely shocked at the moment, totally petrified and disappointed of course.

Not wanting to stay on this ground devastated by the defeat, I will go dance on the dancefloor or I will have much more success! Not really the one I most likely thought of! Indeed, I "received" wandering hands on my back! The first time we think it's a little clumsy. The second time we think there is someone very clumsy or alcoholic not far from you! But from the third it is very embarrassing as I ended up spotting who was at the end of these shameless hands! A man was laughing with another!!! I understood that this world, this evening were not for me. We were certainly not far enough from the Marais. I returned home disappointed.

Hopefully other opportunities will get me back on track. And if we were not yet the gods of video games then maybe we would become because they are the gods of the small screen that I was going to meet after the gods of the Parisian nights! All gathered for a huge banquet.

During the end of year holidays celebrated at a grandiose evening by and for the TF1 channel, I was invited by the management of Sega France to come and hold a room equipped with consoles from home for the pleasure and entertainment of the staff of the first French channel of French television and even the largest channel in Europe (at the audience level).

In the sumptuous setting of the Carroussel du Louvres, several rooms were arranged to offer a huge and lavish banquet. With a gigantic central reception room offering catering and entertainment for several hundred people, in a dim and bluish atmosphere; dimly lit evoking the celestial vault, on a summer evening. It was beautiful, it was magical for all the guests who would participate!

In small rooms various animations were offered. Tarology, Astrology, Clairvoyance; the staff of TF1 could be drawn the cards, make their astral chart, etcetera. It was necessary to be patient this side, a long tail having formed.

And for the younger, but not only, a fully Sega video game space had been installed and I made sure that everything was fine for all those who would come to venture there and test the games present. So I saw the children of the Small Screen Stars. I think I saw pretty much everyone. I will not forget the passage of Patrick Poivre d'Arvor (PPDA), who at the time was truly a living god if not even Zeus himself!

The Super Mega Star of TF1's 20heures, television news, which gathered, it seems to me, every evening more than 10 million viewers for "La Grande Messe du 20heures"! Well, he passed two meters from me! Obviously PPDA has no more today the aura that it had before, following the various accusations of sexual assault brought against him. PPDA must have really taken for Zeus when he received the female audience.

I also remember Philippe Bouvard with his quite surprising physique, for someone who has never seen him anywhere else but on his TV screen. Well, this journalist and animator already in the history of TV will certainly not be for these gamer talents! Many sports journalists will pass, coming from motor sports (auto moto) or football and some even play consoles for a few minutes. I am unable to give an exact list but "in reality" I think I saw almost all the known faces of TF1 at the time (and for some still now): Claire Chazal, Jean Pierre Foucault, Evelyne Dhéliat, Jean-Pierre Pernaut.

There were so many well-known people, men and women of influence, that it was totally surreal for me. I know I was there, I know it was real, but the situation is so exceptional that we must also, once again, pinch ourselves. All these people so seen, so known through a "little box" plastic filled with electronics, were out and found themselves a few moments around me!?! How could this be possible?

Some small screen stars had come to play on Sega consoles, during these holidays, with me! Their children have been more in a hurry. I was not a god, I am probably not now, it was not the center of the world... But for a few moments, maybe only a few seconds, I still felt like THE Sega Master. The TV campaign. Secret and prominent character. And as a professor emeritus, I officiated in my small improvised university of video games as master and absolute expert. Even if, finally, everyone or almost could not care about it, there would always be one, a child, an adolescent, to make me think that here, but no further, the King was me.

This evening which now seems to me as a distant memory, maybe even a dream and that will add to many other memories (so many wonderful dreams) will nevertheless be totally swept away in emotions and intensity by another evening event even more unreal.

Still in my capacity as "Maître Sega", I was invited to hold a new small video game console lounge, but this time in one of the VIP lodges of the Parc des Princes during an International Match of the French Soccer Team: France versus Turkey. The evening was really quiet for me because this match was very intense, very spectacular with no less than 4 goals for the team of France. There were some lost people who came to test the consoles but as during the World Karting Championships, the sensations were really elsewhere! I will meet Philippe Vandel, in charming company, one of the most attached people to PSG. Yes well it's not exceptional: crossing Philippe Vandel at the Parc des Princes is like finding a sausage in a sauerkraut. Philippe was also at that time the "star presenter" of the hard newspaper on Canal +. He will tell, quite recently, that he was a friend with all the football players when he presented this magazine in the evening, very late. I confirm that when I met him that night, I had the "impression" of crossing a prince in his castle (at the same time we are well in the park of princes!) or rather a sultan in his harem! I had met the Prince of the Park, would miss only the King and why not the Gods of the Stadium?!? I had not calculated anything, imagined nothing! They asked me to supervise some consoles during the duration of the Match and BASTA! But at the final whistle someone from the organization came to pick me up to tell me that I was invited to dinner with all the staff! We have dinner and we are debriefing! It must be around 11 o'clock! Ah cool it's nice, yes I come..."

Actually I go there by clenching my ass! Nothing to do with the Bains Douches nor have met the host star of the newspaper Hard. No, I wonder that it was not planned at all! Who would I meet with? Were they going to question me? Ask me for an account on the evening (nothing to report!!!!) I may not like it but my curiosity will take over and I am my host in the alleys of the Parc des Princes. We go down many steps until we find ourselves in front of a very small restaurant inside, in the alleys of the Park, in the basement!?!

It's a little much confusion at this level, the restaurant can probably accommodate between 20 and 30 people maximum! It is full to the max but several people will come out. There are also many people in front of the restaurant and little space! VIP? Journalists? The organisers? And players from the French team will also come to shake hands! The future Gods of the Stadium of a whole Nation! Zinedine Zidane, Didier Deschamps, Youri Djorkaeff in particular. As well as Sabri Lamouchi and Laurent Blanc: Go Auxerre! Guy Roux's team had been crowned Champion of France and even won the Coupe de France for a famous "double" a few weeks before.

Maybe they were looking for their coach? Indeed Aimé Jacquet was in the restaurant. I am then invited to enter it when the Selector begins to leave him. Everyone congratulates, congratulates, compressed over a few square meters and I will shake hands and congratulate Aimé Jacquet! Too funny! I feel like I'm in a movie where I teleported myself! So I shake his hand for a game that I didn't even watch!?! But the coach had not yet won the World Cup! He will shake the hand of "Master Sega", his fate will be totally changed. Aahahhaa... They were not yet the soccer gods we know now but they would become pretty soon.

 Someone offers or coach Jacquet to stay but he will answer that he must join his players! The restaurant is a little empty and the dinner of the organizers and other partners of the FFF could begin. So I will have dinner with them! At the same table as Jean-Claude Darmon! I did not know who he was that day. Better known for being named "Le Pape du football français"! The business man who brought French football into the field of communication, marketing, sponsors and products in the 80s. He is the absolute promoter of football history in France. He was clearly the most powerful man in football, probably more than the president of the FFF or the league. It was not a god but a titan. He had probably decided, or one of these collaborators? To install some Sega consoles during one of these bigger masses ! And he had not forgotten to invite his "Master Sega" to come for dinner after. A moment, once again, unimaginable. And yet.

Chapter 13

The Master's games

It is never easy to choose, to determine the "best game" on which we could have played all these magical years as the number is vast and the games often very different from each other! And it is too subjective: everyone has his own criteria and his way of tasting, enjoying, assimilating. It's a question of culture, references even if for that, we were obviously very well placed, having the possibility to play everything, absolutely everything.

However, due to time constraints of course, all the Sega Masters could not play all the games. I believe that only Romuald and I took the time, at one point or another, and especially outside of "work" hours, to play or test all the games, whether a Shining Force, a James Pond, or Road Rash, Lemmings, Immortal, Centurion, Rings of Power or Thunder Force 4. Other Sega masters will also test a very large majority of games but often block on "pure and hard" role-playing games (especially EA's games, more from the PC universe), fighting games (women in particular!) or sports games (not really essential to know in relation to the others certainly). On the other hand, adventure games and action games like Landstalker, Sun or The Legend of Thor were popular, especially when they were translated into French. As well as adventure and strategy games like Shining Force, Shining in the Darkness and the unmissable saga Phantasy Star who flirted a lot with role-playing games. The main thing is that we complement each other with each other, of course, favorite universes and themes! " What makes the strength of a Sega Master, is the Sega Master who stands on these sides" would say Leonidas, King of Sparta if he had become hotlineur for Sega!

I was known to be the "role-playing specialist" but in reality I played everything. I think I liked almost all genres even if I was not a big fan of fighting games. Except for the series "Mortal Kombat"! Not so much for the violence as for the aura and charisma of the characters: digitized they seemed so much more "real" and immersion, projection even identification more intense! Maybe that was my monomaniac Pit Fighter on Mega Drive!?! But the game was so ugly.

The more we were at the Hotline, the less we had to spread out! Some games were unavoidable and "unmissable": The Sonic and Disney (Mickey, Quackshot, Aladdin...) which will often be sold at one time or another in a "bundle" with the console, the adventure games qualified as "blockbuster" as Landstalker or The Legend of Thor on Mega Drive then Tomb Raider on Saturn, not to mention the "Streets of Rage" which will be all the more appreciated because we could play it together (and like the little recreation of the Sega Masters!). Finally we played on the most popular, best-selling games, so often "the best", and those on which we would have a lot of calls and various and varied solicitations. Nothing that could be surprising or even more simply original, except perhaps for Flicky.

However, it is interesting to note that the greatest successes of Sega were with the Mega Drive because they expanded the traditional audience of players until then! We know that the Mega Drive has significantly increased the average age of users, we probably know less, or we forget to say, that games like Sonic or Quackshot have considerably feminized the audience of the Japanese manufacturer. Among the Sega Masters, and especially among our three historical "Mistresses", Sonic the Hedgehog was a real idol! Sandrine, Aude and especially Bénédicte were all fond of the charming little hedgehog and his supersonic adventures. The biggest fan of the Sega Club and the ultra-fast Hedgehog was actually a fan, who will send us tons of beautiful drawings... And rascals!!!

Sonic is certainly one of the best games on the Mega Drive, the most popular among all players, or almost, but it's even more true in the female audience. Millions of girls will discover the world of video games with Sonic and his band.

So yes, unsurprisingly, Sonic would certainly be named the "favorite game" of the Sega Masters! And it could also be "the best". Because you certainly know, it has everything to please! I'm lucky enough to have a 5 year old boy named Maxence and he loves the adventures of Sonic! In the cinema and cartoon for now only. And when we go for a walk, he loves to think of himself as Sonic by making a lightning acceleration! He sometimes asks me who goes faster between "Flash" and Sonic? I reply that we can't know because they go so fast and far, that we never manage to find them and to decide!

We must also mention Ecco le Dauphin! Who was also appreciated by the majority. An amazing success in many ways due to its quality, originality, sweetness, pacifism (in clear contrast with games often considered violent) and gameplay. He will mark his time and the entire Mega Drive generation. In any case, he will mark the Sega Masters. Our three Sega Mistresses were therefore more oriented towards adventure games like Landstalker, Wonderboy, Sun, The Legend of Thor, Shining in the Darkness. Action and combat games certainly but without being very violent and even less bloody: more "Nintendo" finally!

Then you have to say things as they are, as they were. Among the Sega Masters, you had many passionate video game fans who played a lot: yes. And you had a small handful of "Hardcore Gamer" who played almost all the time (too?) who wanted to know everything, all games, all levels, finish all challenges, all the challenges offered! Approaching in this, a sublimated and mythical vision of the Master Sega of the advertising campaign. And the "Hardcore Gamer" he likes especially what is complicated, very hard, stressful to wish, and that others will not manage to do!!! Or so little.

So I will speak for myself (it is still my book!?!) and probably also for Romuald that I know very well: what was, and what is probably still the grain of salt, the charm of a video game was especially its difficulty. I loved playing Sonic, Quackshot, and other Mickey but they are "mainstream" games! Obviously as for Sonic it's not just about finishing a level, you can beat time records while collecting a maximum of rings! Not to mention some very high levels but we still remain in the register "general public", that is to say that the greatest number must be able to progress without wanting at one time or another, to hang on rage and despair!

The games that will have me most marked will be especially the games that have resisted me the most! Is it useful to tell you that I played without any solution, code or tricks (sacrilege) even if sometimes, for some games, I would have been tempted to make an exception. And what was "wonderful" about the Mega Drive games is that there were only rarely "backups" ! (Apart from role-playing and adventure games). The "best" games were certainly those that offered technically great qualities whether they are playful, visual or on the Gameplay. But what mattered most was the challenge! Like a Revenge of Shinobi (the final maze), a Ghouls'n Ghost or a Mystic Defender! Without matching the difficulty of "Last Battle", "Indiana Jones", "Rastan

Saga" or "R-Type" on Master System, "Atomic Runner", "Batman and Robin", "The Immortal" or "Alien 3": games that can make you completely crazy!

I couldn't see myself playing, so I liked to watch Romuald, from time to time, fighting like a devil on one game or another and not getting there! Not right away! He contorted himself, took the same postures as his character in the game, he jumped, he hopped!

It was almost "VR" and full time before the hour! He seemed to have a suit on him that connected him to the hero!!! Too funny. His face was stretched, frozen, sometimes he grinned. He was in the game. It was impressive to see how intensely and physically he could live the game. We should have filmed it and made an advertisement!

Not to mention the most hilarious, tasty moments when you address directly to the hero you control with the controller! Treating him with all words and all evils. Like when you can talk to your car that does not want to start a winter morning (which is probably now less true with electric vehicles!?!)

I loved, I loved Romuald for many reasons and as a brother, but seeing him play was very often a spectacle. He was one of the most hardcore gamers I know, and maybe even the most hardcore, but he also seemed to be the one who lived his video-fun adventures the most! This certainly explains it. Obviously he is not the only player to suffer as his character, surely there is someone among you? But in our country he won the "interconnection" award!

So we "Hardcore Gamers", we loved "R-Type" on Master System for its technical qualities but also for its difficulty. Just as we would love "Phantasy Star" first of the name on Master System without codes and without solution. I already talked about it but you have to imagine Romuald a time "only Master Sega" to have to deal with "Ultima 4", "YS", "Golvellius", "Golden Axe Warriors", "Miracle Warriors" on the phone of the Sega Club. Not sure that, with the arrival of Fabrice in early 1991, he was properly relieved! The Master System was (and remains) an excellent machine with often amazing games given its limited capabilities! And there are challenges even if sometimes the games are very short.

As for the challenges, those of "Master Sega", we can mention "Fantasia", that Romuald will not fail to put me in my box of "welcome" at Sega in the middle of all the role-playing games and adventures. A game programmed in the old and to tear your head, very hard because not really hyper playable (Thank you "Infogrames" for this "Disney" that few children will enjoy). Then the challenge "Another World" but also and especially the incredible "Flashback" which really created the event at its release! A pure game of "Masters"! Atomic Runner, Rolling Thunder 2, Batman and Robin, Alien 3, Kid Chameleon can complete the list of the biggest challenges to face! If you were looking for more!?!

As for "games for two", I have already pointed it out but "Flicky" (who would have believed it?) will prevail between Romuald and me. Followed much later by Sega Rally. Between the two, many games of NHL Hockey will be preferred to FIFA or any other football game: often good games but too slow compared to the EA Hockey license.

And as for the whole Hotline I think it is "Puyo Puyo" or more exactly "Dr Robotnik's Mean Bean Machine" that will remain in the annals as a favorite confrontation during our recreational moments, before Baku Baku on Saturn! While in co-op mode, unsurprisingly, "Streets of Rage" will impose easily and every episode, as an obvious.

We will also have the opportunity to face each other at least twice in "La Tête dans les nuages", the historic center Boulevard Haussmann. And that's where we could deploy all our talents including a version 8 players network on Daytona USA. My god, it was good to be able to face humans and not a machine. The games were very high as this kind of game allowed players to show their talent as a driver, that one a little less glorious "scrubber" or even bad loser! All moves are allowed to pass or prevent someone from winning. You had to be very good at driving and just as strategist to be "the finisher"! The one who was forgotten and the one who would pass through the net of destruction! Real parties of eight as we will never have. I think I remember that the "R-360" was appreciated among us in various ways! Perhaps a little too much.

Chapter 14

The Secrets of the Sega Masters

Philippe's performance in Guadeloupe will have had a serious impact on all the spirits present that evening. From "geeks", most often proven reputation, we probably had to get closer to "freaks". That is to say a curiosity, a phenomenon of fair, or more simply a person as strange as bizarre, but which, for the most sensitive, would always appear a little as disturbing and disturbing! The Freak is far from chic. The difference, whatever it may be, can be scary. The Freak, like the Punk, questions the uniformity of society and will even push it, or even shake it! In the substance, as in the form.

The Punk of the Pub Maître Sega, perhaps an avatar or one of these disciples, had therefore sprung from the darkness of a room just illuminated by a ball with facets, as other midnight demons in their time, and this, in the middle of gala seminar, happy and cheerful certainly but can be too perfectly slippery. The contrast will be more striking, and the perplexity of the moment will never be matched, during my lifetime.

With a spontaneity and a force that one would not suspect, a Master Sega had struck the spirits by shaking and crushing all protocols. By snobbing and physically pushing away, the time of a wild musical performance, all these colleagues yet all ready to touch each other timidly but affectionately.

But if we had stayed there, all this would probably and slowly evaporate, transformed into an anecdote just "funny"! But alas Philippe had more than one trick in his bag and he would hit even harder and like a rascal. But this time, he would not recover: from wrongdoing we went to the criminal act. And every crime deserves a sanction.

As good Sega Masters we were, and that we had to become a little more day after day, the management of Sega had granted us an extraordinary privilege! We received all the games, on all media! As with a cornucopia that every passionate player dreams of getting, we were overwhelmed with cartridges and CDs. Are we the Gods of video games? Demigods? We were at least extremely privileged and it must be believed that some of us had "the sons who touch" to have as many! (If they had any sons, think about it...)

We had been back from Guadeloupe for a while. One day like another, a Sega Master (I will not know who) then a second will blow in my ear that Philippe sold these games to children or teenagers on the phone line of Sega Master! Obviously they will report this information to Romuald, Jean-Luc and Marc.

It was the amazement. At first I didn't believe! I didn't want to believe it, because I thought it wasn't possible... To be so stupid!

To be honest, I had also sold three or four games out of over a hundred received but privately and to friends or relatives. Games that had no strategic importance for the development of my knowledge (genre sports games...) We had not signed anything on this subject but there was a tacit agreement and so obvious. These games were and should remain tools of work and achievement. This advantage was granted to us all only very recently and should surely suffer from this kind of practice.

At first, and as Philippe's box was just behind mine, I started listening to these conversations on the phone. Quickly I received confirmation of what had been reported to me. I was amazed even though it had been reported! Philippe offered directly and openly to all those who called and had not asked for anything like that, to buy recent and new games cheap!

I will therefore go to Romuald not without going to see Philippe just before, so that he can confirm me, that he admits in person, that he was selling his games well to our young players.

He seemed not at all embarrassed, let alone ashamed. And I was in his place! Because it further damaged our reputation and especially now our integrity! When a Sega Master was misbehaving on the phone, all Sega Masters would suffer. How could anyone be so stupid? I was going to die. Once again, Philippe was fishing. But he fished mostly out of selfishness. Alone and forever against all!?! Philippe will be summoned quickly. By Romuald at first, then by Luc Bourcier I imagine in a second. He will be immediately laid off and fired a few days later for serious misconduct.

It was 1993 and the personality of some Sega Masters, after months and months without stories, were going to reveal themselves. Our reputation would be seriously damaged and take the direction, the trajectory that some had probably assumed! Philippe was certainly by far and by far the one who has most damaged the reputation of hotlineurs. But he will not be the only one. Perhaps Luc Bourcier is not far from the truth when he metaphorically says "Court of Miracles". What if he was absolutely right?

For the sake of completeness, I propose to open the least concealable secrets of the Sega Masters! Finally, probably just a small part: the least submerged probably! The greatest secrets, by definition, will remain secrets. We could be "Sega Masters", but we were still men. More or less fragile, more or less sensitive, more or less weak. Men what!!! with their strengths and weaknesses. Beyond the legend that has been built, and will be even more built over time, with the disappearance of the protagonists, beyond the myth that will feed as much on the legend as on the facts that write a sublimated version of history, there is of course reality! Sometimes so sad, so banal, so trivial.

The mythical heroes, the demigods have a face facing the sky, towards the immortal and a face facing the simple mortal, sensitive, weak and fragile. It is for this reason that we can love and identify easily with the Demigods! Because in many ways they are like us, in what we have of the best and in what we have of the least good.

As I have a great desire to tell you about the glorious hours, and as I have already begun to do so, I would also like to talk to you about the darker, more disturbing hours. If any of these dark hours had been revealed to the general public, no doubt our ears would have whistled loudly, that the family associations would certainly have beaten us! Having already accused us of many evils: violence, isolation, epilepsy... Fortunately these "little family secrets" as there are in almost all groups, have remained locked in their box. For long enough, that now, they can be revealed to you!

It would seem like a "revelation" and yet it is almost a "non-information"! Let's start with a topic that is still taboo and yet widely spread at work: masturbation! Numerous studies, and all over the world, have revealed that more than a third of men (especially 25/34 years old) masturbated from time to time or often at work! Before or with the advent of the internet? While waiting for the Sega Hotline, we did not yet have access to the global computer network, but I could see in some drawers, magazines with "heavily naked women"! And not only women. Finally nothing very banal!?! It is said that there is no harm in doing good, and that "masturbation at work" would allow practitioners to increase their efficiency!?! Getting rid of too much stress! So in the land of Joysticks and Joypads, were wankers kings? Personally, being single at the time, I also had to practice onanism "from time to time"! But I practiced at home! I would have been too ashamed to be caught or suspected, even if it is so common in the end.

Also in the category "revelation" or "non-information", a Sega Master was particularly attached to the games of Mario and Link. He often called SOS Nintendo. Who sometimes also called Sega. He will buy on the Super Nintendo the day it is released. While many of the Masters at Sega were blue and totally blue, others were more... "Purple"! It was probably the most common big joke on both sides. At Nintendo, you probably came back to play the Mega Drive, and at Sega to play the Super Nintendo! That's probably how we could identify the real game crazies!

At the time I was totally blue and my heart would only beat for Sega, Sonic and Mother Brain, but I understood without any problem that you can love Sega and Nintendo at the same time. I will discover Mario and especially Zelda later. Probably two of the best video game licenses of all time but it would not change anything, I remain 100% Sega (or 99% may be just to not die totally stupid).

Much less anecdotal and much more problematic, what we thought would be unthinkable will happen! A red line to never cross, at least among beings who claim to be civilized. Two Sega Masters will come to their hands! I will never know for what different, but the two protagonists, two fans of "Pit Fighter", will also be laid off and fired! Which one of the two would have looked for the other? I was not there that day, it happened, from memory, on a Saturday when we were in half-group. Obviously with this very unfortunate incident, "we" added points to all those who looked at us wrong, when they looked at us... " Court of miracles": + 5 pts! But we were free from at least one troublemaker. The second Master Sega in this matter was, probably, only an unfortunate "collateral damage". But that will remain a supposition.

Let's go even more in range in the nauseabond, and for a few grams of Frisson! The Freak may not be chic but he can harp us like the peaks of the hedgehog. And here, for the moment, it's a real secret! One of the Sega Masters regularly came to the Hotline with a Desert Eagle! A real one! And with these munitions! He didn't show it to everyone, because he didn't really have the right to do it, but he trusted me. He practiced what is called sport shooting. So he had a limited and highly regulated gun ownership. He could move these weapons, unloaded, in appropriate cases, from his home to the shooting range.

So on the day of his weekly session, he had with him, his flamboyant, his Desert Eagle. He was not allowed to handle these weapons outside his home and outside the shooting range, but he was so proud to have this gun with him! So it happened, at the Hotline "once or twice" that he shows me his gun, take it in hand, rather discreetly, but without ever charging it very fortunately! Now, and for having been a military officer in the Gendarmerie when the service still existed: "a weapon remains a weapon even if it is not loaded". For any outside person, it is impossible to know whether it is loaded or not, and being in the presence of a firearm is anything but harmless. Armed or not, anyone can feel threatened and have uncontrolled anxiety reactions. Master Sega will walk on the red line without ever really crossing it. But he loved to bring his gun, show it off, and let people know that he was armed. Perhaps it is what we call a false memory, so many years have passed, but I believe that he also came with another weapon: a Magnum 357. Very impressive handgun with its long barrel!

We were 140 to 150 Sega employees at that time and the vast majority will never know that one of us passed through the offices with a real Desert Eagle. We can always discuss hours and hours, real danger or not (we are not in the USA!?!) but it is factual: someone had a weapon and enough ammunition to commit the irreparable.

I will always remember, in shooting session when I was doing my military service in the Gendarmerie, one of my superiors who came almost to stick to me to stare at me. See and observe closely how I manage the session! My way of carrying, of holding the semi-automatic pistol! My way of resisting the stress of the test! My way of resisting his breath on my face! When you have a gun in your hands, or even just on you, a loaded weapon or one that you can charge quickly, you are not quite the same man. You can always claim that the "sports shooting" is a fun, relaxing, it remains no less potential vector of death. You can't put these things in all hands. Fortunately, there will never be a drama. The concerned Master Sega will keep all his composure, at least when he was not armed with these deadly "toys".

It would not be very honest to caricature us like that, but a bad language could have spread and thus at the expense of that we "Sega Masters" were shady, disloyal, cheater, indecent, violent and dangerous! What I never thought for a second because these are isolated cases! We were 23/24 and 2 or 3 individuals will cause us harm! Maybe there was something worse, but we would never know!

To conclude, I saved the best for last, and this time with a secret certainly incredible but also very funny. A secret also wonderfully well kept for many years! If Sega had debaued a director of Bandai/ Nintendo very little in the same way although calling himself Lavanant of the rest, Master Sega had debaued Mario himself! No, I'm not kidding we had the "real" Mario in the Sega team. The one in flesh and blood!

To infiltrate us, and especially not to make waves, he had changed his name and called himself Martial Sikorski. Which is neither more nor less than the anagram of "Mario Rital ksks". The ksks being the strange little noise that escaped from these big whiskers when it blocked on a difficulty.

You will probably believe the joke, the deception, but ask everyone who worked at Sega and then at Cyber Press Publishing. They will confirm that it was the "real" Mario. In the worst case his hidden twin brother, his doppelganger, his clone, but I know that this is the true incarnation of Mario. One night I will go to dinner at his place and he will make me eat a pizza with curious mushrooms.

Chapter 15

The Sleeper Must Wake

"A Beginning is a Moment of Extreme Delicacy": The Daughter of the Emperor Padishah Shaddam IV in the Introduction to David Lynch's Dune. Here is the extraordinary parenthesis "Philippe Ulrich" and "Dune", at the time of the release, of the second part, of the new film adaptation by Denis Villeneuve in this year 2024. History would be an eternal beginning!

Chronologically this chapter should appear at the beginning of this book. But I preferred to insert a more narrative and especially more sensational passage, with the Formula 1, which fits more with the quest of many players in need of thrills, especially "Sega" players and especially when they were wandering around the arcade. Have emotions, live experiences closer to reality, and go fast, very fast: the F1, a true leitmotiv for Sega as much as Sonic!

If speed is characteristic of the DNA of Sega, we can also find grains of sand, and especially grains of Dune! I tell you this story because it is a little bit that of the Masters Sega, a little bit that of Virgin Loisirs, before becoming a little more also that of Sega through the "MegaCd". The Mega Drive device that would mark a technological turning point with the widespread move to CD players for consoles, as for computers. It's a page in the history of video games, which we were able to witness, incredulous, before our eyes! And even to a page as mythical as mystical with the "Muad'Dib", future "Kwisatz Haderach". Without realizing it: we could hardly suspect it!?! As long as a video game is not playable it's only a vague idea.

When I arrived at Virgin Loisirs in September 1991, I was far away, but then very far from imagining all the encounters I would make. Right next to the Bureau of Romuald, and thus Master Sega, a "little man" with frizzy and wavy hair, so that he could have quite well presented himself to the casting of the Lord of the Rings to play one of the many hobbits. Wearing glasses, he had settled in an office without windows for months, his name was Philippe Ulrich! A name that sounds louder and bigger than the one of a simple Hobbit. A name that even glitters well the Germanic mythology, the

Ring of the Nibelungen, or fantasy as with Elric of Stormbringer: the eternal Champion!

That's for instant fantasies, but what could inspire you more seriously? Probably not much or so little! Well, I was nothing at the time. And yet this "little man" was, and probably still remains, one of the greatest creators of video games of all time! He will be one of the first if not the first great French or even European creator leaving his mark, these marks forever. And as one of the pioneers successfully returned, for many years, in the legend of video games.

He is first known to be the author or rather the creator of "L'Arche du Capitaine Blood" released on Atari ST in 1987. The game will be the best-selling in France the year of its release and the best-selling French game worldwide in the same period, with amazing scores and very high in the USA.

We are talking about 150,000 copies sold which is huge considering the time. SVM (Science and Life micro) will talk about the "Most beautiful game in the world" giving it four pages, which the magazine will never do for a video game. The game will also receive all kinds of awards around the world including a famous Tilt d'Or in France. This playful video adventure is so spectacular graphically, for the time, that Ulrich will see land in his studio, the Matra's bosses, impressed by the result of fractals, they will ask him to develop an animation algorithm: a missile simulation for the French army! Philippe Ulrich, through his company ERE, will also be the first to publish a French game on the Nintendo Gameboy: Bubble Ghost!

Despite the huge worldwide success of Captain Blood, the company of the creator will be liquidated following great financial difficulties of its parent company "Infogrames". Philippe Ulrich will then bounce back in 1989 within Virgin Loisirs, a French subsidiary of Virgin Games which had just acquired the rights to the science fiction bestseller "Dune" by Franck Herbert.

Virgin Loisirs which becomes, in the same year 89, the new official distributor of Sega consoles in the UK and France.

Scalded by his misadventure "Infogrames", Ulrich will work as an independent in the premises of Virgin Loisirs, financed by Virgin Game and under a new label: Cryo (a label only for now, the company will be created later). After the extraordinary success of Captain Blood's Ark, Virgin Games will naturally propose to Ulrich to adapt Dune into a video game. He and his team will not be asked, it is a divine gift! For the record, Virgin Games will refuse to host and finance Paul Cuisset, the future author and creator of "Flashback"! We can only make the right choices!

The project is progressing well but Virgin Games finally decides to drop the case in September 90 judging the development too "French"!?! But Ulrich and his band will continue to develop the game in hiding! Virgin Games cuts the funds but not Virgin Loisirs, then directed by Jean Martial Lefranc, who will become a little later his partner in the creation and management of Cryo Interactive. Clandestinity therefore because for almost a year, they will refine the game without having the right, without having the rights! The boss of Virgin Games finally discovered it, late, and is very angry: we are in June 91. However, Philippe Ulrich manages to convince him that we must (re)examine the file. The boss then gives Ulrich five weeks to present him a playable demo. The Boss is conquered by what he saw, Ulrich can continue to develop his game and employees of Virgin leisure will be able to see on occasion, in the corridors of the company, a small radio-guided vehicle with a camera, for 3D shots that will be used to program and finish the game. Did the employees of Virgin serve as models for the giant worms? The Fremens? The Harkonnen?

The Sega Masters being at the front, we will of course be invited to come and take a look at the latest visuals and to discover the atmosphere and magical music, as some cinematics. The game being very static we could almost already immerse ourselves in it completely: The soundtrack, the "BO" or "OST" for the Anglophones is simply prodigious! She will greatly contribute to the success of the game, both mesmerizing and hypnotic.

And what about the cinematics that bring the video game into a new era more cinematographic of course and immerses you even more in these fantastic universes! We were incredible privileged people and we didn't know anything about it! At the time I would probably have preferred to discover the development of a Sonic or a Phantasy Star but on reflection, this experience was unique and incomparable because "Dune" is unique, and incomparable by its storyline density, fantastic, mystical, esoteric." The Sega

Masters, like the Muad'Dib "Sleeper", should grow up and wake up... but later!".

However Virgin Loisirs will be absorbed by Sega Japan during the summer of 1991 to become Sega France! The Japanese company therefore takes over for itself all the activities of which it has the paternity and transfers the Virgin activities to Virgin!

I remember very well when we come to tell him the news. He was of course confused and very embarrassed: "But how will it go for me then?!" He asked himself all shabby. Sega will then leave the end of September to make these boxes. Almost dismissed as a dirty man, although he was "clandestine" for a while, and even an official "clandestine"!?! It is in fact a separation of all the commonest things in business, except for the person most concerned.

Virgin Loisir, which has recently become Sega France, no longer had to finance it or even accommodate it in its offices. And yet it had become a bit his home, and even his family, his campaign of the time was the press officer of Virgin Loisirs/Sega!

It is this same companion, Nellie, who during the trip in TGV direction Le mans for the World Karting Championships, will modestly make the article to children accompanying her. I was there with him in the car that took us... " He made "Bubble Ghost" on GameBoy, and the Captain Blood's Ark...". I did not know either or very vaguely. Sacrilege: I may have even thought at the time that it was a second-zone creator. And yes, a game "Gameboy" in addition, among sworn enemies!!! It was still the first French game developed at the Japanese giant.

On 27 September 1991, almost at the time of his departure from Sega France, Virgin Games USA signs with Sega an adaptation of Dune on Mega-CD.

In retrospect, it's terrible for a video game enthusiast like me. I spent a month a few meters from a legend (even if it was not as much as now) without ever being able to appreciate its true value! He wrote some of the history of video games and I will only realize it much later! Two years exactly, discovering and playing Dune Mega CD version. An incredible game at the time, taking us into a new dimension of video fun. A new age, a new era... " A beginning is an extremely delicate moment"!

I do not know where he will find refuge but what is sure is that the game would be released on PC in 1992 but still in "floppy disk" version. Cryo, the company, would finally be officially launched with his ex-partner, former CEO of Virgin Loisirs Jean-Martial Lefranc and with the success that we know him for many years! Dune will be the first game to be released, with The Seven Guest on PC, in full CD-ROM at the end of 1993. This is the beginning of the end for floppy disks, which will very quickly disappear in favor of CD-ROMs. The Sega MegaCd version also comes out at about the same time with a lot of advertising. Sega will even pay the luxury of a unique TV ad of 3 minutes on TF1. The Mega-CD will not be a commercial success but the manufacturers of consoles would soon offer themselves a new battlefield with a new fighter of importance that will do much harm to Sega. Of course it's Philips and its CDI! No, I'm joking, you will all understand that I'm talking about Sony and its Playstation. Sony which will prepare its entry on the market in several years but waiting for the advent of CD players on consoles in mass market!

Sega has won battles, lost battles, and will lose the war against Sony. But the society will have had the merit, all the merit and the honors of being and remaining at the forefront and standing up to the end as long as there was a modicum of strength and energy left. Like Leonidas and his 300 fighters against the army of Xerxes: to be defeated without danger, one triumphs without glory.

There is no shame in losing to someone much more powerful than yourself. Especially when this fight requires you to be as inventive, creative, always be bold. That is also why I was and will always be a "Master Sega". To be able to compete with someone stronger than oneself, and only with someone stronger than oneself whenever possible. Whatever the cost, whatever the outcome. It is the only way to rise higher, always higher.

Chapter 16

What is it then, Master Sega ?

It was not three months that I was at Sega that I was asked to accompany the press officer for a radio and live show, to present new products and especially to talk about "Master Sega". The advertising campaign is a hit with both young and old and arouses much curiosity and interest in the media, it will even be quickly parodied by Canal+ via "Les Nuls" by Alain Chabat.

Appointment is taken at Radio Nova at an advanced time: Too advanced probably for the many commuters who have a lot of transport before returning home! The Parisian radio is then very close to Place de la Bastille and therefore not far from my home. I will stick to it willingly and as a neighbor, even if I strongly fear this great media premiere! Nellie and I meet at the entrance of the radio station. Time to brief each other on our roles. She will present the new products and I will probably be questioned as "Master Sega". Attention: not as a "hotlineur", animator or advisor but as a media curiosity! Singularity that will last as long as it must last but I am invited to present myself as "Master". Big pressure but also colossal excitement! Nellie does not make any recommendations, I am free-wheeling, in perfect improvisation!

That's what I would love for years at Sega and above all! Confidence or unconsciousness, unless we are not taken seriously enough? I will always be given maximum freedom! We were, we would be and we would remain the official voice of Sega, or rather of Master Sega (the difference is tenuous especially for children) for many years in "off" but sometimes even in "On"! Patrick Borg and Richard Darbois were the voices of the TV advertising campaign 2/3 years, we would be the voice of Master Sega for more than 10 years otherwise! Live or recorded, by phone and in interviews on TV channels, radio, shows and private events! Oh sure you could read the chronicles of AHL, JM Destroy, Banana San or even Marcus, but nothing was worth a phone call live to know immediately which game to choose between "Flicky" and "The Immortal" (if it is possible to ask this question, we must believe that our Sega fans had a sense of humor and challenge! Or were they just looking to test our knowledge?) or how to beat the last boss in Ghostbusters.

Total freedom that I surely owe, retrospectively, to Romuald, who in his work of representation of "Master Sega" has always been able to play perfectly balanced with all the good levers of communication. Relaxed but professional and never failing to add a touch of humor, mysticism, provocation, not forgetting the end of the end, the edge of laconism!

Because it is also that "Master Sega", it is probably even his trademark which lends itself wonderfully well to short format ads: You want to play with me? Did you come by bike? You may be called Michael but not yet Jackson! You will laugh, you are second last! And the athlete, what is important to participate? So you have little wires touching?"

Master Sega recalls in this the greatest warriors of the archaic but especially classic Sparta! Enjoying a reputation, barely usurped, of unbeatable fighters or even indestructible, the Spartans allowed themselves in all circumstances, even if conditions did not allow it, to mock, to make fun of those who dared come to challenge them, with such confidence, the smile in the corner, that even the most formidable opponents, the largest of armies, were more often to doubt, before trembling or even abandoning the battlefield! Julius Caesar himself, much later, Hellenist and especially laconic at will will use like no other of this sharp and striking rhetoric.

The "Sega is stronger than you" is just as fully assumed in provocation, triumphalism and then authoritarianism as the "Veni Vidi Vidi" (I came, I saw, I defeated) of the most famous imperator of Rome. At least from the point of view of "Master Sega" of course because the "it's stronger than you" also reason as a personal and individual challenge uncontrollable and infinite. But in both cases, the pride and the pride of the players are deeply affected, and the student will always try to surpass the master, whatever it costs him! This is the huge victory of Sega: to become the ultimate challenge, probably unsurmountable.

I have been practicing "role-playing" for many years, so it is always a joy to get people, listeners into the improvised stories, that they finally want to hear! Nevertheless I am an employee of Sega and I cannot completely tell anything... Unless: they stretch me the pole? You are a player or you are not! If you are looking for a "Master Sega" there is a good chance to find it!

I will always remember the seconds before the take-off! On the radio (as on television during live broadcasts) you have a countdown that starts at 60 or even 120 seconds to reach zero. It's the moment of emptiness where everyone must be able to concentrate one last time, or remember each other, how it should, how it will start! For the first time for me in Live, this countdown is totally hypnotic, a little stressful and at the same time it captures all my attention! Fascination! Nellie and I are sitting in front of the radio host. We are finally live and our interlocutor immediately takes the floor to announce to all these listeners that he welcomes tonight the press officer of Sega as well as Master Sega himselfsame: Enormous pressure but also delicious and formidable adrenaline discharge! I'm on 50,000 volts! It's totally unreal!

Just four months ago I was playing at home, all alone, in the province, in front of my little tv connected to the Mega Drive (or the opposite) studying more really pimply if not those of the gamepad, and now I am "Master Sega" and I will address tens of thousands of listeners! I will later do recorded interviews for TF1 or FR3 but it will never be worth, in emotions, this first time live!

I was so excited, tense, excited that I can't remember the chronology of the show very well, but I still remember it as if it were yesterday when he asked me: "We talk a lot about Master Sega right now, "blablabla", tv, radio, press... But what is it then, Master Sega? A sect? A knight's order? Do you end up in secret caves or at the bottom of an abbey?" Do you sacrifice Polish plumbers? Or Italians?".

BINGO! We are in humor mode it will do but we do not forget to specify what our missions are. I go in Jedi order mode where Teutonic knights, with a great master or a high priest I do not know anymore!?!

"Yes we are warriors, eternal fighters appeared at the dawn of humanity and we train day and night, we must win or die, and re-win before rearing. We are immortal anyway." Smiles. No need to add, never do too much, the humor mode must cover with a light veil and keep the mystery that surrounds us!

For years, I will be asked the same questions over and over again. The children will ask me how we are to be Master Sega, and the adults: "But what is it Master Sega?". More than thirty years later I believe I can give several answers according to your level of curiosity, the time you give me and all the more your passion on the subject.

The first answer, minimalist, very down-to-earth and for those who don't have much to do: the "Sega Masters" were young men (and sometimes young women) often very passionate about video games, that one could contact by telephone or minitel in order to have all the tips, codes, solutions, information on products distributed by Sega. Yeah, yeah, yeah... that's right!

A second answer necessarily more literary and therefore more flattering, generated by marketing and communication around the Mythology of Master Sega through its various advertisements, will invoke Sega Masters knowing everything, absolutely everything, omniscients at least as far as the Sega universe is concerned. They are the strongest, most talented, most fierce players in the world (and even the Universe as Romuald claimed) The Krachs of video games and all-powerful on Sega machines. We found a good part of them playing on Nintendo consoles and so depressed, so frustrated not having the challenges they needed, that they heard the call of the Master and went to challenge him!

We can concede that the trait is perhaps "a little" exaggerated!?! In fact Master Sega the one and only exists indeed, but through us all: forming like a impregnable Greek phalange! Nothing can resist them! Like the Spartans of antiquity, they will be the first to be "warriors, fighters, professionals"!

The Hotline of Master Sega is the first army of trade, professional players! Who do only this and on the hardest games that are, because often from the Arcade and therefore intended for those who have already chin hair! I hear you think: what about Nintendo? You wouldn't forget SOS Nintendo? The collective unconscious that we share will draw them more like firefighters or plumbers, circulating in truck probably red, when the Masters Sega take, they, the train of the European challenge refereeing and designating the greatest players of the old continent. Bandai/Nintendo executives, not the least of them, will leave Mario for Sonic. The reverse won't happen, not in those years anyway. Two of them, defectors, will even become "DG", one after the other, with more or less success! I take the opportunity to salute Bruno Charpentier who, in addition to having done an excellent job in the various positions entrusted to him, was not lacking curiosity and interest for the Hotline and its Sega Masters.

We the Masters were dedicated only to this: to advance and triumph over all dangers and all adversaries! Sweat and blood: sometimes real, sometimes virtual.

Mythology? But yes, children aged six to fifteen will believe in Master Sega, as others in the exploits of Achilles or Ulysses. Sega has become a master among the masters in the art of "Story Telling" via video games! The first source of entertainment and inspiration for hundreds of millions of people now around the world! Sega will tell hundreds of stories! And the one from "Master Sega" will style them like that from Shéhérazade and 1001 Nights! As if Arabian Fight was superimposed on Arabian Nights. Master Sega is a living and enduring myth thanks to the passion of thousands if not millions of nostalgic gamers. And that make me, at this very moment through the writing of this book, come out of a long retreat! When I say "retirement" it is the Sega, because I have never stopped maintaining my rank, my level wherever I go. But it is, or rather they are, other stories!!!

I could repeat it a hundred, a thousand, ten thousand times! What's incredible about this story is that the Sega Masters were tremendously passionate: they saw the light and they came back... But "you" the young "Sega Maniacs" of the time are often even more passionate than we can ever be! TontonSega, Spartan, Negan, Alexandre, Mathieu, Steven and so many others! You would have probably been excellent Masters! And you are certainly already!

I can offer you a third, more "personal" answer! More philosophical, more metaphysical, while striking it with my immoderate taste and my insatiable curiosity for ancient civilizations. Starting with the Spartan civilization you will have noticed. I speak for myself and certainly for Romuald. We the two Sega Masters who have almost gone through the whole history "Sega France", at his service, for better or worse, on thirteen and fourteen years! We could have been the Remus and Romulus of the Sega Masters but ancient Rome won everything, everything. Sega was more a Challenger if not even the number one challenger: very strong, very powerful locally but never tough enough to hold an Empire! And like the classical Sparta, it will one day reach the hegemony around the Aegean Sea, thus crushing the Athenians at home, before collapsing only a few months, a few years later! It is always much more difficult to keep a title than to take it, to tear it away.

We would be rather the "Castor and Pollux", the illustrious Dioscures of the archaic sparte ("Trojan" era) and who will inspire to this legendary "City State" a double authority through a diarchy: two Kings at the same time! One ruler in his kingdom while the other one plays the ambassador around the world when it's not about war! But if I make this analogy between the Spartiates and the Sega Masters it is that there are probably as many misunderstandings about these "champions" on both sides!

We know the Spartans to have been soldiers, warriors undaunted, almost invulnerable! Which could also suit the "Sega Masters"! But the strength of both Spartans and Sega Masters was not simply in their ability to fight the enemy, to triumph! The spartiates, like the Sega Masters were certainly more combative (they almost systematically won all the Olympic or Pythian events during the various games organized at the time) but they were also and above all versatile and formidably resilient! Curious about everything and insatiable...

The Spartans were not so much the greatest warriors of antiquity or even all times, they were also and above all men, and women, the most educated in the world! They all knew how to read and write (rare for the time), learned to sing, dance, play musical instruments. They were learning drama and comedy. They learned history, philosophy and rhetoric, that of their native laconia or the art of expressing themselves in few words and in a striking way! What we could call "punch line" in our time. The illustrious Socrates said it very well: "when you meet a Spartan you first have the impression of falling on a man not evolved, he listens to you for a long time, then in the end, in a few words it is he who shows you that the child: it's you"!

A Spartiate, alone, is not necessarily the strongest, is not the most intelligent, is not the most skillful, is not the most spiritual, but gather several and they become quickly unbeatable! On everything! "The strength of a Spartan is the Spartiate who stands by his side," will say Leonidas. From agogy to pedagogy, the Spartans were champions of education and teaching. And they were trained in a steel mind! An unshakable faith. To men and women: historians, even contemporary, will not emphasize it. The war, the battlefields, were forbidden to them and therefore few women will go into history except for Hélène, Gorgo and Cynisca.

A Sega master can play Flicky then Road Rash, Gynoug, Phantasy Star, Megalomania, Terminator in the same day... Before returning to Flicky! And finish them one after the other! Real war machines on all games. Or rather on all challenges whatever they are.

Spartan like Masters Sega never retreat, never surrender, if they fall, they immediately rise up, we have thousands of lives and almost as many challenges. Resilient and versatile, they take on all the challenges that may arise! Nothing, absolutely nothing should, can make them "afraid"! They will repeat the same thing a hundred times, a thousand times as long as they have not exceeded it! That's the big difference with most players! We never let go of anything and we will never let go of anything because we were (or not!?!) the Sega Masters!

Chapter 17
How I became Master Sega

In the previous chapters, I wanted to focus on what is now known as the "Roaring Twenties" of video games, both in an effort for memory, entertainment and pure nostalgia: a cuvée as exceptional as fantastic for Sega in France, in Europe and everywhere in the world. And if there was only a memory of the great epic of Sega in France it would be obviously that! If the rise of the waters had certainly started vigorously in 1989, let alone 1990, it was especially during the years 91, 92 and 93 that this rise turned into a tidal wave taking away everything on its passage. In the abundant foam of this boiling ocean agitation sprang, as frantically as proudly, "Master Sega". It will shine like the sun, marking the hearts and minds of the public, players and non-players alike.

It was very important for me to convey, share and perhaps even, for many of you, to relive those years of maximum video fun illuminations, full of parties, meetings, joy lived by millions of young people, as younger players, through the eyes of one of the greatest, if not the most privileged in France at that time: the "Sega Master", of which I was one of the avatars, and for whom I remain one of the most faithful actor and now narrator. We carried and fulfilled this mission most often with passion of course, an intense and contagious joy, a certain ambition, an absolute motivation and sometimes even devotion.

I therefore spontaneously told the beginning of my Sega story, partly from the point of view of "Gaming" of course, but probably too succinct for many "player readers", because I really wanted the madness and generosity of the years 91/92/93 to be at the heart of the first Tome, and that they are perceived exactly as what they were and will remain in the collective unconscious: absolutely demented and especially wonderfully human! As if it were perhaps also a question of answering, and twisting the neck once and for all, to the sad gentlemen, to all those who have never understood anything about video games and will never understand anything, who have tried to vilify him, To put him in the same line of accused, of the same evils as those that have fallen before on literature, music, radio, cinema and television: these news and therefore these "sub-cultures"! Before they gain respectability and before they permanently upset the hierarchy.

Video games are now recognized as a major art, no matter how many people like it, but they have been since the beginning, even if it was not necessarily the most obvious when two rackets, or rather two large luminous bars frantically returned a small square, on the background of a screen still too dark! Art and major entertainment that are absorbed, shared and passed on... But as anything, it is not to abuse, and a fortiori it is to continue to cultivate its curiosity, these desires without that any can eradicate definitively the others. Without any one can take all the space, and leave nothing to the others but maybe a few crumbs. This intense passion for video games, which sometimes made me play twelve hours a day, six days a week over small periods of a few weeks, never prevented me from socializing, even if not as much as I would have liked, having unfortunately not the gift of ubiquity but often fighting my shyness, precisely by this passion through events and shows.

My passion for video games was unlimited for almost twenty years but it never evacuated, never replaced, my eternal passions for cinema, tales and legends in general, Greek mythology in particular, astronomy, astrophysics and the sciences of awakening and life. An insatiable curiosity that has found in and around the world of video games, many years, discoveries and challenges of all kinds, architecting with happiness and delight my little neural circuits, The intellectual scheme as the emotional lift of my thoughts and consciousness! Always higher, always farther, always stronger. Although I will never deny a part of "Mortal Kombat", "Streets of Rage" or "NHL Hockey", I got fed up and filled with strategy games, puzzles, adventures and roles. Megalomania, Sim City, Ultima 4, Phantasy Star, Shining Force, Landstalker, Rings of Power, Bubble Bobble, Centurion, Dune, Tomb Raider, Bust A Move, Dr Robotnik's Mean Bean Machine, Ecco le Dauphin, over and above. As before I had been able to get enough of the tales of Andersen (Hans Christian and not Marc!!!), of those of 1001 nights, of Grimm's tales, of Charles Perrault and so many others. So many video games that open many doors of our imagination, thus offering the possibility to open new ones. If video games are an art, it is also a huge, continuous and shared celebration, in a living room or in a playground, and I hope to have paid him the sincere tribute that he will always deserve to give us so much happiness.

But gaming is going to come back to the heart of the action and strong. The Game: this so powerful engine, this inner form, which can sometimes turn into addiction, even a real Demon, in many gamers, especially in Sega enthusiasts, and not that of the Masters, amateurs more than any other strong sensation, and at least at that time... So here, and in detail this time: Or, When and How the Demon of the video game took hold of me. Pushing me inevitably to the fate that will be mine: that of a Master Sega, marked with red iron and forever.

1978. Claude François dies electrocuted in his bathtub. Carton of his song "Alexandrie, Alexandra". Dorothée launches and presents Récré A2: First broadcast of Goldorak, millions of children, like me, completely hooked! The Giant Robot Song, performed by Noam, is one of the best-selling 45 tours of the year. The film "Les Bronzés" comes out to cinema (he has a malaise the bathrobe?) Premier Paris Dakar. First success for the singer Daniel Balavoine and "ça plane pour moi" for Plastic Bertrand.

And it will be high for all the geeks around the world. I discover the first video game console for the general public, the Magnavox Odyssey, so this is my first big "injection". Will follow the Game & Watch of Nintendo, in playgrounds with notably Donkey and the Plumber not Polish, then the Commodore 64 in the early and mid 80's and in salons. If the sensations and pleasure were already very intense, they had not prepared me for the shocks that I was going to live eight years later in two times and three movements! 1986 will be like the big, the very big injection, the mega shoot historic, overdose to the limit, mystical connection, and that will make me totally hooked, and in conditions that will flirt with sin!

I had heard about the arcades, these magnificent and spectacular furniture installed in bars and other cafes, often offering playful video adventures as intense as colorful, as rich as wonderfully sonorised and rhythmic. Had I probably ever approached them closely, had I even played them on occasion, in various and varied circumstances, devouring ghosts of all colors on Pac Man or blasterizing hordes of flying saucers lined up like sardines in a supermarket as in the game Space Invaders. Always accompanied by adults, certainly my parents, because children alone were not allowed to come, and especially to stay near these infernal machines. Experiences already hypnotic but too short to dive into completely. It will be quite different in 1986.

"A NOUS LES PETITES ANGLAISES"

1986 the happy, we get there. Year of the first cohabitation under the fifth republic. Jacques Chirac becomes the prime minister of François Mitterrand. The FN of Jean Marie Le Pen enters the assembly with thirty-five deputies: it is a shock for a large part of the French population. But we are then especially, us young people, teens, turned to music, the party and its many "Booms"! And it is good because it is also the madness of the "TOP 50" and he invited all the youth's for a particularly prosperous year music side, French artists as foreign with notably the New Wave and Depeche Mode in the lead. The number of night clubs explodes and so I will go to the wall, on occasion and like many others, with my older brother, literally with a ladder, and to get out of my room on the first floor, then at the back of MTX Honda and to go dancing in clubs more or less lost, around Auxerre, and well before the unavoidable and monopolistic "Styliss" in Rouvray.

It is a year of confirmation and even consecration for the Top 50, with the emergence of cinematic quality video clips, Rita Mitsouko, Midnight Demons, Eve Rise Up, Like a Hurricane, Mylène Farmer and her Libertine and through Indochine. Catherine Lara sings "Nuit Magique" (she will soon become addicted to Nintendo consoles) and a young boy named Marc Lavoine gets known with his "Parking des Anges" (A very happy parking that I will find also this year!?!). The singer also of "Eyes revolvers", will become Sega Maniac and spend an entire afternoon enchanted with us, the Masters Sega, a few years later. We'll slap him in Street of Rage. It is also the disappearance of Daniel Balavoine in a helicopter accident on the Dakar and that of Coluche to Moto. And I can close the parenthesis with the card of "L'Aziza" of Balavoine, as a voluntary and assumed response to the rise of the National Front.

I am a teenager, and like most of those around me: in full emotional overdrive, we are then in search of XXL adventures. My classmate Julien Xavier and I are on a school trip at the end of the school year, near Oxford in England, and we had the wonderful idea, for some, the very bad idea for others, to whistle and call out happy and playful "little English" in front of our hosts' house, the first or second night of our arrival. An initiative that came totally from Julien but I will accompany him and encourage him very well. The local girls seemed particularly receptive to these proposals of interactions and connections diverse and varied and we really thought we could improve our language skills by this meeting as exotic as spontaneous!

The channel tunnel does not exist and the important Anglo-French population transfers on both sides have not yet begun: we are therefore fully benefiting from this reputation of "French lovers" as well as a rarity effect! "A nous les petites Anglaise" (To us little English girls), a very light French comedy of morals from 1976 and still popular ten years later, must have resonated in our carefree teenage heads, in full explosion and other hormonal disturbances! The trailer of the film was very clear: "Send your children to England" with an extract from the most catchy movie "Since I tell you that they f..k the English it is known! There we will only have to lift a finger!!!". Not sure that the film has met the same success on both sides of the Channel but in France, it was a long time "reference" (good or bad) for many teenagers, not yet "finished", just started!

Our prospects on the subject seemed to want to be crowned with success and we would also have "our little English", but it was not counting our host family, like those of the neighborhood and therefore those of these naive British, and it would end rather: "No, no, no!!! The little English girls" ! We had crossed a red line and then immediately became the danger of an entire neighborhood! We were going to pay him immediately. To be sure we wouldn't do anything stupid, our two hosts will take us both, all evening, in their pub! But as we are not adults, they will abandon us, lock us in the evening time in a small room next door, with a ridiculous package of chips taste vinegar!?! A drink and with, for only distraction, and for several hours: an arcade! That I had not really calculated in the first minutes of our arrival, because it was inert, disconnected as we could be ourselves at this moment: empty.

So it is a little, much, the soup with the grimace, when we arrive. We settle down, but after having blown many times out of spite, even despair, thinking back to these young and beautiful English girls all excited, I discover all the potential treasure and the extraordinary mysterious power of this playful video furniture that is there, close to me, but which shows no sign of life at the moment. I remember so precisely that incredible moment when I was physically, totally, attracted by this fantastical object! Vibrations, waves of unimaginable power were then exerted on me and like a magnetic magnet, I will advance towards him as a mystic lover. I will have to meet the most smiling and attractive woman, later, to make me at least as much effect. The situation was memorable because I was alone physically, or almost, completely psychically naked, free of everything else, of the slightest parasite, and therefore totally open to this machine that seemed gigantic to me, taking over my entire field of vision. It seemed to be only for me in this tragi-comic moment, or I abandoned illusions as more or less "romantic" impulses! Time was suspended and it will remain in a corner of my memory, almost forty after.

I was like Indiana Jones finding the Ark of the Covenant or the Dial of Destiny. I was like Arthur Pendragon approaching the Excalibur Sword planted in his rock. An extremely powerful and vibrant magical aura surrounded this technological artifact and it seized me, penetrating me and already changing me deeply. It was visually exactly like in the Walt Disney movie "Tron," where the hero would walk up to this machine, a computer, to go through, to enter another dimension." I was always dreaming of a world that I thought I'd never see, and one day something happened, something extraordinary..." As "Kevin Flynn" will tell, the hero of Tron has his son Sam. Also talented, in the footsteps of his father, he will also advance to the door of Tron, after passing through many old machines of dusty arcades and disconnected.

The Borne straight out of my dreams, totally supernatural, appeared to me as the most incredible and fascinating of all Graals: bigger than I was from the top of my thirteen years, and even more, that at this moment, she slept like a sleeping dragon in the depths of her hiding place, in a cave as deep and dark as it is secret, and it was not certain that we could wake her up, make her emerge! It was not connected but I was excited, the current between us, would necessarily pass. Between the day of my birth and the day of my death, Destiny, impeccably and still so majestic, had invited himself, and he was coming closer to me than ever. I easily took my courage to two hands to try to revive the sleeping beast, by connecting it to the sector, and then revealing me, in what fantastic universe, it was going to be able to make me tip over.

My whole soul would fall to the overflowing if it were not already so. The adrenaline gushing in profusion, time had stopped again, I was transported by a thousand sensations and so many emotions for a trip probably without return.

It was really like a dream and finally it would be: we get closer and caress perfection! Because a few seconds later, I was going to discover in a greater happiness than the Everest itself, I was going to be able to take and dress, the shining armor of King Arthur! Not without having slipped a first coin. The legendary Arthur Pendragon who is looking for his dulcinée, crossing ruins, cemeteries and underworld populated by flying demons and other hordes of living dead, King Arthur associated with the fabulous history of the knights of the round table! I was fascinated, as many others probably were, by this legend and I was still filled with the vibrations and emotion of John Boorman's highly-acclaimed 1981 film, but seen personally very recently. I knew by heart the magic formula of Merlin the enchanter (Annallnafratt...) the very powerful breath dragon. I knew all the protagonists: Perceval, De Galaad, Morgane, Guinevere, Gauvain, Mordred, Lancelot, Uther Pendragon, often played by young actors in the making such as Gabriel Byrne, Liam Neeson, Patrick Stewart, Helen Mirren and many others.

I was discovering the incredible, and now mythical all over the world, video game "Ghostn Goblins" of the no less mythical company "Capcom". Javelin, dagger, axe, torch, shield and crucifix will allow me to fight and get rid of my enemies, and may be find my tender and very beloved Guinevere, who expects a lot from me, to pull her out of this very bad step. Because yes, in pure hypnotic magic, I became instantly Arthur Pendragon! The game is as fantastic as it can be difficult, and even very difficult. And he had suddenly transformed this moment so lymphatic as tragi-comic in pure moment of Happiness, Evasion and Exaltation! Opening a new door to my imagination in search of adventures and challenges and immediately getting out of my glass bell and therefore prisoner. With a joy and an unprecedented zeal, if not those of the infant, opening these wonderful Christmas gifts. I was five or six again and addicted: clear, clean and definitive. I will never be Nintendo, I was not yet Commodore, not yet Sega: I was just CAPCOM at that moment!

These magical furniture irresistibly attracted every child or teenager passing by, otherwise it was still necessary to be tall enough to lean on the screen. When you did, you were most often seized by this hypnotic power which was very difficult to get rid of once it had penetrated you. Fortunately, these machines were difficult to access. They were, on the one hand, reserved for adults, except to be stuck with them in exceptional circumstances, and especially intended for those who were able to feed it by many pieces, because these were eaten in no time. The arcade posts quickly became, and often a ruin for those who put their hands on it, because they would put their hand on your wallet. Thus limited access and most demanding, both physically and economically for a teenager, yet unless you are locked in a bar or cafe, this equation to three unknowns, or, when and how, would be solved soon, in the most singular circumstances: unique!?!

We would return to Auxerre, with images "so british" full head, memories, most often, very culinary: horrible things to eat, sweet with salty and breakfast, chips in vinegar, tartines of jelly, jams and meats! BOUAAARRRRKKK! But I came back especially with this taste of the Adventure embodied by this good king Arthur jumping and gesturing, with or without armor, in all directions to get rid of these dark pursuers more villain one than the other by their natures. My life would be permanently and totally changed: undoubtedly, my Future!

This first fall "to the bottom of the cauldron" from which I did not recover, would be followed very quickly by a recall, even more powerful, much more violent and destabilizing. I will then be penetrated in every single one of my cells! If Eternity can be a day, it must also be a fraction of a second. Emotion transcends time and space. I was not yet fourteen years old, the age of many torments, and I was going to discover my first arcade room, my first great chapel and in a dizzying emotional elevator, as for my true baptism and through the very joyful funfair of end of school year that was installed, as every year, on the large parking lot of "La Noue", between my college, which I will attend from 6th to 3rd so, and the Stadium of the Abbé Deschamps, the football (soccer) temple of AJA and its magician: a certain Guy Roux. Another Absolute Master in his category; who will show that passion, youth, ardor, work, blue and the D system can take everything away and reach the heights, Glory and success, at least for a few moments, but moments engraved for eternity.

College student in the small town of Auxerre, and from different windows of the rooms in which I studied mathematics as the Latin, I will see every year dozens and dozens of fairground in their big and beautiful trucks, on this parking lot of La Noue, huge parking lot, which also serves to accommodate all vehicles of football and AJA fans. It will then, little by little, turn into this vast party that every young person ardently wanted to attend, and more than anything else, in one way or another: ghost trains, Palais des Miroirs, bumper cars, cotton candy, love apples, pirate boats, Giant wheel, I pass and more sensational that filled the bellies or emptied them! It would soon become "my Parking des Anges".

Although I love all these rides, my attention would be quickly and even very quickly taken by new attractions: video games! Especially arcade machines that then begin to offer furniture offering real physical sensations as new as exciting. If on the one hand I could play video games on "standard furniture" like Pac Man or the already very famous and very sought after "Ghost'n Goblins", a very important video game company offered much more advanced and therefore more immersive terminals, for experiences that seem much more real! It was left to me to check it out for myself. SEGAAAA!!!

Yes Sega appeared to me for the first time, with these large and beautiful letters in blue, and immediately offered me these very valuable advantages: starting with the sensational, the unique, the irresistible, the absolutely phenomenal HANG ON, One of the first 16-bit arcade games, technology then offering a palette of 32,000 different colors! It is also one of the first games called "Taikan" by the Japanese manufacturer, which allowed to reproduce certain sensations of a motorcycle race, directly riding a reproduction of a GP 500 motorcycle and not any, that of the world champion of the time: Freddie Spencer, or for the race queen of motorcycle competitions. An SICK experience at that time, a madness for teenagers, if you had not yet had the chance to drive one of these infernal two-wheeled cars!

There would be a before and after Hang On for all those who would be and those who will want to be! Hang On, the first game or your feet would not touch land!!! Literally as figuratively. The first game Whaoooooouuuuuoouuuuuuuhhhh accompanied by this moisture that begins to cover your eyes before it turns into this little tear of emotion and absolute happiness. It's too good, it's too strong, it's too much sensation, it's like the golden key to a fabulous first treasure. The Blue and the immensity of the Ocean would also be those of "Sega"! " Sega Hang On" to begin, and accelerating like never before, as no one else will for a very long time. Hang On was absolutely fabulous because disruptive but as incredible as it may seem, it was only a appetizer, the Aperitif of a gargantuan meal that would last a good ten years in Arcade.

It's the first "master" shot of the designer and brilliant creator "Yu Suzuki" in 1985, and at that time, we are certainly closer to the magic trick than the video game ! " Suzuki" in Master of the Moto GP competition at Sega!?! We could say that it is not invented!?! Suzuki would be blue like no other: from the multiple world GP champion to that of Sega, a great enthusiast of motorcycles and speed competitions who immediately marked the history of video games with this sensational first creation. In 1987 he would put the cover with Super Hang On and its turbo button to exceed 300kms/ hour! If he had not invented the "whaaoouuuuuuuh" effect, he would lengthen it until you lost your breath, with shivers from head to toe, and he would try for years to renew it again and again, taking thousands with him, millions of enthusiasts and lovers of sensations and speed! Hang On will be the first incredible arcade of the "Taikan" series looking to reproduce the physical and bodily sensations of racing machines, driving and later those of mechanical, aerial or ground fights. A first earthquake in the history of video games and which would have many aftershocks.

As early as 1986, I tasted in the arcade for the first time this stunning experience of Hang On: riding this superb motorcycle representation of the great "GP" races. To put it simply, I had just passed again into another dimension: I already liked video games in general, but if they also became a "physical" experience with sensations of this nature, there is no doubt that it was then, To reach very high levels of pleasure, competition, frustration and satisfaction. The impression of speed was really bluffing and the rest even nearly forty years later, with as bonus these almost natural movements to make it lean left or right, and even though we were still quite far from reality: we believed it! I was already Arthur and Capcom and will remain so, but I also became Freddie Spencer, Suzuki and especially "SEGA", and a little more at each game, at each new challenge, knight and warrior on one side and speed rider motorcycle on the other.

I will not deny my pleasure except by the fact that these parts were relatively expensive! Which also participated in the excitement and emotion of being able to participate each time, again, sporadically certainly, but finally necessary to keep and maintain a certain frustration, we now in a never completely satisfied desire. I also found my very precious "Ghost'n Goblins" in unconditional Heroic Fantasy lovers and for some parts always as frustrating as satisfying!?!

This first real arcade discovery 1986, totally breathtaking, Sega colors, Suzuki colors, Hang Hon colors, was ending, closed with the departure of the fairground, for another city, but it would leave behind, a giant open door, a new dimension that would very quickly expand and flourish like an immense web of spiders woven by the hands of Masters of the arcade, by the Masters of illusion and also now by the Masters "Taikan" ie physical and bodily sensations. There had been Atari, Capcom, Namco or Taito as well but now there would be SEGA. Now and forever!?! With in particular Suzuki and its fabulous AM2 department. The new bodybuilding gods, overpowered, undisputed of the Arcade offering incredible and unmatched sensations and for a good time. I then really and irresistibly became SEGA and even SUZUKI but this time the manufacturer! A few months or rather a few very small years later, my first real bike will be a RG Gamma historical colors Moto GP race and these gradients of blue and its all firepower! To which I will add a new pot of relaxation Polini in order to have also my Turbo mode! I will then abandon my first Honda MTX all Red! The red frankly it does not go as fast as the Blue!!! Pffff... But I will park anyway, at the Fourrier high school, my RG Gamma, the only one, next to the NSR Honda, the only one, they can always tell racing stories. Riding it, I can then remember my first Hang On parts when I will be running several speeds and the scenery will run faster and faster around me. But in the meantime, I was going back to my studies and would wait wisely for the new season of the video game Arcade!

"Sur le parking des anges plus rien ne les dérange. Quand leurs corps se mélangent dans la lumière étrange..."(Marc Lavoine French Singer). A year had passed and, again, the fair was going to land on the parking lot of La Noue, so we are in 1987 and my waiting will be richly rewarded. SEGA has been successful all over the world with its Hang On. The demand is such that they have trouble producing all the units requested! The explosion, the

Taikan earthquake has just begun! Before the "Home Consoles" years, Sega will have some extraordinary arcade years, from Hang On to R360, Space Harrier, Out Run and After Burner. Many "players" of the video game never fully grasp what was really SEGA to be totally missed or through these years Arcade. "The Arcade" being then for them, at best, only an adjective like another, or a kind of spice that would be sprinkled from time to time on the plate(e)s consoles to enhance the taste, flavor.

Sega will then surbid very quickly, and every year or even every semester, advancing new pawns, new limits: for new and ever more extraordinary sensations. Sega emotional lift and accelerator as there will never be more powerful in such a short time. They are going to conquer the whole world, and they will break the house, blow everything! Competitors will only have the crumbs of this market. This divine wind will blow very strong on the Master System in Europe, but also and especially on the Mega Drive throughout the West with its brilliant central processor "68 000": that of Hang On arcade!

Almost already cult and bestseller as soon as it is released, we tear it apart despite its price, the thrilling, the breathtaking "Out Run" racing simulation or rather driving as Yu Suzuki himself will specify. You take your seat in a complete and faithful reproduction of the Ferrari Testa Rossa convertible and, icing on the cake, you can choose the music that will accompany you during this experience. Not a self-respecting arcade, will miss this new extremely qualitative jump into the Future! And to make sure, Super Hang On and its turbo mode as well as Space Harrier, first post with seat and hydraulic cylinders will complete this wonderful triple "Taikan": always stronger, always faster, always more sensational. Sega/Yu Suzuki set the arcade on fire with these machines that crush or completely kill the competition! I am, and probably like many people, totally amazed, from the top of my fourteen years, by such productions! I like video games on consoles or on microphone but impossible to compete with such proposals that explode all the counters, create and push immediately new limits! How far can Sega push the plug? When other moustaches are reduced to repair or go through pipes?

These new horizons and more distant videos, will not prevent me to continue playing on more standard games in 2D, like Rastan Saga and Black Tiger: two other productions "Heroic Fantasy" and as a fan of Conan The

Barbarian I am! They are much less spectacular at first glance, definitely not so sensational physically, but once inside, the magic works wonderfully and just as well. It does not prevent that if I can finally play these arcade games without being accompanied by adults, at least in the framework of the fair, their use is still significantly limited by the cost of use. And it is perhaps in these limited conditions that a "Master Sega" will be born because "the end often justifies the means" and I was going to check it.

Excited as ever by this incredible Gameplay that explodes everything we could have imagined just two years ago, but rather reserved for those who can afford it if you quickly become addicted, and that while I was broke as wheat and like most 14-year-olds. I had to find a solution! Make money of course!!! But unless I have a real job, I will never get enough!? And here, I must confess, I have surely become "Master Sega": in sin! The video game would transmit me a disease or even worse: the Demon of the game. Everything would then become a game and would be no more than challenge! And if it were only in and through the video game, it wouldn't be too serious.

Among the new features inside the arcade were furniture that was very different from the arcade stalls. Under windows, more or less in the shape of a flying saucer and therefore in half-sphere, large rakes advanced and retreated in a continuous back and forth to push forward, moving bright tokens relatively close to five francs coins! These tokens are countless, stick together, mount on top of each other. On these tokens were carefully placed lots, either physically, like watches, audio tapes, Game & Watch and all kinds of "small objects" often electronic, or larger lots in volume but marked by a plaque, Then we could exchange with the fairground. The goal of the game was simple, it was necessary to slide new tokens with a handle or rather a slide, which was oriented manually at the beginning of this sofa bed of tokens. These new tokens shifted the bed a little, much or not at all, and ended up rushing the tokens and the nearest lots into a small pit by ebb and flow on the outside of the saucer, in which they could then be removed manually.

Obviously to make the most exciting lots fall, you had to send a maximum of chips, most often and finally pay it, because these chips were bought, one franc per unit! But the cleverest would wait for other players to pass before them and "fail" not very far from the goal! All that remained was to put a few extra chips to win the bet. It was therefore above all a game of observation and patience, that is to say that you had to learn the mechanics and the dynamics of the system by observing it for hours and hours to know when to enter the game properly! The players in a hurry would slide and throw their chips to learn, and some more envious to "buy" their lots, and the less rushed to win the bet at a lower cost. Finally, it is mainly the fairground who wins the bet, he is there for business and not really to offer gifts, as it is difficult to make the prizes fall, and contrary to what one can think at first glance.

I'm going to try this game just to see if I have more luck or if I am smarter. I will especially have confirmation that smart or not, you must put a lot of chips even when it seems to be very close to the goal! I will give up all the same, very quickly, any hope of winning an interesting lot without making me empty my pockets! Nevertheless, while playing and therefore being in the handling of these chips, I noticed two things. The first is that these tokens were really very close in size and weight to five frs coins while they were offered at one franc per unit! The second is that it was often better to aim, to play the piles of chips close to falling into the pit rather than the lots themselves! Playing chips to win chips!?! At first it was the best strategy.

The coin being quite close to the five franc coins, I tried very naively to slip one into the slots of the arcade machines. Failed of course, the chips were a little wider, but not much. After a few games of video games and some chips slipped in the pousse pousse chips, I went home, but having kept a chip in my pocket! I was watching carefully: the alloy seemed very fragile, I do not know what material(s) they were made of, but you will now and certainly guessed what could well come to mind.

In the cellar of my house, in the DIY corner, I took a file and reduced the size of this token all around, by one or two millimeters! The operation was relatively long by hand, it took five to ten minutes to complete a full tour. Nevertheless the token was filed and had now the width of a five frs coin! The last possible obstacle could be on weight but the token seemed to be very close. It's 1987 and the automatic machines are not yet ultra precise as it is the case today and certainly for a long time! Since, certainly, small smart "gamers" and more simply scammers or other scrocs have been able to proceed in this way on fair tokens as other various and varied tokens and not worth the sum thus misappropriated!

The next day, after class, I went back to the party and in the arcade to try this pirate's chip! With my heart beating and a bit as if I was going to rob a bank, I slip my chip! I am well aware that it is a theft, a grivellerie, a scam, more simply a robbery! However, at that time I did not measure very well what harm, what wrong I could do, or so little. I became a trader twenty years later and finally learned what it was like to be robbed, and I have, perhaps, repaid this "debt" eventually.

I am not at all proud of this story and fortunately it will no longer encourage anyone to try to replicate it, because today's machines are now extremely accurate, and unless you have the exact weight to the thousandth of a gram, it would not work, It would not work anymore! Except that on this day, my chip light to one franc will pass as a coin of five and therefore credit me with three units on the game "Tron", a 3D game. After the stress hit it is total excitement! Playing video games would now cost me five times less and I was probably going to get fed up! I had then probably become like a kind of Junkie allowing himself some crimes in order to meet his insatiable desires. I will have to buy tokens discreetly, use some of them in the sight and knowledge of the fairground who traded them to me, while using them in an "exponential" strategy as I described it earlier! I could not have bought quantities of tokens and regularly without being spotted quickly, it was now absolutely essential that I can recover through the "shoot", more tokens than I leave directly on the slides! Start for me then an incredible cache game between fake coin maker, or rather fake chip maker, that of hard core arcade players, and the casual player and especially very opportunistic "push push push chips"! I will then play five to ten minutes on an arcade machine while keeping an eye on the chip machines, which I will come to examine quickly and regularly between two different games, but without ever dwelling on it. I will go home with the full of tokens to file, but these last required me too much time to be transformed, manually filed and completely a token, for this guilty pleasure of violation, transgression for an even greater pleasure, to play more and more.

Also I put the perfume of one of my good classmates, Olivier G, who had an electric "grinder" at home, and a crazy desire to play on the terminals. We would go to his DIY cellar to file and prepare our fake coins, in a chain, in one or two minutes for each. What became perfectly "suitable", cunning and apprentice counterfeiters that we had become very spontaneously, but I reassure you, for a very short time. We were going to make almost industrial quantities, dozens or even hundreds and I was going to be able to play every day, especially on Wednesdays and Weekends, for hours and for a little more than two weeks!

So I will be able to play now like a hitch, like a madman, almost unlimited, but nothing should be noticeable from the outside, especially the fairground that managed the room. I will go to make change, a lot of money, every time I pass through the room and I will slip some tokens from time to time in the gift furniture shaped saucer. The subterfuge will work perfectly, I'll spend hours and hours in the arcade and nobody will put his inquisitive look next to me or behind me. The manager of the room will come to see me, at the very end of the session Auxerroise, when I was playing on Tron 3D, where I had certainly slipped the largest number of pieces limed, whispering something in the style "if I catch the little cunts who eat me, they will spend a dirty quarter of an hour", but maybe more vulgar, dissuasive and scary! Which I answered quite and falsely puzzled by asking him to explain what he wanted to talk about!?!

I had certainly dropped the fairground into a quantum riddle like the Schrödinger's Cat. He often saw me playing Tron 3D, as he often saw me asking for money, and I had paid a few coins but very little, nothing compared to those that were misappropriated. He probably thought it could be me, just as he thought it couldn't be me, given the number of tickets I'd be losing every time I passed by. Then I could have been ashamed or scared, but not at all, I was totally absorbed by the games.

Tron 3D was far from being among the best games in the room but it presented itself in a 3D of the most beautiful effect: holographic memory! The Holograms matching few colors, it was at least perfect for a game like Tron shooting mostly on the Blue and some gradients. It was a high-flying "record fight"! The player had to throw his famous blue disc in order to touch and explode these competitors on the other side, while dodging the red discs of these same opponents. It was a game of speed, skill, precision and reflection because to take over your opponents faster, it was better to imagine many bounces and deviations on the walls or the floor, a bit like billiards, in order to surprise and neutralize them.

I was, I remember very well, totally mesmerized by this game, its atmosphere, its setting. The bollard was almost physically closed and could only be entered from the sides, left or right for an almost total immersion. In the evening I will make my own "records" houses, my rings of power, with my comrade Olivier and his grinder, and I would use them the next day with their full powers, those to open and keep open another dimension, in the late afternoon, in an incredible challenge and face the mythical TRON. The game that brought these players into its matrix and transformed them into a program on the sole condition of always wearing and keeping a record to live and survive. And when mine would be destroyed, I will then make another appear, and yet another! I eliminated the day by the discs that I filed at night. I felt more like Flynn, the hero of the film, who designed, played and hacked the system he invented. Him, me? We would end up being a prisoner. I really felt like I had entered Tron and had the keys. I had become the offspring of Flynn, the offspring of tron and I played, replayed and replayed with my chips, my re-chips and my re-chips almost to infinity. I did the same things over and over again, to reach a certain form of perfection. Hundred times, thousand times to not know finally who is really the machine. I lived, I die, I relived, I revisited... And Caetars. I was building in me a form of extreme resilience. Dying, even symbolically, thousands of times but always getting up and immediately: never give up, never give up, choose and forever "Continue" rather than "Game Over". I even have the impression, now, that it was me who physically jumped from one bridge to another and who sent all these forces his killer and destructive disk! The 3D dimension or almost already "VR headset", with a tight frame, put you at the heart of the game. Part of me will remain forever in this 3D Tron as I could take a part of it; engraved in me.

TRON, the film, its universe, are two major competitions: the athletic and warrior fight with the records and motorcycle races. I will do both more or less alternately for hours, for about fifteen days and at a low cost. Champion of the video games Tron and Hang On!!! And champion of the gruge!!! Triple Champion, I had "hacked" this space rather simply, to make it my training camp. And as the very young Spartan warriors at their agogé, more than two thousand years ago, all means, even the worst, were allowed, for a day, perhaps, to reach the heights of their Art. The end as hunger justify all means.

I chained, in sin, dozens and dozens of game, probably hundreds, between memorable races on Hang On, on Out Run or playing on Black Tiger, dressing myself in this blue suit, which I covered so easily, so regularly and so intensely! And I was already fighting opponents dressed in red, a symbol. I chained again and again and again... To become at first and most likely the one and only "Master of Tron". I bounced the disk and destroyed the red like no other very certainly (it should be noted that "the intelligence of the opponent" was still very limited and therefore repetitive) while flipping gracefully from one platform to another. Without knowing it, I then began to carve, to burn, to chisel the future Master Sega, 100% Sega, Grand Master of video games certainly but also and especially that of the Arcade: the training room for gamers category heavyweight championship. Consoles, commodore or CPC it was good, it was even very hard sometimes, but the gameplay was still too limited at that time.

The Arcade still showed Tron strong but I was slowly and surely rising to the rank of Champion of Champions with a desire and determination without any fault. I can doubt and question some things in life, even today, like the Doc of Back to the future (Time, the Universe, Women...) but never oh great ever when passion pushes me and assails me with so much energy, I will never let go, and if there is a "summit" it is that it is made to be reached, sooner or later! It is then only to train, fight and do nothing loose. First party, first arrived? It will just need to be confirmed every day, every month, every year and every life!!!

I will still need to "hack" the system, shake it up, but in a totally playful and legal way, Score Game, Micromania, La Fnac, the boutiques Boulevard Voltaire, Cdiscount, Amazon, Sony, Sega (not?!?!) and so many others: they will all taste more or less bitterly in my very sharp sense and therefore very spicy of the absolute game, as soon as I am no longer officially a Master. But these times, and unlike my limed pieces, they can never stop me from taking the game, understanding it, turning it over, dissecting it before taking it into their hands and absorbing all the best, legally. Flirting often and irresistibly at the borders of the Law, one will not be able to "at best" only look at me from the side while staying sometimes stuck. This is also how we can recognize a "Sega Master" because he probably never stops looking for his own Master, through the game, through challenges.

Tron was not a Sega game, but they will be the only ones who can offer me regularly the challenges I could dream of! Dozens? Hundreds? Nintendo? Anyone talking about Nintendo? No but seriously, Nintendo it's fine maybe in another way, Myamoto is a genius, but it's too sweet, it's too slow, it's for children who play quietly in their rooms by being able to play with one hand and taking breaks from time to time, It's not fast enough!!! And yet his name smelled as good, like Yu Suzuki, asphalt, leather and engine oil.

The years 86/87 are indeed very surprising retrospectively in more than one title, if not to have more than 50 years! Because the "war" Nintendo vs Sega did not exist! Not yet! Not at home! Their consoles are not yet sold in Europe. There are the Game & Watch, it's very nice and I will have four or five of them including a plumbing game, but as far as I'm concerned the video game is mostly SEGA, and don't talk to me, not for long, of Nintendo because there is no subject even the beginning of the beginning of the appearance of a hair of moustache Italian! Because at that time, the video game of "salons" is mostly Atari or Philips, and they are at the end of their lives...

Chapter 18

ADN Virgin Loisirs and Sega France

When the first Japanese consoles of Nintendo and Sega appeared officially in France the same year, in 1987, it was necessary almost immediately, and against all odds, to prepare for the most urgent and as the challenge that we expected more, The real Big Bang video fun!!! Whereas the consumer society seemed to be barely recovered from the historical crash of the previous generation, in 1983 in the USA and to a lesser extent the following year in Europe, it thus appeared to most that this "new generation" of consoles would probably, if not certainly, be a new mirage. And that, therefore, nothing, really nothing, would hurry, finally... The last link of the distribution chain, most often the large distribution, even had sometimes important stocks of unsold consoles (Atari more often) to recall the historical debacle with notably these millions of "E.T" games unsold, because really rotten, they will end up compacted and buried in a desert in the United States. Much more than a shock, the awakening would then be all the more violent and will surprise almost everyone, including the "distributors importers" themselves, even if they were the most enthusiastic, the most optimistic and therefore the most waiting for this new wave! Simply, no one would have imagined how gigantic it would be: a real Tsunami that would overturn everything.

A certain Patrick Lavanant (yes, the brother of Dominique Lavanant, you know "No but is it not going well behind? He has an unease the bathrobe?" and "I don't drink, I don't smoke, but what can I suck like Sucs des Vosges!") starts in this business via his company ASD (audio sound distribution) specialized in the marketing of "brown" products. He feels the good, the very big deal and he wants to be in it immediately. To get the distribution contract of Nintendo consoles, he is then in competition with (or against) Bandai and like the fox cunning, hungry, and long and pointed canines, he will present himself with improbable orders stamped Fnac. The subterfuge will work: it will then touch the Holy Grail, sign the distribution contract certainly, but the latter is "to the highest bidder", understand here rather "at least looking". This contract, not negotiated but on its knees, is very binding, obliging it to pay for the equipment immediately upon order and therefore with a slow, very slow return on investment. The large distribution still pays most often 90 days after sales to these suppliers. A dry and sharp contract that imposes very important financial means to launch and before the financial machine deigns to return its investment then these first profits, more on games than on consoles everyone knows.

To make matters worse, the first order will be two months late on delivery and, with a lot of bad luck, will soon be followed by a historic financial crash in October 1987, which will bypass ASD's main financing: the Worms Bank. 15,000 NES will finally be sold in France in this financial storm: a figure very insufficient for all stakeholders, the 8-bit console of Nintendo is already selling millions of copies in Japan and the USA. The company goes bankrupt and Bandai finally takes matters into his own hands, with the same Patrick Lavanant who still has teeth and sharp claws, and who will take over the Marketing and Sales Department of Mario's products. This business man has committed himself to Nintendo as he could have, as he would have wanted to commit himself to Sega, and the fate of the latter in France would probably have been very different... But, fortunately, the company with the blue hedgehog had already concluded a distribution deal with a subsidiary of Virgin named Virgin Mastertronic, with Martin Alper and Franck Herman at the controls. British people who, throughout the empire and the personality of Richard Bronson, were ostensibly more oriented towards adult culture and entertainment than those of children: through the mature industries of music, film and video. The opening of the "Virgin Megastore" on the Champs Elysées will be a kind of apotheosis of their conquests on French territory! In any case this first Megastore will become the Temple, the Mecca of Culture and its innumerable various products, these derivatives, for many years. I will even spend several evenings officially as Master Sega and for the launch of the Mega CD, when the video game department was then in the basement, just at the foot of the escalator on the left at the entrance, in this room with treasures with a singular atmosphere, of secret location with its huge round style bank vault door. As "Master" of this highly, even eminently magical place, I felt then a little like the father Fouras at the top of his lighthouse in the Fort Boyard and as the mystical guardian of immense knowledge. I will be regularly posted in "VIP seller" especially for different Fnac but these sessions "Virgin Megastore" will remain the most striking. The Virgin Megastore had become, from its appearance, my third home after Sega France, and I was delighted as never to be able to pass there as a professional, all the more so as a recognized master of video games!

This British DNA, "so British" and one can no longer dominate, will be passed on irresistibly in the choice of the first men of the French subsidiary with notably the first of them: Jean Martial Lefranc! An incredible talent that will reveal itself a little later, almost as much as producer and distributor in video games, as in cinema, he will distribute the Japanese animated film "Akira" in 1991 in France. With his friend and partner Philippe Ulrich (a French legend and perhaps even the first video game legend), they will lead one of the greatest success stories in video games in France and around the world with the company "Cryo" since 1992 and therefore well before Ubi Soft.

Sega will benefit more from this profile, which is more focused on creation, art, innovation and geek culture than a more standard, sanitized profile that is simply focused on commerce, business and money. And not to mention this lead screed "toy", or as a huge ball that will weigh both directly on and around "Nintendo" but can be even more through "Bandai". Who certainly found it the easiest way to measure and control this wave, which was in direct competition with part of his range of toys. The best way to avoid, to circumvent or in any case to absorb the frictions of an inevitable "War against the Toy" that was announced, and on which I will come back. Arrived at the right place, at the right time, for him, as for Sega, he will finally be the only real Gamer, a fortiori Geek, to be in charge of the distribution of Sega in the 80s and 90s. It could not be better. Jean Martial Lefranc will be a Masterpiece of the appearance of Sega in France, its identity and its explosion! It is he who will validate, with Luc Bourcier, "Sega is stronger than you", "Maître Sega" and the Punk campaign straight out of Mad Max Fury Road! Jean Martial Lefranc will end up on the sand immediately after his time at Sega, even diving from head to toe in the sands of "Dune" by Franck Herbert, when the passion for cinema joins that of video games and through his new company called Cryo. We are then light years away from the sand, and the clay of Rolland Garros that Patrick Lavanant so loved (I will also come back to this). It is said that the devil is in the details, it is probably and to the smallest grain of sand.

In this year 88, the structures of Virgin Loisirs (name of the French subsidiary of Virgin Mastertronics, distributor of Sega for France) and the dedicated one of Bandai for Nintendo are still reduced, emerging market or rather (re)nascent obliges. The number of employees on both sides will be counted with one hand in the first year. Only now, sales are starting to accelerate seriously and the players most in trouble in their games, but not the less clever ones, find themselves trying to contact distributors directly to solve their problems. And some will succeed!!! The very charming Eve Lise Blanc Deleuze, head of marketing, communication and consumer services will be, despite her, most likely the first "hotlineuse" of video games in France. The dedicated hotlines do not exist yet, it is indeed who will respond to the first shipwrecked Mario or Zelda on the NES console. Whether she can cope with one or two calls a week more or less easily (and maybe a little more of the rest), this new demand from consumers will have to be addressed very quickly because otherwise the moustachu in red overalls might come to squat his office more often and even settle there. Then abandoning, scattering some unfortunate hair of moustaches on the elegant clear suit, and now sown, of the young woman. The first official hotline operator of SOS Nintendo, Josué Césaire, will be recruited at the end of 1988 by replying to an announcement specifying and thus luring the hoodlum, by a formula that might seem suspicious at first sight, but which will nevertheless be, finally, unequivocal: "Earn your living by playing" !!! While Eve Lise had to face the shipwrecked of Zelda, at Sega, it is certainly Luc Bourcier, director of marketing who has had to face the lost of Golden Axe Warrior or those of Miracle Warriors (a most hypothetical situation but if it had come true, I would give some coins to see this moment as unlikely as tasty). It is therefore very likely under the pressure of the most misguided consumers, but also the most clever, and as the piquant of the prods, that the Hotlines of Nintendo and Sega were imagined and thus naturally appeared!

After Josué Césaire in October or November 88 for the SOS Nintendo, it is therefore Romuald Merdrignac who will open the Sega Hotline in March 1989 without adding a more fantastic, fantasmatic and finally heroic dimension: that of the Master Sega. The first stone, the first milestone of a road that will be studded with countless challenges awakening and stimulating any adventurer who would have fallen asleep on the sidewalk of a path too sweetened. And even then, and especially even?!? When you could also be a discreet and unconditional fan of Zelda! However, there will be less differences between Josué and Romuald than between Patrick Lavanant and Jean Martial Lefranc, if not always at least a gap: that of the Passion. Yesterday, today and tomorrow.

In 1988, Sega sold about 40,000 Master Systems for a NES of 45,000 and generated 50 million francs of turnover, compared with 60 million francs for Nintendo (the average price of games was considerably higher at Nintendo than at Sega). First round won by Nintendo without triumphalism, quite the contrary, given the global performances elsewhere, but it is especially on the Hotline side that we can note a difference as singular as characteristic. Nintendo will recruit first and will be able to grow this workforce much faster than Sega. The reason you may know it or can guess it easily, in fact there are two and they are called "Mario" and "Zelda". Two of the biggest and also the best licenses of all time in video games (and before toys, even before cinema very recently...)! Like or don't like, especially if you are "Sega" but it is factual, Nintendo (Bandai) had these two blockbusters immediately on release and it will be all the more remarkable for Sega, afterwards, to recover this handicap. Because if Sega also has many hits, they are far from being as prestigious, we can not lie thirty five years later!

The Nintendo vs Sega Match had started, it was very tight and would remain for several years at least in the main market of Trade Shows consoles, because there was not really a match between the Game Boy and the Game Gear. And it is precisely because the match was so close that it is wonderful to dissect, to analyze 20, 30 or 40 years later! The devil is in the details and it is often true. This Homer battle has often played out on little. Sega, who was only an outsider in the world until then, quickly becomes the official challenger of Nintendo with two or three shards. This one-on-one event highlights the men and women who have contributed or not to the success of Nintendo and Sega. Especially since, finally, not many people have substantially pushed Sega and Nintendo a little higher as sometimes a little lower. Because, and I already stressed it in Volume 1 with the sales of Sega, the product was plucking! It sold like rolls and sometimes even "too much", and that it is promoted by Dupond or Dupont will change nothing or so little. But it is also on the thickness of the line that we can measure talent. An

Olympic 100-metre race is played and sometimes won on a hundredth of a second!

And it is not to devalue the quality of work of each other, who will all make a more or less positive contribution, but what sold and still sells consoles are well on games! Essentially, inevitably and most fortunately: THE GAMES! The main merit of a successful console is to be found in game creators, even if for Sega, as for Nintendo, the console component is also a powerful argument because the quality of a game is, or rather was, also due to its technical prowess. But the machine is and always will be more in the service of games, rather than the opposite. Nevertheless, there are most likely, at least in the beginning, two different approaches that have a lot or even a lot to do with the DNA of the official distributors of Sega and Nintendo. Bandai who is one of the kings of "toy" and Virgin Loisirs, subsidiary of Virgin of the incredible Richard Branson! The one who will sign, among others, under his music label the "Sex Pistols", the sultry Punk Rock group, if you see where I want to go! It should be noted that when Sega France launches the campaign of Pub "Maître Sega" with the Mad Max colors Punk, it is said that some British people saw a kind of subliminal mockery of the French Staff towards the British authority! In truth this unique and fantastic campaign that no one will forget will be especially envied all over the world and particularly in London. The British also married the rebellion, a little later, with their "Pirates Sega" (Canal Sega in France recognizable with its skull).

These radically different states of mind, which will project and stick to the main targets, will also be reflected through consumer services and a fortiori the Hotline. Before all teenagers were equipped with smartphones, before the internet was available in every home, consumer services were, if not essential, at least necessary to support the development of the console market! The sometimes quite expensive games, could not, should not turn into a graveyard of dreams, passion and illusions for anyone, players must be able to progress, continue to have fun and be able to exploit the entirety of their games, before you can move on to the next without regret or bitterness.

We say "Who looks like, gathers" and also that "Dogs do not make cats". They are found naturally, with very strong signs of compatibility, and they will go as far as marrying: on the one hand Nintendo, a toy manufacturer and distributor named Bandai and rather docile players, well behaved and perhaps a little less passionate. And on the other side SEGA, a music producer and distributor and a handful of hardcore gamers who are rebellious or even indomitable, a pack of lions who only think about playing, fighting, competing, measuring each other. We finally just installed our different totems: Nintendogs versus the Lion King.

Presented in this way, we would be irresistibly closer to the "Buddy movie", unless it is rather a revised and corrected version of the "Bad Cop - Good Cop"!?! Vision necessarily manichean and therefore very exaggerated, whose main purpose is to oppose two styles, two universes to better distinguish them! The question is who is good and who is bad and if they are really. While this view may seem a bit caricatural, it remains that the two companies will cultivate their differences both in the image they give of themselves and in the management of their affairs. So yes, let's continue the comparative test.

For the salaries of the Hotline advisors, they were relatively close. Has the advantage of Sega at first with a fixed salary of 8 to 9000 frs gross per month against 7 to 7500 for Bandai/Nintendo/Stock services which certainly caught up over the year with different premiums and profit. At the level of the work environment in general and offices in particular, the comparison is cruel. You just have to look for the videos on youtube and photos of the reports published in the specialized press: at Nintendo we had the impression of being in a rabbit or chicken farm! An open space all in length where the offices were glued together with 80 cms of width for each advisor! A feeling of isolation and confinement that could also be accentuated by the total absence of windows!?! Claustrophobes pass your way. Reality seemed to exceed fiction, as soon as you arrived at SOS Nintendo you must have found a key, a secret passage or a pipe to escape! Of the "offices" that Josué Césaire himself will call from the rest as "cabins", like those of showers or fitting? Offices unfortunately connections with the external frame: a kind of warehouse in an industrial zone from which it is impossible finally not to think about something other than a "factory work" and chain, in a closed space, a cabin!

The working environment of the Sega Hotline was very different. First of all it is also important to point out, to remind, that we were not separated from the rest of society. We were in an open space with offices that were as open as they were spacious: furniture mounted in "corners" which did not give us the impression of being locked up and crammed into each other, one after another and in rows of onions. Everyone, each had a large and sufficient space, just for themselves and therefore without ever having the impression of being in a battery farm or in a factory on the chain. I'm very surprised to have to say it but we even had natural light, a lot of light through huge windows, whether in the premises near the Aqua boulevard on the 15th, before Sainte Croix street, or later at Cyber Press Publishing in Clichy, with breathtaking views of the 17th and especially the Sacred Heart, because we were even on the end, very high. The outdoor setting was very pleasant, whether in the Marais first rue Barbette and rue sainte croix de la Bretonnerie, then near the Aqua boulevard in a second, the lunch break at noon was particularly sweet and relaxing.

Bandai, a global toy giant with very heavy logistics, and therefore necessarily at least slightly decentralized, had thus imposed an industrial framework to its "division" video games Nintendo, and therefore the Hotline. When on the other hand, Virgin was more cultural, more event-oriented, more urban, more people, cosmopolitan and above all lighter and more festive, it chose the warm or even burning heart of central Paris, before Sega France moved, certainly into the 15th, but it is still Paris! Nintendo/Bandai was mainly aimed at children when Sega was aiming for the floors just above: the biggest and/or the leaders! It is therefore probable and even almost certain that the recruitment of both sides will also be done by two approaches, two different conceptions which could move away from each other by a concept holding in two words: that of "Master Sega", the ultimate hard core gamer.

Romuald has imposed by his presence, talent and passion, an essential character in the Marketing and communication of Virgin Loisirs! It will even become the central element with the various advertising projections and the Sega club. When Fabrice, the second master, will join him, he will also fit perfectly into the structure! The two Sega masters weave slowly but surely the web that connects them to marketing and communication managers. It is not yet known at that time, "Master Sega" will become the champion of brand communication but also a whole generation of enthusiasts. And as much as I tell you the things as they were, Sega will take advantage of them and not always leave them locked in small or larger offices! The Sega Masters will be a force, a major asset, super ambassadors, the "Mega Force" like Romuald. Sega had found these super champions, these opinion leaders and gave them ALL the necessary means to try to knock out Nintendo.

Master Sega, Romuald, had become a powerful symbol but also the mascot of Virgin Loisirs, his favorite lucky charm. The next Sega Masters will be these students, or even these (spiritual) children. We would all end up being the X mascots of the Society, maybe as much as Sonic, at least in these years 91/92/93 while Punk came to challenge Master Sega in newspapers or on TV. Between Sega Masters we formed a first family of ten to twelve people in the middle of a larger family, that of marketing and then the commercial management, who would give us, which would give me many tasks, often delicious, to accomplish.

At Nintendo or Bandai, it is much harder to talk about family, otherwise can be recomposed!?! The Hotline was already physically separated from the other offices! But the separation was not only physical! The technical advisors never worked directly for Bandai a fortiori Nintendo, they worked for the company "Stock Services". A company, a service provider dedicated to Bandai's service and then to that of Nintendo for the brand's video games! Only the SOS Nintendo managers will be employees fully integrated into the parent company: Eve Lise Blanc Deleuze and Stephan Bole at the start-up and on the marketing and communication side, Pierre Muzas for the technical part (minitel) and Denis Ducommun later the Boss, The Department Warden. A difference that will leave a very bitter taste in many SOS counsellors.

It is understandable that Bandai, at the very beginning of SOS Nintendo, wanted to create a light structure, dedicated, in parallel with their historical activities of the toy, while surely having in mind that this distribution contract was not at Vitam Æternam. On the other hand, why did Nintendo not pass under its flag those employees totally devoted to Nintendo except for Denis Ducommun? For me the answer is simple and easy retrospectively: the activities of Hotline do not yield anything directly, before the surcharged numbers, and the staff is not considered definitively strategic. This means that in the event of economic difficulties or a market downturn, it will be much easier to reduce the wind on this side. Of course I can be wrong but we can now look more closely at the organization of the different hotlines.

For Sega it will go very fast. The goals were only qualitative! Even though we were asked to avoid "chatting", not to stay too long with the same interlocutor and when calls were made many, we never heard of numbers and therefore no demand from near or far on this subject. Jean Luc Hadi and Marc Leroy, our two "Saturday Hotline managers" kept an eye on us, or rather listened to us from time to time to check that we were doing our job properly, but they also participated in the Hotline.

At Nintendo, and as I also point out about the mysterious "46,000" calls, there was a general but also individual count. But it did not stop there, I will be told that the responsible "Denis Ducommun" had a mission to monitor constantly and therefore "fliquer" in the words of an old man of SOS Nintendo. He also passed between the technical advisors by exclaiming generously with a "that dissuades"!?! But dissuade what? To stay calm, to remain calm? The surveillance still did not stop there and I kept the best for the end: I fell out of my seat when I was first told it and then confirmed because I could not believe it! A person at Nintendo was paid (a certain Colette) to be able to listen continuously the different advisors in a completely secret, Soviet way. All the advisors were aware of this "quality" monitoring! Following these wiretaps, she then referred files, detailed reports on each other to Denis Ducommun and the management. Vibe! Of course the best of them would be rewarded with bonuses, well when I say the best, it is according to the supposed objectivity of the censor and will be questioned by some advisors! And not necessarily the much less rated!!! It is difficult to avoid cronyism a fortiori the favouritism. Colette was not a bad person at all, quite the contrary, but she had a sacred and heavy responsibility, probably that these abilities of discernment were very high, without lacking kindness most of the time.

So yes now I understand better the introduction of a number of the magazine Player One and their report on the Nintendo Hotline: "they seem relaxed" ! The Nintendo Hotline had its own advanced monitoring and control system! One could obviously discuss it hours on the pros and cons, but one must be particularly docile and/or resigned and/or philosopher not to be at least a little embarrassed. Let's even admit that I am not at all objective about it and that it is even more normal! I come back to the Hotline to say again and again how my greatest pride at Sega and that finally we have always been taken very seriously in our work and our commitment! If the framework is important, if the remuneration is important, it is above all respect, consideration and trust that grow you more and allow you, in a virtuous circle, to gain even more respect and consideration... Despite two or three accidents in a few years, the Sega Masters will not pass this tipping point where we go from confidence to defiance and surveillance.

At a time when, in the world of work, many people suffer from this lack of consideration, we "Sega Masters" were often perceived as geeks, sometimes freaks, but all the time like the missing link between the passion of children and the top of the pyramid: creators as merchants and leaders. I have already reported that we were the heart of the Passion but we were also a kind of center of gravity! Nothing to do with "the center of the world" or this world but the center of gravity in the sense the center of stability. We were the heart and a good part of the soul!!! Sega's success, and some executives, like Bruno Charpentier, had probably understood it, could be measured by the intense vibrations that were created, or not, in the Hotline. At the expense of Nintendo, we can always grant them that we do not manage, that we do not supervise forty people as we supervise a dozen, it is obvious. But having known people on both sides of the Atlantic, I can still tell you that on the one hand we trusted, and rightly so, even if two or three of the 25 Sega masters will cause some problems, and be thanked, whereas on the other hand it was considerably less so. Trust versus surveillance: two systems that each have their strengths and weaknesses.

To conclude this demonstration, certainly charged but factual, and changing slightly register all the same, I can also tell you an episode equally quite incredible and that I will call more grotesque than everything else! Although even in Hotline we could be more or less monitored, directly or indirectly, by people not necessarily the most friendly and neutral, even if we would be a little, much or not at all considered, we had at least one indisputable duty: that of knowledge to serve the best all those who contacted us. It could seem like a princely advantage, maybe it was the case, but let's not be mistaken it was above all an advantage to serve the principality. At Nintendo and Sega, the advisors received all consoles as well as all games distributed so that they could play them quietly at home. AND YAUIIIIII!!! Stock Services at the time "Bandai", they will even have toys Turtles Ninja, Power Rangers and everything that the manufacturer distributed iconic!

An advantage in nature as extraordinary as necessary! However, Nintendo will want to take this advantage away from the technical advisors of SOS Nintendo. And this is the opportunity for me to introduce an incredible character that I will name no more and no less than "Captain Nintendo"! Because even at Nintendo, there would be one to stand up as a hero and refuse "The cost killer"!

Chapter 19

Captain Nintendo

In France, "Maître Sega" penetrated the collective unconscious of millions of French children through an extraordinary communication campaign on and around the explosion of eight- and sixteen-bit consoles in the late 1980s and early 1990s. What you probably don't know or don't know very much, and I only found out myself very recently, is that Nintendo also launched in the United States, on television, at about the same time as "Captain N, The Game Master"! A cartoon series featuring young Kevin, Captain N, in the fictional world of Videoland. The series contained many elements from the most popular NES games of the time, such as The Legend of Zelda, Kid Icarus on his mountain, Mega Man, Metroid, Castlevania or even Donkey Kong. Master Sega in France, Captain N in the USA, two virtual characters who could have faced each other, amicably, but the Ocean as their very different uses, will forever separate them from each other.

When I started writing these columns a few weeks ago, I didn't think for one second to talk about the Nintendo Hotline, the Nintendo SOS, except in a very anecdotal way. Being "Master Sega" and still very deep blue in my heart and in my mind, the slightest criticism can then probably seem as very objective but to address me to an audience totally acquired at Sega. And I thought that I would have, a priori, more than enough to tell the stories of our Hotline rather than the competitor's. The truth is that, even if for me it's really far from worth Sega, especially at this time, I also like Nintendo games, especially the adventures of Link (Zelda). The universe of Mario and all these friends is very (too?) essentially childish and therefore intended for a younger audience, but this does not prevent the quality and a certain fun to play, at least in small doses and as, probably, a kind of exotic adventure or extra conjugal in a forbidden territory! And as with and after each more or less forbidden outing, to finally return home. Most often with more pleasure than ever, satisfactions and freedoms!

As I have already pointed out, for me, Sega and Nintendo are certainly, or rather were, opponents, but they were also and above all antagonists! The best that can be on this field. The question then, not so much to know which brand or console could be really better than the other, but to know at what level of reality you wanted to get closer in video games. Sega endeavoring to push all the cursors of realism to the maximum and assuming in particular a level of violence never proposed, seeking in this an audience of older and more sure. Strategy often criticized, by Nintendo mainly, but not that. Sega responding and then pointing Nintendo by: "baby games"! The two returning the ball again and again at once, to stand out, but also and above all simply exist, while walking both almost side by side, hand in hand as two children of different education and ages.

Sega was the undisputed emperor of simulation especially in arcade rooms. Simulation rhymes with sensation and perfection, which must be always brought closer to, violence would then become the scarecrow that we would wave as we had already waved it in literature, radio, cinema and television. Violent video games make children violent? Should violence be banned, or at least considerably limited in the sphere of children? Absolutely, but the "simulated violence", in small doses, can also serve as an outlet for this more or less great propensity of aggressiveness that lies dormant in each little male wishing to confront, assert themselves and become "strong" in this! Stronger!!! And for some it would never be strong enough, at least for me it will never be.

I am totally and definitely against violence in real life, but we must also learn, and have learned to channel it, perhaps even get rid of it. Otherwise, we can always dream of becoming the next Teddy Riner, our Teddy Winner!

 Even though I could enjoy a number of Nintendo games, I would never leave my place at Sega to go to Mario. Not a day of Sega exchanged for a week or a month at Nintendo! First of all because my experience with the Sonic Team was simply wonderful, in every way, far beyond anything I could have imagined: The dream big, the dream giant and therefore, difficult to imagine even "better". Romuald affirmed "The job where we go every day running", I will complete with "the one where we already want to return, the day just finished"! The "Monday" became the best day of the week. Every Monday, Tuesday, Wednesday, Thursday, Friday and Saturday will rhyme with Défi. On Sunday I will be able to make mumuse on Nintendo by sneaking into pipes. Thirty years later, and based on several internal testimonials, comparing now and retrospectively two consumer services that at first glance could look alike, I can therefore more than ever confirm how happy we were at Sega! Because we were, if not gods, we were treated, most often, as Kings! The Kings of video games of course. By researching information and interviews about Sega and its Hotline, I inevitably consulted a lot of documents on our competitor, awakening all kinds of memories, good, very good and sometimes much worse! Measured or crude propaganda, approximations, caricatures, lies, the whole panoply of a business like any other finally, delivered to tricks of masters or genius but sometimes also to viler moves, smaller than others, petty and sneaky! It is not a question for me to force the line because retrospectively and "finally", this confrontation between Nintendo and Sega was rather, on the whole, regular, at least on French territory and in the staff. Which does not exclude, on the contrary, some tasty anecdotes that I will have the pleasure to tell you! And there I would like to tell you: "Pleasure to tell you" as much as for you "Pleasure to read it" because: "OUIIII! THE WAR IS OVER". Thirty years is not nothing! We just celebrated the 80th anniversary of the landing in Normandy: D-Day and the Germans are now among our best and closest friends and Sonic and Mario face each other amicably at the Olympics.

But it was unfortunately without counting the dishonesty of some testers, sometimes claiming to be journalists, that is to say, minority but influential, of the specialized press of the time, while they have never been able to relay information correctly and as their profession required: that is, objectively, as much as possible, and factually. I see today, as thirty years ago, that corruption (they call it cronyism, with the "little" gifts that maintain friendship) remains well established and for good reason, The video game world remains a golden goose that many influencers want and can come to caress in exchange for their good graces.

It is however in the May 1994 issue of Player One that we can find a first subtle hint, a nuance concerning the differences between the two hotlines and all the more Sega in Nintendo. The article specifying as well as at Sega, "the first stage": "The atmosphere is cool, the majority of hotlineurs are young" while for Nintendo the first words are: "Hotlineurs seem relaxed". Without being an expert in semantics, we will immediately notice a more advantageous rhetoric for the blues with in particular two clear and sharp statements against a simple hypothesis, little telling and therefore not convincing, for the reds! One might even ask, by an excessive deduction, if the Nintendo advisors were not too old!?! Did they all have a moustache or a beard.

To stay in the semantics, the Sega Masters were officially recognized within their company as "Consumer Advisors" while for Nintendo, and before Bandai, and finally "Stock Services" we will speak of "Technical Advisors". I find the term "consumer" quite, even very pejorative, but it was certainly difficult to find better. If the children were very numerous to call us, we had in charge of the whole population and all the requests, therefore far beyond the only distraction and pleasure of playing. Nevertheless, and even if the job was almost the same on both sides, the "consumer advisor" had the merit of placing our interlocutor, our young player, or less young but passionate, at the centre of our job and our raison d'être. We could have dreamed of a "Master Sega" stamped on our pay sheets but it will be nothing on this side, the collective agreements of companies being very little sensitive to titles so esoteric for ordinary mortals!

The devil is in the details (bis, ter...) so let's be as meticulous as suspicious as would an investigative journalist or even an anthropologist looking for two almost extinct species: Master Sega and SOS Nintendo Advisor. Moreover, stay well seated because this investigation, these investigations will exhume a character quite incredible, unimaginable and never imagined! And that we could name, to return to the beginning of this chapter, as "Captain N" or rather Captain Nintendo because "N" in writing it still passes, but in oral it is more ambiguous especially if we add that we work for "SS".

Originally, it is confirmed on both sides and I emphasize that it is the two standards of the two commercial companies that are first attacked by consumers lost in their games. On the one hand, Eve Lise Blanc Deleuze is drawing Josué Césaire and on the other, Luc Bourcier answers to him by Romuald Merdrignac a few months apart between late 1988 and early 1989. Hotlines are officially opened under relatively similar conditions. However, and probably more than a detail because quite decisive, the Nintendo Hotline, then distributed by the toy giant "Bandai", will be covered and managed by a company called "Stock Services" while the Sega Hotline will be fully integrated into the Virgin Loisirs company in a first time and then Sega France in a second.

We will be physically detached in a different building from the head office but temporarily and for a few months and because of the rapid acceleration of the number of employees and pending new offices larger and able to accommodate the whole of these new Sega employees. We were the "Masters of Sega" and totally attached to the marketing and communication department. We will meet every day, all the time, this allows a communication more than fast: instantaneous and also offering some emulation between passionate players profiles and more technical executives, more commercial even if mayonnaise would not take for everyone. This is not a detail, but it is of the utmost importance for the quality and efficiency of our work. Not that we would necessarily do it better in these conditions, but the latter were more numerous, more advantageous because at arm's reach! Only timidity or lack of curiosity could prevent us from doing so.

Let's go back to our first heroes of the Hotline. At Nintendo, Josué Césaire is very friendly and even quite jovial! He has, from this point of view, nothing to envy to Romuald Merdrignac. He loves to play, he likes to communicate, these human qualities and listening are undeniable and he will be absolutely perfect in his mission of technical advisor in a first time and trainer in a second. The anecdote is quite widespread, they will even call regularly to help each other on the games of competition! Romuald being a fan and even a lover of "Zelda" and "Link". The anecdote in the anecdote, Romuald will even buy a Japanese version of Zelda to play before everyone else. And I take the opportunity, if you had not understood it, or did not imagine it, to emphasize again that Romuald was a real Hard Core Gamer! He played everything, all the time, on Sega or Nintendo, in French, English or even in Japanese!

And it is also on this point that I draw your attention to the DNA of Sega France versus Nintendo. It is absolutely not caricatural to report that Nintendo was more and almost completely immersed in the world of "toy" and therefore of childhood. Virgin Loisirs then Sega France have attracted profiles much more Hard Core Gamer, more Geek, it is indisputable and at all levels, although there were not only Geeks at Sega, They were significantly more numerous in proportion and therefore to influence the course of things, in their style! Whether it was Jean Martial Lefranc as the first DG and therefore now the first hotlineur, their passages, their presences would not be without consequences in the recruitment to come. And I must add that it is Romuald himself, who has self-proclaimed "Master Sega"!!! He will even blow "Mega Force" to Marc Andersen. Opening a magnificent corridor to his destiny or even his legend, as to the fate of Sega in France. A fate longer, further and therefore "out of Ducommun"!

His love for video games, his unquenchable thirst for adventure and mystery, his overflowing imagination, had infused him with this extra soul and fantasy. No doubt that if he had returned to SOS Nintendo, he would have then proposed himself as "Master Nintendo" and no doubt also that it would have been refused, even though the idea would have amused most of the leaders! At Nintendo, you'll see, we don't laugh. Not too much anyway. I believe that if, at Sega, we have been treated so well and for many years, it is because Romuald had totally imagined himself and incarnated in "Master Sega". In addition to his cheerful and very endearing personality, he had established himself as THE Master! In fact, because he was the first, let alone for a good time, it probably became a symbol, the flag, the winning standard of both passion and skill. The Mascot!!! He appeared as a savior for all the children in distress but also for the members of the marketing and communication teams who were mostly overwhelmed by all this madness as furious as sudden.

While Josué Césaire was certainly very good, even excellent in his tasks, and therefore he did the job, for Romuald it is quite another thing, on a completely different level: as enthusiastic as imaginative or visionary, as Hard Core Gamer as competitor elsewhere. The job where you go every day running" and that he finally never really could invent and that he will have simply suggested, because in fact, "The Master", it was already before! By immediately touching his first Master System controller, he immediately became the Master of the System, the Master of video games.

If the average profile of Nintendo's technical advisor was probably and significantly less player than that of a Sega Master, it does not prevent that there were also several Hard Core Gamers ultra passionate, or ultra competent, or even both at Mario. Moreover, and this is particularly facetious on my part coming back to it, Romuald Maître Sega could also have been "Master Nintendo", at least unofficially. He will never hide his love for Nintendo games although he would remain very discreet about where he worked! He bought the Master System early on as he will also buy the NES to be able to play Zelda! He will also buy the Super Nintendo, on the day of its release in France, with F-Zero and more tense than ever before receiving, finally, his new baby. In an ITRW published in issue 26 of Pixel'n Love, he will not fail to highlight this "second love", and I think I can confirm that it is Zelda who is, at heart, the game far above all others! It is thanks to him that I will eventually buy the SNIN so I can discover Mario and Zelda. I had a good time with the moustached plumber but I will still come back soon enough to my Sega games. But for Zelda, it was really sensational and magical, unquestionably. There is a prescription today but the legendary leader of Maître Sega had converted the Master Sega by far the most "Sega", and who will remain (I have not yet finished telling you why, I am just starting) but at Nintendo, at least to Zelda! The "Arthur Pendragon" of Ghost'n Goblins is probably not far from all this.

Although I had already compared, at the time and on various occasions, the Sega Masters to the Jedi Knights in their mystical and mythological dimensions, thinking about it again now, more than ever, in fact, I think I can say that Romuald Merdrignac, in the Jedi Knights would have been Anakin Skywalker! Later known among the Dark Jedi or rather Sith Lords, under the name of Darth Vader! He would be both Jedi Knight/Master Nintendo and Black Jedi/Master Sega. He would have allowed himself to be invaded at the same time, by both sides of the Force while diverging substantially towards the dark side that extended his arms. Because Sega, it was on the dark side of the video game and he would be one of the Masters if not The Master! But as for Anakin Skywalker/Darth Vader nothing would ever be totally blue or red! Romuald Merdrignac was finally blue on the outside but red inside! He will prefer a hundred times more Mario than Sonic! And will even talk more about his passion for F-Zero than for Sega Rally in his last great interview!?! TRAHiSON might think some of us first!?! Not even, just a wide and infinite passion for video games as it should be most often. A virtually fictional ambivalence created by a more or less factious war but which will generate 100% blue and 100% red, all ready to fight with the other clan, because after all, it is much better when there are rivalries or antagonisms! As illusory as they may be.

And now that this secret has been revealed twenty, thirty years later, we can finally reasonably imagine what Romuald would have come to whisper in the ear of Luc Bourcier, the director of marketing at Sega at the time: "Luc... I am your father!!!" Which Luke will answer immediately, bending his knee and lowering his eyes: "Dear Master... My Master... I am at your command!!!". And Luc Bourcier, with Jean Martial Lefranc and the agency Lintas will anoint for eternity "Master Sega" in an advertising campaign now Legendary. Romuald Merdrignac was probably more than "Master Sega", he might even be "the game master"!?! The master of video games forced to choose a side, at least in appearance!!! But if Romuald was Darth Vader, what Sith Lord, what dark Jedi could I be? Aahahahahahah!!! At SOS Nintendo, you would find Claire Saunois! Second employee of the Nintendo Hotline after Josué césaire, she will be named and sign her contributions "Yoda" a little later at Player One! If she was the small, but overpowered, green Jedi, who could be or impersonate Obi-Wan Kenobi?

It's a great moment for me, as well as for you, the one I was waiting for from the beginning of this chapter, because it's time to come or rather to return to one of the greatest masters of video games of these 90s and 2000. Not totally unknown by the most passionate among you, it remains undervalued. In any case, he does not have the place that should be his in the ancient and sacred pantheon of video games and those first phantasmagorical heroes. For this great Master, undoubtedly, has very clearly the Etoffe of heroes, and it is most likely too great a humility, compared to others, that will distance him from the spotlight and therefore honors even "posthumously" (to consider this time, today, as very distant).

At SOS Nintendo, he will first be known and recognized as the "King of the binders". He was perhaps not the most "Hard Core Gamer", though, but he had an increased awareness for access to game knowledge and its dissemination to these colleagues. I could say more simply that he was a great professional of the Hotline and that he had a keen sense of duty! Well done. This rigor combined with the taste of challenge will win in one of the most extraordinary adventures of Nintendo in France: The super Nintendo Tour with the Nintendo truck traveling all over France, him and four or five other employees of SOS Nintendo. This adventure will be well told by the one we will name here, right now: "Captain Nintendo", in an interview conducted by Florent Gorges on his YouTube channel. I already tell it in "Volume 1", this Captain Nintendo will be driving in his red truck and for several months, when we, Sega Masters, would do our tour a few weeks, much more quietly, in our very pretty and spectacular gray and blue train! Two adventures that are certainly parallel, adversaries, but which will eventually cross each other or even overlap a few years later. But before we get there, this brave Captain Nintendo will be distinguished in a Homeric battle but above all to merit! His, but also that of all those companions of fortune embarked on the same boat, who will be surprised to take such a powerful grain of sea while the latter seemed so quiet and so sweet. The grain had pierced the boat, which was taking water, and it is indeed Captain Nintendo, rising immediately without doubt, who would try to save his crew!

At Nintendo, as at Sega, we had a huge and absolutely sacred privilege! A privilege, a right, a particular advantage granted in the favour of the compelling need for our sustained knowledge, our extensive knowledge. Totally indisputable in the substance but in the form this privilege had a significant cost which made it, or could make it fragile, and put it into question. And there, again, after more or less denouncing a surveillance system at Nintendo, where one might think that the most important and determining factor was "the number", offer all games for ten to fifteen people, It is not the same as for thirty to forty people! Nevertheless, after a good 90/91/92 when the incredible and irresistible rising waters allowed all expenses, the belt finally tightened, but not in the same way on either side. The Passion dominated on one side, when on the other everything would be only Reason!?!

At Sega we would keep our privilege until the end (despite a very unfortunate incident reported in Volume 1 and around Philippe the worst Master Sega of our history) and we would never know, or not for a long time, how, in the end, we were and remained privileged. However, at Nintendo during 1993 it is the stroke of thunder, the management wants to remove this advantage to these technical advisors. It is the dismay for everyone of course, because it is as much a benefit in nature important, that a logistical and technical help one can not more virtuous! What happened at the management level? Cuts in expenditure, budget, savings to be made? Increasing power, taking power of "filing cabinets" and other detailed solutions "home" or specialized press on the background of important turn over? It turns out that the SOS Nintendo would be seriously affected by the "Philippe" syndrome but in XXL version! Nintendo's management will find that many of the games offered to advisors are immediately sold on Cergy's flea markets! For a number of Nintendo advisors, this endowment could certainly have seemed like a salary supplement, an opinion very far from that of the company's executives! The penalty will be quick and severe, advantage removed and replaced by a mini award of three games per month, or 36 in the year. A lesser evil but a very heavy or even too heavy sanction for some. Two technical advisors will then stand up and protest, especially our "Captain Nintendo". The latter will even propose, to all technical advisors to strike! Never seen and almost never known outside the Hotline! A showdown began.

The timing is random, but the election of staff delegates is coming up shortly, just before the holiday season. The HR department of Stock Services will then call our Captain Nintendo and suggest that he run to be elected among these delegates: he would be a proud and worthy representative without doubt! Did the HRD hear about this fight against management? Necessarily, and becoming a "staff delegate" would then confer the Totem of immunity to one who is engaged in such delicate matters, but he would not tell him explicitly. Our captain Nintendo will refuse for the first time, perhaps he was too confident, he who had already given a lot to the SOS Nintendo and who had been relatively well rewarded. Too much confidence, naivety? Honestly it's easy for me to put myself in his shoes, because I ended up having about the same status at Sega as he did at Nintendo. That is to say that of a serious employee, committed, having made himself otherwise indispensable, at least as a "master" piece of the Hotline. I do not know if I would have been the "leader" of the protest, but I would have taken a large part in the struggle since it was supported by at least half of the hotlines and without this being too much of a concern for me. All this to say that I could also have refused the job of staff representative without any concern, I mean without stress. However, the HR Director of Nintendo will insist on Captain N to run for election, and that is far from trivial, but our Captain Nintendo will once again refuse without suspecting a second what could be going on behind the scenes.

We are in the last days of the year and a few hours or days from the New Years Eve. Captain Nintendo is summoned by Denis Ducommun. He announces that he will be laid off and then simply fired for his sling (and unofficially, most certainly, for daring to defy his sole authority). The SOS official claims that this announced strike and which they are, he and a second advisor nicknamed "Snake", the leaders, absolutely does not like the

Japanese!?! Nevertheless, he has committed no default, no serious fault to justify a dismissal, so it is an amicable arrangement that will be found! But finally our Captain Nintendo was offered the exit on the sole ground that he refused to be taken away from him, his colleagues, an advantage in nature, an advantage in knowledge and culture, a work tool. For me it is a serious mistake on the part of Nintendo not to keep the most motivated and committed employees. And even if we can understand a little, that they wanted to reduce the canopy to follow these wild sales and not really discreet! The shock was certainly very difficult to take by most of the Nintendo advisors. But the historical figures were already gone: Josué for Acclaim and Claire for Player One. Our captain N will go to him for the group "Mega Press", a company of Marc Andersen, which publishes notably Mega Force and Super Power. Alain Milly, since it is him, and you will have recognized him all the more easily that he has accepted to write the preface of this Volume 2, our "Captain Nintendo", will become in these two magazines: AL1 Vincible in one and Logan in the other, Generating and participating in dozens or hundreds of game solutions, for both Nintendo and Sega.

Extraordinary irony of the story. Mega Press will become "Cyber Press Publishing". The Sega Hotline will be relocated from Sega France to Cyber Press (a story, a new Tome later). The head of the Sega Hotline at this time, Marc Leroy, will be fired because he is not offering anything productive and has become a total slacker within the Press group. Romuald, who was totally assigned to the Sega Club in recent times, but remaining integrated into the Hotline group, will be offered, like the other Sega Masters, new activities, but without really and officially the general framework. And it is Alain Milly, ex SOS Nintendo, the commander of the Super Nintendo Tour, who is chosen by Marc Andersen, rather than Romuald, to take the direction, supervision of troops and activities! " Captain Nintendo" will become the boss, the superior of the Sega Masters! And it will not pose me, it really will not pose us any problem, because as he says himself in his introduction: "We do not have the same swimsuits, but we have the same passion"! And we still had Mario (the real one!!!) in our MS team (we will find his photo next day!!!).

But it's not over yet!!! The height of irony, a few months later, Marc Andersen will ask Alain Milly to kindly receive with him, Denis Ducommun still boss of SOS Nintendo, and in the possibility, The possibility of relocating also and completely the Hotline of Link and Luigi within the Cyber Press Group! The Sega Masters were going to merge with the SOS Nintendo? Were we finally able to find out who had the longest controller? Who was really the fastest on F-Zero or Sega Rally? And especially who was able to answer the largest number of calls? And probably that the players, consumers would know nothing about it, or so little. But this grouping, much more incredible than improbable, will not happen, because there were still too many at SOS Nintendo, probably more than fifteen, and the revenues generated by the telephone and minitel were on a downward slope. Cyber Press had enough staff for the continuation of Sega services, also declining, but also and especially to develop other services, in all directions video ludiques! I would have liked the best players of SOS Nintendo to join Cyber Press and be able to participate, a few years later, as forty-four pro players from many specialized publications, in the trophy of ultras gamers! Which would have had, then, only more value.

Chapter 20

The 46,000

Nintendo vs Sega: Technological war, playful war, marketing war, communication war and numbers war!

When Nintendo, through its dominant and charming Eve Lise Blanc Deleuze, announces a record 46,000 calls to the Nintendo Hotline on a Saturday in "very high season", that is around Christmas, the figure is not false, it's just too flashy to seem even a little honest! It is certainly in communication, but much closer to propaganda than information, because it does not specify what exactly this figure corresponds. Before interpreting, explaining this pharaonic figure, we must first ask ourselves what could have pushed her author to make it real by disseminating it to the public? What can be the motivation to spread it through the press essentially "economic", as in the magazine "Capital" or newspapers like Les Echos, La Tribune, "La Vie financière" or the Economic Figaro?

Nintendo and Sega are global companies that are listed on the stock exchange. They are therefore constantly scrutinized by the economic and financial circles. With agents who can potentially sell or buy the securities of companies almost at any time. All highly competitive and open to capital markets environments are under the scrutiny of these agents who seek, scratch, the slightest gestures around the world and which can translate into a possible opportunity in one direction or another. You should know that on the stock markets, you can buy securities when you think they will rise, you can also sell your securities without having them directly, by borrowing them from banks, if you think they will fall (and this is called short selling). It is a daily pressure that weighs more or less on the managers of companies because the companies listed at all fortiori to the "open" capital are potentially prey, and the slightest misstep in terms of communication can be extremely damaging. If a company's price falls more than reasonable, it can then become the target of a takeover bid.

Nevertheless, this extrapolated economic dimension is probably the most important, the most justified and the most visible, must not make us forget a first dimension more ego-centered and therefore very human: pride! Whatever this extraordinary figure is, it's big, it's beautiful with these five digits and these three zeros! By the way, speaking of zero how is it possible to have a number with three zeros? Children are most often calling and each of their voices, their chronic playful distress is a fight, a challenge that the hotliners of Nintendo as of Sega must meet, so that the child can be replenished with happiness and energy, Looking for the Triforce or Mother Brain! But maybe this figure has been rounded by the diffusers of information!?! So the pride of being at the head, let alone also being the artisan, of very efficient and highly demanded consumer services!

The SOS Nintendo was probably like a child, like Eve Lise's Baby, and she must have been very proud of it! She who selected her first champion: Josué Césaire, and most likely participated in the selection of the next ones. And when you are a mother, you are so proud to see your child grow up and reach certain heights that sometimes, often, you will make some arrangements with reality! 46 000 incoming calls (but not processed) it still beats better than 9764 calls processed (estimate a little too precise on my part certainly, I will come back to it) and therefore more than 36 000 who will have thus been stuck on music and other messages of expectations ("all our lines are busy, please wait...") before trying again later with more or less success. A great pride, probably but not only: presenting such a figure also allows to perpetuate, to confirm a whole strategy put in place in front of his direct superiors to whom one must be accountable. SOS Nintendo first Hotline of France is certain: for the number of unanswered calls, and from very far away (Yes I know I'm very nasty!!!).

As I read a lot of the business press at that time, especially when it talked about this fascinating fight between the two Japanese manufacturers, I immediately came across this figure that literally stuck me! I knew that at SOS Nintendo there were more people than at home: the Sega Masters. We often talk about forty people for Nintendo, perhaps a historical and seasonal peak at 48 individuals, even if it seems to me a lot, while we were at that time (92/93/94) between twelve and fifteen at the consumer services of Sega. Nintendo therefore employed three times as many staff to handle these calls. For me, at that time, I thought they were between thirty and forty so a quick calculation made me appear a score of more than one thousand calls per person! OH MY GOD! They are much stronger than the Master Sega had me then I said without thinking! Immediately, and this is a very important point, I set myself a double challenge.

The first would be to count my calls: the calls treated as if it was not the only thing that really mattered!?! And here I would like to be extremely clear, and for having covered the entire history of the Sega Hotline in its "open bar, open to all" versions with or without consideration, that is to say free number and communicated to the whole population or surcharged number on the end (the famous 3668): we were never asked, oh great ever, to count or make count our calls. They have never been counted individually, and we have never been put in competition with each other. There is no question for me to make a judgment on this subject and moreover, if I thought about it well, I would probably be in favour of a count! Although it could have been very handicaping as far as I was concerned, having been the "role-play specialist" for the whole period, with calls sometimes very long and not really easy to deal with, I always kept the taste of competition, a fortiori when it can create an emulation.

So the question is not to say whether this counting was "good" or "bad", I just have to note and let you see that at Sega, we never heard about it, while at Nintendo, there was indeed a counter or even several: a call counter "general" and an individual counter. Everyone is absolutely free to think what he wants (of course). Josué Césaire, the first full-time employee of SOS Nintendo, in a youtube interview with the unmissable video game historian Florent Gorges says that Nintendo advisors made on average between one hundred and two hundred daily calls! Figure which is perfectly matched with those of Sega. Rather one hundred for the low season or when the children are in school and two hundred in high season a fortiori on Saturdays. He also states a record number of 250 calls on a Saturday: figure that will be confirmed to me by my former colleague (future colleague at this time) Alain Milly because it is him who will make 252 calls very exactly on a Saturday around Christmas. I know Alain very well, he has always been very professional in everything he did, he hits fast, masters most subjects well and is not the type to get lost too often in chatting. The "King of the binders" was of maximum efficiency. So not surprised a second that he is holder of this "record". Before I continue, the most gifted of you in mental calculation will have made appear in their head a more "real" number of calls processed, far from the very questionable 46,000.

However, I come back to my two challenges of the moment! The first is to count my calls, on a Saturday. It's still very strange for me to count the calls. Nothing to do with the fact that it is good or not (a concept most often) but it changes, it distorts the perception I have of my work. I am neither Candide nor a Bisounours but this count acts as a bias, a distortion of my commitment and my will: the quality of my work can never be measured by the number of calls. An aid on Rings of Power Mega Drive or Ultima 4 on Master System will most often, playfully and humanly speaking, be worth much more than ten or twenty calls for codes on Sonic and Aladdin.

Second challenge: be as efficient and accommodating as possible but never flunk a single call. So exit the unnecessary chatter, Sonic's vacation at the beach or hiking in the central massif, my favorite character in Streets of Rage, the reminders of the style "you have another question maybe? This last point may seem extremely professional and friendly, and it is, but in reality more than nine times out of ten the answer is "no that will go thank you"! Nevertheless, when the calls are few, these "chatter" become very valuable because they create a bond, complicity and therefore fidelity. And I don't forget all my spontaneous fantasies about Sonic, because the players were very fond of it and probably still are even now forty years ago!

In "record" mode I clear all the frills of the low periods but while delivering a welcome at least friendly if not even friendly and warm. It is about being extremely focused both to answer correctly and totally the player, without ever losing a second, and without pushing or pressing my interlocutor. A record yes, a record of rushed or burned appeals: no. So it's off to a very intense day or clearly I would, hanging on my last call, feel like I was, at least that day, a kind of machine, an "AI Master Sega". I would then make 330 calls not in sprinter mode over 100 m but rather runner of the 1500 meters hurdles! Almost without having time to catch my breath or so little. As I thought after the event I probably had a little luck that day (like Sonic codes day) and I lacked reference, I reissued my record counting operation a second time (a Saturday or a day full of school holidays) to reach this time 310 calls. Precision of the most important to reach these "records", I did not play, I no longer play at all so that I can be totally focused on the call, nothing but the call while remaining as zen and welcoming as possible! We can obviously play and answer at the same time but we are necessarily losing speed and efficiency. Nothing very embarrassing in fact but to want to establish this record!

The difference between my 330 then 310 and 252 of Alain is very certainly due to two elements. The first, I had put myself in "record" mode absolute and competitive, while Alain probably did not look for it. The second, the Sega catalogue is not the Nintendo catalogue. Sega has neither Mario nor Zelda who concentrate on them both a very important (majority?) part of the calls. At Sega we also have Phantasy Star, Shining Force, Landstalker, Thor, Sun I can't say the best but nothing to do in terms of sales and calls compared to plumber red and green adventurer. So we come to the final count. In busy times, hotliners will likely answer 200/220 calls on average! Even a 48-fold increase does not go far beyond the 10,000 mark. This figure is still much less spectacular especially if it should be no longer five but four figures!

Last point to close this small, even anecdotal but very symbolic polemic: where can the figure of 46,000 calls come from? It's very simple, these are all the calls received at the standard without any distinction. And in times of strong affluence, the vast majority will not be treated because "all our lines are occupied, please wait or call back in a few moments..." On a standard you have a number of open lines on telephone combinations and others that are virtual lines like queues on which you can have music to wait. These unprocessed calls are counted in the same way. The more a standard is saturated, the more the number of such unprocessed calls increases. If I was a little naughty (just a little) I would definitely return the figure by pointing out, insisting on: Nintendo record of unprocessed calls in one day: 35,000 lost calls! That is almost 80%!!! So see how one can treat the numbers to his advantage depending on whether you are on one side, or the other.

Obviously Sega was certainly not exempt from these small arrangements with the figures. And I remember very often being surprised by the figures released on the Game Gear console. We still had a pretty good market share while we were getting fucked by Nintendo in volume. It is that, and for the Game Gear alone, we communicated market share "value" and not volume, the console being sold twice as expensive as Nintendo's, the gap was less important. PDM value that Nintendo also took for the SNIN versus the Mega

Drive and which masked the fact that the 16-bit Sega console often sold better than its competitor.

Chapter 21

Bruno Charpentier

Bruno "Segala" !

As much to continue to say things as simply as possible, even though the vast majority of Sega's executives will have done their job properly, or often very well, I did not hold them, and still do not hold them, today, in very high esteem. I had been, I remained and will remain very marked by the comments of the salesmen at the first seminar that I attended, purely national, namely, and as I told it in Volume 1: "we do not force, we do not force anything, the product sells itself so if we can avoid that we ask for much more next year... !" A real shock for me at the time: these salesmen had just broken my Arthur armor, ripped off my Hang On helmet and reduced my Shinobi Shurikens to dust!

So without being as severe in their regard, as could be a good number of editors of the specialized press, AHL in the lead, and finally like most Gamers, known or not, and without even wanting to denigrate them, because they had all the same and obviously many qualities, I often wondered what all these technicians, all these "operators" of sales and communication could really serve!?! Otherwise grease the paw and thus ensure the "benevolence" of all their interlocutors and especially the media in which they deployed!?! Like, more broadly, oiling and watching over all the wheels of this irresistible mechanical that seemed, in any case, to want to advance on its own? Even if it were, it would be little or no assistance. Operators and managers more than narrators or visionaries, companions more than conquerors, and even if for me it was too much for the price, it was still without measure with a Nintendo totally locked in, prisoner in an absolute conformity, Crossing time and generations, certainly relying on the one we can consider as the messiah of video games on console: Shigeru Miyamoto, the creator of Zelda and of course Mario. Such a genius, in the genre, can then dispense completely marketing and communication. Nintendo had its messiah, its religion, its dogmas and therefore its immobility. For years, decades and maybe even centuries! AMEN... but very little for me. I would rather ride a crazy comet, a spinning and whirling star for a few moments, than stay perched on even the most sacred cow.

Bring "bread and games"! "Panem et circences" in Latin, could already be said since antiquity in Rome! The result is still visible today. Millions of players will play all their lives the same game(s): Mario or Sonic when you are little, Street Fighter, Mortal Kombat or Virtua Fighter when you are big but also and especially football, soccer and even football for some. Marketing will then have nothing else to do, and as in real life, than change the players, jerseys and composition of teams! There is nothing personal for me here, so what could be the use of Marketing and Communication? What could be their margins of manoeuvre? For Sega? As for Nintendo? And a fortiori at that time "blessed"? Without forgetting some great media hits that still reason thirty years later as the now mythical "Sega it's stronger than you". But how many players will have bought this or that console by being influenced by advertising? Of course you have to be there, and occupy the ground of media space, which will immediately double with a physical space (even if it is less and less true today) that is like a spider web, if you do not weave any, It is obvious that you will certainly catch fewer flies. It is certainly there, the real and indisputable effectiveness of advertising: opening additional points of sale.

In this video game world, at least in the early 90s, where the first consumers were most often what we still call "Gamers", that is to say ultra-passionate players who rush on new experiences and/or their favorite games, what could be the impact of marketing and communication? When everything is finally so frozen at the level of choices and consumption? Especially when these gentlemen of advertising often remain a little or totally foreign to the emotions aroused by their range of games? For them more "products": when you hear this rhetoric, you have understood everything! For some simple "parodies" and even for the one I would consider as being the best! I bought myself a Japanese Mega Drive in import with two or three games, with as only compulsion, the irresistible desire to satisfy my passion for games that made me really and terribly envy, namely first the mythical Ghouls'n Ghost and the legendary Shinobi. I became in a split second the most glorious of warriors of tales and legends: Arthur Pendragon son of Uther Pendragon and friend of Merlin the enchanter. Or I became Joe Musashi, the most formidable, indomitable of the "Shinobi", better known and identified as "Ninja" in the west, with his incredible throw of Shurikens and his physical and athletic performances that made him the ultimate killer. It was not useful for me to add more because the video game creators had touched me at heart and deep down, everything else would seem a little ridiculous even if, as for many people, ads with humorous and offbeat tones would be highly appreciated!

However, in the case of Sega and like that of Nintendo, they can at least be attributed to them, I the first, even if they inevitably imposed themselves, they can be credited with the paternity and the training of "consumer services". The Clubs of course, with information letters, codes and tricks and more unnecessary contests, but also and above all of course direct assistance with the now legendary "Hotlines"! If the public service had for many years its "SVP" by phone, known to the entire French population, the hyper-specialized hotlines emerged and exploded with those dedicated to video games. An indispensable "SAV", at least at that time, and which was one of the biggest files to be treated, for the two Japanese manufacturers, Place des Vosges for Sega and Luc Bourcier, as soon as sales began to fly. The video game console format needed these Masters of the game immediately to, in a first time, not lose any player and accompany them, and in a second, to retain them. So I would be very ill-advised, and above all, very little grateful not to give them some credit at that level. Recruitment was not absolutely perfect, on the number there is necessarily a little waste (two or three individuals maximum) but Romuald will have had, most often, the hollow nose (but he was obviously, and he remains, a true passionate, a pure Gamer) and marketing will only be able to see this. Master Sega and his personal line would give the thrill more than any other (e) other! It was an unforgettable experience, especially as I recalled in Volume 1, if you called the dark and powerful Master Sega and fell on Sandrine or Aude!!! (How many will have hung up!?! Before redial the number...).

If I did not really wear all these frames, like all these gears fixed but turning, in very high esteem with respect to this mission that was theirs, as my but for me the most sacred one, namely to bring Sega to the highest and conquer the world without fail, there were some of them with certain talents and even sometimes really bluffing efficiency in the execution of their tasks! And so now I will introduce one of the key characters in the history of Sega France through a quote from David Ogilvy, one of the world's advertising popes, and that this flagship character of the Sonic team will have taken as its motto: "If each of us hires people smaller than ourselves, we will become a dwarf company. But if each of us hires people bigger than himself, we will become a company of giants." An amazing motto if we only take it to the first degree, and therefore without taking all the metaphorical and philosophical measure, because Bruno had worked for both Mario and Sonic! We have known much bigger by size but rarely as big and even giants by their talents! But it does not take anything away from this motto that reflects well the man who wears it and will make a large part of its originality.

Bruno dreamed of being an advertising agent: curious, empathetic, creative, intuitive, sensitive and communicative as he was naturally! Listening to him recently in a video interview about his career ("it goes live" by Simon Collot) he makes an absolutely delicious lapsus (7 minutes and 20 seconds): "I wanted to be an advertising man, it was the time of "Segala", from Hollywood...!! This guy is obviously "Jacques Séguéla" one of the biggest advertising of the 80s and 90s. But Bruno will not be advertising, but commercial, because it had to earn his living and the ad often imposed years of internship "free", his parents did not have enough means to finance him and you had to eat well.

Before we tell you more about it, let's give back to Caesar what definitely belongs to Caesar and even to rehash him a little too much! Unlike Nintendo, we the Sega Masters were fully integrated into the distribution company! No "Stock Services", we were at first "Virgin Loisirs" like the others and in a second time "Sega France". We were fully integrated into the marketing department and our offices were adjacent to those of the product managers and management. Which allowed each other to help each other, to be very effectively informed because we were very complementary. Jean Luc Satin, Philippe Deleplace, Cédric Maréchal used to come to the Hotline regularly to see Romuald, most often, but not that. The other product managers should probably be more shy!?! Although we were installed in "open space", we each had a large office, "corner", in which we had all the necessary place to work and so play and for some sometimes: fall asleep! No one will pressure us to achieve numbers. In times of high affluence, we have just been forbidden the "chatting" but it was so obvious. So yes, within the "Marketing", there were consumer services and the Hotline that will have delighted and accompanied thousands and perhaps even millions of children and adolescents! They can also be credited for having validated the campaign of Punk and that of "Master Sega". As you probably already knew for a long time, and recalled in the Chronicles Volume 1: a fabulous advertising campaign to the credit of creative agency and com Lintas (one of them was a gamer and it will probably make all the difference!). It is in retrospect, and all the more remarkable to see year after year, at that time, that Sega will have known its culmination in everything and for everything as a manufacturer of consoles: during the years Mega Drive! No more communication campaigns will have the same success, no more will have the same impact as in these crazy 16-bit years!

When the heyday of Sega France is propelled by an incredible precocity!!! It will be necessary to wait many years to make the observation. The Sega adventure of that time will probably remain as a kind of Big Bang in the video-gaming universe. What could marketing and communication have done after such a bang? Success is so fragile that it is better, of course, not to be too hasty in achieving it. When you fly up to the sky so quickly, it is very difficult to put your feet on the ground. If some things imposed themselves, it was still necessary to accompany them with talent, curiosity, sincerity and generosity, especially when the wave began to fall. If I have already told you about Jean Martial Lefranc, Luc Bourcier, Jean Luc satin as the first craftsmen working in the development of sega in France, it is time for me to talk more widely, from my point of view, about the best of all: the well-named "Bruno Charpentier", far from being as well known as "Joseph", he will be no less mythical at least for Sega France. Master craftsman or "commercial developer" as he likes to say and present himself. The one who will have been certainly the most effective in setting up the technical elements and the new set of wheels so that the machine runs wonderfully well and has the best oils as the best cooling liquids! He will have made sure that Sega is in the best of form, its representation everywhere in France. The last, and probably the greatest "Master of Sega", purely technical and commercial.

Still a young man at that time, with a few years and also a few centimeters taller than me, Bruno had an unquestionable allure! Very tall, straight and determined, always neat suit, tie and hairstyle, sometimes slightly rosy shirts, he exuded as much strength and conviction as sweetness, delicacy, and was equipped with the fatal weapon indispensable in business and communication: Smile at the President! A wide and omnipresent smile that will be of all the discussions and all the fights. In the warrior metaphor, Bruno was clearly a Paladin: this knight as bright as powerful, as generous as he was valiant and who never doubted one moment of his strength and talent, because in reality, he was, and remains, an eternal optimist is an irresistible force of conviction. His natural empathy and a restrained, measured ego will add to this quiet power an incredible 360° vision, and perhaps even an increased sense of clairvoyance.

However, the first time I saw it in the corridors of Sega, in the last months of 1993, I confess to have thought of a brand new and very powerful Troll! If it happened that a rancid smell of seafood spreads in the corridors of Sega after the passage of the miserable crustacean shamefully crawling, hidden under his cap, I was afraid of the influence of this new character who seemed too red to go blue. A little thin and especially a bit too smiling for a Troll worthy of the name, but I saw in him, if not an evil being, at least a disturbing element! For he disturbed me! It should be noted that it is our new CEO, ex Bandai, ex Nintendo, Patrick Lavanant with whom he had already worked so, who has got him from Nintendo, as he himself was but by the Japanese of SoJ! Those defectors from Nintendo to Sega didn't mean anything to me, but I was wrong, at least half way, at least on the side of Bruno Charpentier.

I saw rather stupidly, you have to recognize it retrospectively, because I was probably a little too much in binary mode, in "conspiracy" mode I perceived a new and potential "traitor"! But Bruno was neither "red", nor "blue" or even "violet". In hindsight I could easily confuse him with some kind of mercenary, but he was a Paladin in the "Dungeons and Dragons", a conqueror, an adventurer who always advanced against all winds and against all tides to bring greater luminosity on everything that approached it, is its wonderful nature, and on the condition that these challenges and adventures are renewed and offer new horizons!

My first impression was therefore totally distorted, by the a priori of young man too passionate about his job, extrapolating probably a little too much the spirit of family or "corporate" as that of clan, and although I stay and would remain, even with so much hindsight and years past, "99%" Sega! Impression Kiss kool which will be the best for, as an absolute surprise effect, finally discover a man with a brave heart as I liked to have them by my side in this immense battle that held us, and would still hold us in breath for months and years! The "Game" will never be as big and as intense as with

Bruno! It will often give me the opportunity to dive or reimmerse myself in the heart of the most intense, the most bitter fights, which certainly "the worst of my memories"!

During our great seminar evening concluding a magnificent year 1993, at least in appearance through record volumes, and in the very first days of 1994, Sega France employees were invited once again to meet up and feast at the cabaret "Brazil Tropical" at the foot of the Montparnasse Tower. We were then, but we did not know it, at our Apogee! Economically, artistically and humanly, we had reached all the heights and we were going to enjoy it among ourselves! And it is probably also in this that the arrival of Bruno is remarkable and to be noted. It was, it happened a little like the cherry on the cake! He did not know himself at the time, who will bring and contribute very significantly to our company, but it is also him who will sign the layoffs of more than half of the staff, in a little over two years, including that of Luc Bourcier! Or the other side of a medal that he will have acquired nevertheless formidably well. He was the last great, the last giant of these historical years and it is he who will have the dark task to thank almost all the others and even often the "first"! His arrival marked the end of the "roaring years" but it was better that Bruno be on our side than that of Nintendo for years much less easy, but equally exciting.

However, at that moment, in this intensely Carioca universe, it was again the perfect joy and happiness! We were going to have a dream evening, a magical, magical evening, as we had already tasted on multiple occasions. We started in 1993 in Guadeloupe and we would finish it in Brazil, at least in one of these little pieces, and in a really extraordinary show, as if we were participating in the Rio Carnival with all those dancers and all those Samba dancers! With these fire-eaters, these spinning athletes and performing truly incredible physical prowess! Carnival, circus, show were all around us and we grazed while we ate and we would feast for example with more than fifteen different meats served!?! As if we were to be terrible carnivores like T-Rex or Carnotaurus and having two or even three stomachs!?!

We were about 130/140 employees (our top) and about twenty tables had been reserved just for us, but without any table plan! We have therefore settled down more or less spontaneously and happily, but in this slight confusion of improvisation and a flurry of selection, where one tries at the same time, more or less consciously and logically, to get closer to the people one likes most, but without snooping others!?! A Cornish choice in reality? On the surface? But fortunately there is also and always fate! I could have been next to my best friends, my brothers in arms "Masters Sega" like Romuald and Jean Luc but no, that night I will be at the same table and even quite opposite... Bruno Charpentier!!! The infamous, filthy Troll reddish or pink, gluey and repulsive from Nintendo and maybe like a kind of growing allergy to crustaceans and all those who would make me think!?! The one I would probably have placed in the last, if I had made a list, a desiderata, but how could I have talked so much about him without approaching him at some point? And to say that that night I had taken out my very pretty cashmere jacket paid a fortune but I had instead given up my pink shirt: unlike Bruno! Maybe he had carried in his wake, and therefore at our table, two people I really liked: Véronique Cosatti would be just to my left and Philippe Deleplace just to my right. Just Magnificent!!! I could have sat even in front of the Prince of darkness as long as I was surrounded by so much! Véronique and Philippe were also among the last important recruits of Sega France and of this glorious and triumphant time. This totally improvised table composition proved a radical and very happy change between the first generation of frame and the next. We can always discuss hours and hours on the reality of the gap that separated the Masters Sega from other employees of Marketing, especially since it is obviously never to generalize to all individuals, but it was good day and night between a Bruno Charpentier and an Olivier Creuzy!

The party would not be spoiled on the contrary, Bruno was curious, jovial, affable, funny, generous. It is probably the "tie suit" that we will see most often pass the Hotline just for fun! I read it in an interview written on joypad.fr by Régis Monterrin, Bruno says he loved to go to the Hotline out of curiosity and surely to peck, feed our passion. He also talks about the confrontation of the two worlds, mentioning Marketing and the Hotline! An often electric confrontation, a brothel organized that also amused him a lot. As what, it really was not only one point of view, my mind, or that of the Sega Masters...

He came to incruster five, ten or even fifteen minutes, as we "Masters Sega" could go and beat us, individually or in several, in the other offices from time to time and according to the affinities of course. Obviously he exchanged with us to get our opinion on a 100% sega subject but not that. What I will also notice is that he could sometimes come and listen to us for a good while without saying anything! He listened to us for five or ten minutes, smiled and left looking happier than when he arrived! He was not the only one to spend time at the Hotline, but for me it is quite clear that it was him who got the most profit! It could be seen, felt and his natural smile was growing! If I talk about it now with so much happiness, we must recognize that it contrasted not bad, it contrasted the most with a good part of the other frames! Even if Jean-Luc Satin, Philippe Deleplace and Cédric Maréchal were also "naturally" very close to us and they were not the last ones to want to have fun, smile, a little!

The one I had seen as a kind of traitor or troll was finally this valiant paladin: determined and combative but in joy and good mood and for the happiness of all. Everyone can be wrong and in this case it was so joyful to be able to admit his mistake. I will see it during this wonderful evening until no time: Bruno was a sweet and charming character with many talents. He was therefore largely of size against the historical Titan of Sega France: Luc Bourcier with whom he would compete as much as he would compose. Because they were going to share the work in the strategy of development and conquest of the general public. Luc kept the marketing and media communication and "gave up" to Bruno the more commercial part in direct relation with all our "big clients" and other big accounts.

Bruno started his career by spending a few years as a buyer, on behalf of Auchan and developing the "gray ray" for the famous "brown" products!?! Booming as TV, VCRs, computers and therefore also the first consoles. He met Luc Bourcier for the first time in 1987 as part of a negotiation to refer the Master System at Auchan. The "Plug and Play" side pleases enormously and immediately to Bruno who takes over the Sega console and makes distribute it in more than one hundred large stores. Sega enters Auchan while Nintendo will remain at the door for a long time, because the "NES", being distributed by Bandai rather in traditional toy stores like Played club or La Grande Récré, offers sales conditions and margins too little advantageous. Bandai wanted to protect, in any case prefer a model 100% "toy" and in which he was immersed from head to toe! Not only were they not very accessible to expand their distribution network, but the day the dams start flying in pieces, they will continue to play with carrot and stick with their official distributors as they always did. Basically, to sum up: sell more Nintendo, consoles and games if you want to have Bandai in good conditions (various and varied games, figurines and merchandise) and vice versa. This policy, conservative and unduly restrictive, and too pro-specialist toy stores, will be double-edged and will eventually turn against Bandai. If it can be optimized in a universe, an eco-system "toys" as for 8bit consoles, it is eventually condemned to become a drag in a universe of mass consumption and larger public. The large distribution so-called "food" will eventually accept these conditions but sometimes by having their ear pulled!

This was also the case for Bruno Charpentier who will tell this wonderful anecdote about the temporary absence of Nintendo consoles in the shelves of Auchan. He will receive a phone call from the assistant to the CEO of the group (Gérard Mulliez): "Mr. Mulliez would like to know why you can't find the Nintendo console in Auchan stores? Because his grandchildren asked him!" To which Bruno will reply that the conditions of sales are not interesting. But Auchan will eventually refer to Nintendo because the heirs of the big boss wanted it, whatever the conditions...

Sega will take advantage of this partitioning voluntarily "toy" associated with Nintendo, opening, or rather by expanding this very large distribution gap and thus take a little lead over its rival while activating an important and decisive dynamic when the arm-wrestling really takes place. Especially since the distribution of the NES will be disturbed by the passing of witness from the first company to distribute it to the second: Bandai (Thank you Patrick!! One point!!! Sorry 2 or 3 points even with the debacles of ASD).

Sega and Nintendo will be almost equal in terms of sales in France on 87/88 while the reputation of Nintendo is very much higher than that of Sega at that time, with almost 90% of world market share! Almost a monopoly! Bruno Charpentier had already scored points for Sega. But also and especially for Auchan who will be momentarily the leader on this niche, ahead of Conforama and others and before being caught up and surpassed by Fnac or Micromania a few years later. End of 1990: Association with the magazine Tilt to distribute in the 120 Hyper markets the special issue "100 best console games". Several hundred thousand copies! A Master's move for Bruno and Auchan, a formidable publicity move for Tilt which, if it were not already the case, will feel the pressure "console" increase even more and at a prodigious speed to the point of launching "Consoles +" a few months later.

That is to say, he knew this market well and how much more could be done at the next level! Initially, and for a year, he became sales director for Bandai then Nintendo (92/93)! He had long fought with the Japanese manufacturer, through Bandai, in the time of Auchan, and it is for this reason that he will be contacted. Bandai wants to break, too, if not push the boundaries of video games. The NES would no longer be merely a toy, Bruno Charpentier would be the architect of its development in all channels of mass distribution, which he knew perfectly. Nintendo will emancipate itself from Bandai, the toy merchant, and give themselves the freedom to not, to no longer let Sega lag behind on Salon consoles in other broadcast channels.

Bruno will develop, in partnership with the retail networks, the Linear!!!! Its presentation, organization, demo consoles, anti-theft systems... Everything he could learn, develop and test at Auchan in "Leader", he will pass it on to Carrefour, Continent, Mammouth, Cora, Leclerc, Fnac, Darty, Printemps, BHV etc... And it works! Success was inevitable but it was wonderfully well-accompanied. Nintendo will speed up with Bruno but he, will be a second time, to be debunked by Patrick Lavanant, after being debunked from Auchan to Bandai! And now it is Sega who will then take advantage of this "fatal weapon"! The biggest specialist in the video game market in the large distribution, with his sting as fast as that of a scorpion! The Pioneer, the Adventurer, the Promachos, the one who always arrives first!!! Veni Vidi Vici.

He knows everything about the big distribution and he even forged the new shelves! He rubbed off on Bandai and then Nintendo from the outside as a buyer, looking at and measuring all the strengths and weaknesses on one side of the mirror often generating, at least frustration, on the side of the dealers. Then, by going to the other side of the mirror he was able to definitively validate these strengths and weaknesses while introducing the NES in all distribution channels including the "GMS": the large specialized stores (Darty, Printemps, Fnac) and finally, by introducing himselfeven everywhere!!! With the referencing of the NES everywhere in France, Bruno Charpentier had become the expert and even the King of the Video game trade in large stores. The Trump, the Master. He was going to use all his knowledge and all these contacts to make Sega the "perfect Nintendo"! Cad by working hand in hand with each distributor! Listening, being very attentive to all requests. Nintendo was absolutely not doing that, totally convinced that he was the only Master on board, that he would stay on board and never have to discuss. They have the Messiah of video games in their team and everyone will continue to bend the knee.

Bruno was clearly the Fatal Weapon and in probable avatar of Sun tsu (the Art of war) no other more than he could personify this elementary principle to win a war: "Know your opponent and especially know yourself and you will be invincible". Bruno like the Titan, the Promethium of video games was going to succeed what seemed impossible! Bring together young and old, marketing, communications, players, Sega masters, resellers, consumers to audit them but also and above all so that everyone can listen and be heard by others! He would share and make share all the knowledge, knowledge and fruits of Passion to reach the Best! The shelves will be perfectly equipped with superb furniture, sometimes accompanied by trained and passionate demonstrators, and Sega will flood these shelves with console + games packs, the most expected, the most requested! Sonic, Aladdin, The Lion King, FIFA, Streets of Rage, Street fighter 2, Ecco le dauphin. Sega will be the king of the Hyper sexy console pack.

The demonstrators at the point of sale: a first in France with Sega, after the successful tests of the Sega Masters on one side (for Fifa Mega Drive from memory as far as I'm concerned) and that of "Captain Nintendo" on the other with Super Mario 3! Home and CDD demonstrators, specially trained for end-of-year sales or new product launches. In Paris, the Marketing will regularly employ these Sega masters for major events, but obviously we were not enough to go beyond the peripheral or too long. Bruno understood the first, all the impact and effectiveness of having these ambassadors at key moments! Tilt the undecided as rearrange the ray to the advantage of Sega!!! Some more Sega consoles in front of those of Nintendo, and in this corner more passing or more "visual"! We were making sure of a better visibility when it was needed to Sonic, when Mario on the contrary, seemed to have disappeared again in a pipeline!?!

The commercial management will also send Master Sega to convince the department heads of large specialized stores. But this time, it will not be a great success, on the contrary, and as you will discover in the chapter on "forgotten war"!

Chapter 22

Forgotten Words.

Forgotten Wars.

The return of consoles in Europe at the end of the 80's and beginning of the 90's, was so sudden and so violent, the passion generated so intense and so radical, that it would almost pass for a wonderful magic trick! ABRACADABRA!!!

And as with a great hat of magician placed just before our eyes, top-hat of the most standard with its high and cylindrical cap, first deeply and singularly empty, before that at once, in one single stroke, but magic wand, and under our applause, It comes out a beautiful and very dynamic rabbit who would jump from everywhere and in all directions! A two-coloured hare: blue on one side and red on the other, leaping and zigzagging one shot to the right, then one shot to the left before going back to the right in a crazy race or nothing seemed to be able to stop it! Shoving, trampling, stepping on feet and throwing in the air everything that could be in his path, without caring a bit about it. Perhaps, or certainly, he had not even noticed anything in his amazing acceleration!?! It's all the art of magic and prestidigitation: hypnotize you on a very precise point to see nothing else just around.

Was it a blue and red rabbit? Or a moustached plumber in blue overalls and red sweater? Or a blue hedgehog ultra-fast and red shoes? What is sure is that it was red and blue, that it jumped and bounced on everything and everywhere without ever wanting to stop! The great cleansing had begun. As we know, nature hates the void, and before going on, and communicating with game consoles, children had other occupations: most likely more peaceful, much less addictive and therefore more varied. The almost magical and instant reappearance of consoles, especially Japanese machines, was not without its setbacks, because they were confronted with a particularly robust competitor, ancestral and thus appearing totally invincible, in any case unremovable. But as an opponent indeed overpowerful, it would be better to speak and nuance by evoking a colossus certainly, but a colossus with feet of clay.

The Toy"! Yes the eternal, timeless and irresistible Toy, it has everything from this huge but fragile colossus as it has everything from the very wide and very deep "Legion" but always flirting with division even the explosion. To continue and end in metaphors, and especially those generously drawn from the tales and legends, "the Toy" would also be a little, much, like the famous Hydra of the Greek Mythology. Cut off one head, and two will grow! 2, 3, 4, 6, 8, 11, 22! The beast seems to be more and more powerful, but in reality we are closer to chaos: the command is divided and dissolved, the beast can no longer be controlled! This forgotten war that I will evoke is, and will remain, we can no longer "mythological" as the years are stretching and memories are scattered! How many of you know or remember that it existed? How many of you could assess how much damage it had caused, even scratching out many French "SMEs", toy manufacturers, sending back many employees looking for jobs!?!

The reality of this war was already debatable and discussed, and therefore more or less contestable and disputed, yesterday as today and probably tomorrow. The toy", that is to say the toy said "traditional" was already seriously attacked by electronic toys most often from Hong Kong and more generally very cheap toys, often plastic and coming from Asia. Cut off one head, and he will grow two!?! And for many, over time, and now definitely, we will withdraw the video game market from that of the toy! Too different, the video game will slowly but surely incruster in the shelves of "brown" products (TV, Hifi, microphones and co...) especially in the "GSA" (large food stores like Auchan and with the fabulous epic of "Bruno Charpentier" that I mentioned earlier) before also deploying in the "GMS" (large and medium-sized stores) and department stores such as Printemps, the BHV, the FNAC, Darty and the Samaritaine. It was a great battle, another one that the Sega sales people and Nintendo were fighting. The video game market has become both global and transgenerational, but it was not always so.

An encounter that is sometimes violent and almost completely forgotten today, for not having been, perhaps, very commented on at the time, and which will certainly leave few memories, because it was prior to the advent of the internet and all these huge DATA. It is, however, a real and intense war that I will exhume as I have had to revive memories buried deep in my mind. I had almost completely forgotten them until I looked back on this glorious past! Our subconscious gives pride of place to very good memories, evacuating or rather repressing the worst and least important. A natural selection and healthy for our mental balance, in any case if we always prefer to see the glass half full rather than half empty.

I can do the devil at leisure with hedgehogs, plumbers or rabbits and I can do it all the more willingly, I hope most often by chance, to bring out all the pathetic dimensions and sometimes even a little tragic, of a world that replaces another without realizing it, or so little, in any case without caring. Which would not be very revolting in itself, because that is how the cycles of the economy go, let alone the cycles of life! Except to touch directly the sacred and ultra protected world of children, their learning, their cultures and their developments! The toy being one of these most important vectors, to save and guarantee cost what costs, value what value. You can always replace the pedal truck with a bike, the bike with a scooter, the scooter with a moped, the moped with a car, the car with a train or plane or a flying saucer, but "Le Jouet" is and remains particularly conservative for the first and the most tender years of our lives, probably under a powerful effect of nostalgia on the part of parents, and I will learn it quite dear, at my own expense. Because yes, I had passed myself, completely by this aspect of things, being a teenager and then over the age of 18, I was totally out, at least I thought so, of the world of toys. From one dimension to another, I had forgotten the whole substance and importance of the first, before I was, therefore, confronted again but without having been warned. Although even Sega in a first time and Nintendo in a second, but with less convictions, will seek and succeed to cut the bridges definitively.

Belotte and therefore rebelotte thirty years later!!! This war that I initially thought rather to be the fantasy, the anecdote, or "at worst" of the simple "collateral damage", therefore probably negligible, this forgotten conflict also surfaced and surreptitiously from the bottom of the magician's hat to remind me in a scathing way and probably even more striking than when she touched me several times now thirty years ago! If this confrontation, yet long course, was and remains "forgotten" it is very likely that for most of you, of us, it has probably never existed! But for others it was if not the Armageddon, at least the Apocalypse and all these upheavals.

Some things appear to us so suddenly, and so obviously, this probably explains it, and vice versa, that they do not bother, or so little, small damage and collateral damage that they can cause! Subjugated, hypnotized by a new experience, the latter takes over your brain, and it takes at least for a time, total control. Your old concerns, your previous interests are pushed back, temporarily or not, into the lower floors of your memories and thoughts! As in Toy Story and with the arrival of Buzz the Lightning, it is all the former tenants, including poor Woody, who are then relegated to the depths of oblivion, at least temporarily.

But in this case, it's about much more than that. It's about much more than that. The "Novelty" will take everything away for the greatest number, leaving only crumbs to the oldest, and for a long time and sometimes even permanently. Because yes, the video game has heckled, pushed and sometimes overturned THE TOY! Not all "The Toy", and not for everyone either: girls resistant more than young boys, as long as they were not offered games more adapted and often just less violent! You will probably be surprised and cautious yourself!?! A war against the toy? " But it's not the same at all" some will say! " It's another market", "parallel" and "never heard of" will say others! Nowadays, the two markets have diverged seriously, even if the gateways exist, and these two worlds are often completely separated physically in large specialized stores or not. They have grown so far apart that even now they like to get together with some juicy licenses like the one of Lego. The reality of the war of toys against video games, is neither more nor less questionable than the war between Sega and Nintendo. It's just a matter of perspective. I was not up to the task, much less in the right place to appreciate even the tiniest trace. Until under the leadership of the commercial management of Sega, and therefore that of Bruno Charpentier, I was sent to the front and even in the first line.

Today, almost everyone plays or could play video games, at least on mobile phone, while the toy is almost entirely turned to the child, but not exclusively with Lego or Playmobil selling now a lot to "Kidultes" : those nostalgic adules who want to remain children and enjoy collecting. The game consoles are out of the toy department to join that of the Hifi, video and more generally "brown products". War underestimated, undervalued and forgotten also because one of the two protagonists is not really "One". Never unified and because it has been, and remains a fortiori very divided, with compartments that will be, sometimes only very little affected while others will be purely and simply eradicated. This colossal opponent has seriously trembled everywhere, so that it even dropped some pieces, most often "national", and it is in this that one can count the torture after the fact, the injuries, even if he will eventually recover from them and sometimes even be stronger. Anything that doesn't kill us...

There are one or several federations to defend games and toys, but it has been very difficult and even futile to try to rise up towards this cultural and generational clash of an unprecedented violence because terribly disruptive, between an old world and the new. It is extremely difficult to measure the intensity of this war. We can always observe and analyse the evolution of each other's turnover, such as the disappearance of many toy manufacturers, the most fragile, and often the most "French". It was only in 1994 that I could measure how much this war existed!!! That it even existed "still"!?! The Nintendo and Sega consoles were already there for several years and the Toy resisted well or badly. A new world and seeming without any limit trampled the old world without even looking at it. No contempt, nor arrogance, just the indifference proper to Darwinian evolution.

THE DISASTER!

When Bruno Charpentier joined the sales management team of Sega France in late 1993, he was going to take very seriously and very concretely to optimize Sega's sales. From the large distribution, buyer for Auchan, to the commercial management of Nintendo/ Bandai, he knows perfectly all the workings of the system and will grease them to the maximum: for the better very often and sometimes for the worse. As part of his strategy of conquest, I was offered as "Master Sega" to accompany Véronique Cosatti (then responsible for the "GSA as GSS" key accounts, food and specialty stores) and to assist her in a new and exciting mission. It was a pleasure to work with Véronique, always positive, dynamic, very smiling and pedagogue! No wonder she became Bruno's right-hand man in the Commercial Department. She was really sweet and I think she liked me too. I will discover very recently, that after many years spent in commercial and marketing positions, she will be retrained in national education as a Teacher of schools! What a wonderful, wonderful choice of life!

Our delicate mission would be, more or less, to train, at least to sensitize, the chefs and other managers of department stores in Paris such as La Samaritaine, BHV or Printemps to Sega products, consoles and games and especially new products. Under a growing and exponential demand, as a little in all the distribution channels, the shelves, the linear Sega of these large stores, were taking up more and more space and the commercial management of Team Sonic wanted to play on a relationship of proximity and accompaniment of these department heads, as it already did successfully for the GSA: the large food distribution, these heads of department are not always, far from it, "Gamers". Bruno and Véro were very attached to this direct, frank, friendly relationship in search of a maximum of listening and interactions. They wanted to maintain and develop this more human, less commercial relationship, to make the difference with a much cooler and especially too vertical Nintendo company. Bruno had acquired this exceptional vision in four dimensions! Bandai + Nintendo + Sega and of course the big distribution. He was always one step ahead because he saw the market better than anyone else and therefore, for the most part, he would invent it! As a true Promethean Titan he had become: taste for action, faith in man, big and small, he will bring and enlighten Sega as all his partners by the sacred fire of his knowledge and deep generosity. And yet he will not see, he will not imagine a single second, an enormous disappointment in which I would be plunged from head to toe.

Véronique told me that we would have several meetings, one per week, for several weeks, around lunch time on one or two hours, to present the new Sega, praise the merits of the best productions available, often the best-selling products of the moment, and those that would soon be available and likely to have some success. She would do most of the work of presenting products, rather in a technical and formal way, as well as strategies to be implemented with demonstration furniture, POS and all other accessories available to potential buyers. My role would be very limited and in "support", I will confine myself to answer any questions more technical on games or consoles in my capacity of ultra gamer and therefore as the Master Sega that I was, and that I incarnated wonderfully, when I found myself in front of amateurs more or less enlightened but always curious. A new mission full of promise and gratifying that I could nevertheless grasp neither easily nor with difficulty, just what it takes to concentrate and be up to the task! We would both go in the car of véronique, to join these department heads of big stores, in premises, in the center of paris. From the historic BHV? From the Samaritaine? From Printemps? I don't remember the order and it will ultimately remain without great importance after hits.

We park, get out of the car and join a meeting room. I have not imagined anything, nothing prepared, my role is limited and reserved for the gaming aspect as I can do every day at the Hotline on the phone. I have no reason to worry, everything will be for the best and in the best of the world, that of entertainment, games and therefore fun. Yet, upon entering the meeting room, I immediately feel a little unwell. Something, if not abnormal, at least extremely curious, and deeply destabilizing, jumps in my eyes and pricks me as rarely! The room is full of WOMEN! Women, nothing but women, a good dozen, probably a dozen and rather age wall! Expected, unconsciously, "leaders of the ray", expected "men", expected rather "young" or even "geeks": I found myself in a configuration totally opposite!

Although this observation is tremendously striking, I do not take full conscience because I am surprised, shocked and probably a little upset at the bottom of me by this unimaginable situation! They are "only women", I mean human beings! Certainly civilized and therefore safe, but I am KO standing, anesthetized, lost and finally disconnected! By talking to children, adolescents, by meeting more often boys or young men, I had certainly masculinized the universe of video games, without forgetting girls as women, We even had two at the Hotline. I had not imagined anything but especially not to find myself face to face with so many women so mature! Namely probably between 40 and 55 years. It was the world, it was my world but upside down and like a dream or a nightmare, like in one of those of the movie "The Forbidden Experience" with Julia Roberts, when one of the protagonists emerges in the middle of an assembly totally made up of women, at first all friendly...

I was losing my footing, although fortunately no one could notice it. Moreover, Véronique took the meeting and information in her hands and I could regain my spirits, albeit a little bit jittery. While she was demonstrating I could quietly and discreetly observe our interlocutors, or rather our interlocutors. I had not imagined anything, and so much the better, because I could never have imagined this unimaginable scenario and almost Science-Fiction! It's as if I went to Greenland to meet, after hours of patience and hope, polar bears and finally I met giraffes, gorillas or lions.

I was like falling into a parallel universe, a slight distortion of my reality, or what I thought it was or could be! But I was only at the beginning of this very amazing scenario. Véronique conscientiously unfolded all her work and her reflection, around the novelties, the furniture to be exploited, the commercial operations planned. It was perfect for her and maybe even a little too much, her audience seemed to understand everything, accept everything, validate everything. No one will ask him questions!?! This was becoming particularly suspicious but I will not think about it until well after this meeting, when my mind will have fully recovered. Once its demonstration is complete, it will propose to all those managers and other heads of department to ask her questions, or even to ask me questions about the games and consoles. A small adrenaline rush runs through me, electrifies me and therefore wakes me up and I prepare to be asked about Sega games and consoles! " What can you say when asked if you should buy a Sega console or a Nintendo console?" ? " Is Sonic better than Mario" ? "Will Street fighter 2 be released on Mega Drive" ? "Should I buy the Mega-CD" ? " What can we offer as a game to an 8 year old girl"? "To her 35 year old dad"? Will there be 32X-Mega CD games? Will Zelda be released on Mega Drive? Will there be a new Sega Train? What is the best game on Game gear? Can I play Mega Drive games on Master System?

I wait, I wait, I wait... I'm hot burning and overvoltage. I'm still waiting.

The eyes of all these women are more or less focused on me but their looks seem to me, for the most part, empty or lost! Although sometimes the face of some seem to suddenly go from spite to anger! It is not humans who are in front of me but zombies, spectres and ghosts: not the beginning of a glimmer of life and energy in them! I was discovering in that very moment, the whole width, the huge gap between the children who were so passionate about video games, the banana on my face when it came to evoking Sonic, Mickey or Alex Kidd and these women completely and desperately emptied of the slightest trace of energy, electricity, the smallest will in any case when we mentioned video games! Maybe they all liked Luigi and Mario!?!

I could wait a long time, and certainly thirty years, because there will be no question!?! Neither for me nor for Véronique. Enormous malaise!!! I'm in apnea and close to syncope! I am decomposing!!! Maybe they had their tongue cut off? I feel like I'm in a trap! Some big blah? Like hidden camera? This is probably the greatest moment of solitude in my life, at least at that time, and at least of everything that will be later on in my entire professional life! We "Sega Masters" inspired most often the joy and good mood in our interlocutors, at least curiosity and questions about the "phenomenon" video game in general and Sega in particular. The often crazy effervescence of the salons, the Sega trains, demonstrations in prestigious sales places, radios, televisions: there was really the pompon for me: the void, a black hole, the interstellar nothingness can no longer be destabilizing.

In my heart, I will ask myself, and therefore without questioning Véronique on the subject neither now nor later, because she had particularly well prepared and done her work, how I could have found myself and how I could have participated in such a fiasco! I was no longer in my bearings, I was even really very troubled! Also, I had to say myself in a reflex of self-defense and to reassure me that it was "no luck", it would happen one day, I had fallen on an audience very unresponsive to video games: female and rather elderly. The pro-Nintendo and even the Sega Trolls would seem to me then a few moments, just a few moments, almost friendly! There is nothing worse than indifference, in fact there was probably even more than that, but I could not guess yet. The answer I had found at that moment would be more than enough for me. This experience being really new, and so far out of the frame of what I had known, that I will integrate it, a little forced, to the spectrum, to the field of vision now much wider, of my knowledge. Véronique seemed satisfied with this performance, I did not dare to tell her what I thought of it... And besides, it was better for me as for her, that I do as if nothing had happened, because we would still make several meetings of this type in the weeks and months to come! I was not so excited anymore.

I cannot detail these sessions independently of each other, because ultimately, will you believe it? I still have trouble believing it myself: they will be absolutely and totally compatible copies of each other! "Pasted copies"! BHV? Samaritaine? Printemps? We would find ourselves every time, every time, in front of a women's assembly! More or less the same generation: always women, still women, nothing but women, with more or less the same profile, it was just hallucinating, delirious and hopeless! How is this possible?!? I did not understand and will not understand, even much later, because I had not looked: a situation that was completely beyond me, invariably. We did not share anything at first sight, and we would not share anything, although we were asked!?! How could such a terrible situation have been made possible? How? By whom and therefore why?

If the presentation of véronique could change a little or much over time, incorporating the latest potentially decisive information, the interaction between us and these women remained close to the marjords! Apart from the polite exchanges at the entrance and exit, I would never hear the sound of their voice, just may be some acquiescence, obviously the most polite, although sometimes perhaps, even often, a little embarrassed, extremely discreet, pinched or muffled! My journey in this other dimension continued, and fortunately, in some sufficiently spaced episodes in time, while remaining themselves; of quite short duration.

This experience was becoming more and more like a nightmare! Not that it was as terrible as that intrinsically, certainly not at all pleasant and even very embarrassing, but because it repeated and would repeat again and again without varying by an iota!?! HOW IS THIS POSSIBLE? As a kind of time loop like dreams and nightmares can have the secret and in which you end up feeling that you will never get out, like "A Day without an End" or rather in my case "Happy Birthdead". The time becomes much shorter when you know when an unpleasant situation will stop, but here this infernal scenario continued and repeated. There was something important, and rational, that escaped me!?!

Although these meetings were never too long, one to two hours, they seemed to me to last much longer! In some circumstances time is compressed, the seconds appear minutes, minutes hours. It's a bit of the elevator effect when you end up with someone you don't know and with whom you suffer the weight of silence, of that time that compresses and you with. Many times I would have to endure this terrible moment of solitude or I face a gathering of women who clearly did not care much about being polite! Looking at me really very strangely, as much distressed, as embarrassed, that sometimes can be annoyed!?! This experience left me a very bitter taste because unpleasant, disconcerting, hurtful or even humiliating. Véronique thought she had a good idea, asking me to help her, but the exact opposite happened! Nobody would ask me anything and I didn't exist. It was to deny my skills, my knowledge and trample on my passion, my enthusiasm, my reason for being in this company.

But I will find out much later, much later that my diagnosis was not the right one! Let's say it was inaccurate and far from the truth. I was really far from understanding who these women were actually in front of me! Véronique had perhaps clarified it to me!?! Perhaps not, not enough, which is on what I had measured nothing, for lack of having visualized a single second, their historical framework of work. It will be only very recently, and in the context of writing these chronicles of Master Sega, that I will finally understand the reason for this huge fiasco! Thirty years later! Watching "INA" videos on youtube, I discovered the backstage of the BHV through their "heads of department" of the time! I rediscovered with astonishment these faces of these women, these profiles often very close and that I had met! And I fell on my back! Thirty years later! And like an almost mystical Revelation!

In a few seconds, I understood, finally, that if I had been presented as "Master Sega", all these women of a certain age would see me, they, neither more nor less, than the Antichrist or one of the four horsemen of the Apocalypse! I was the embodiment of absolute evil, the Prince of Darkness. He who corrupted, perverted and sent the souls of the youngest to the dark side. The management of Sega, in its strategy of conquest, had succeeded in making me meet the people who would be most hostile to me, because they hated, they hated everything I represented! In the depths of themselves, every day and forever, I was and will remain the incarnate evil, the champion of chaos and destruction that slowly but surely ate them!

Because in reality, "Heads or managers of departments" as they were really, obviously, it would have been necessary to specify which departments they were! They were therefore "Rayon Heads" but Rayon Heads TOYS! In large stores such as BHV, La Samaritaine and Printemps, the linear "video game" had been certainly and systematically given to the toy's managers! And the least we can say is that these women who had ten, twenty or even thirty years of shops did not welcome them with enthusiasm! It was even the opposite. These women of a certain education, of another generation, who have always revered the "beautiful toy", classic, made in noble materials, and often "French", were most certainly the last and greatest guardians! Paris city rich economically and historically still offers magnificent toy rays in sometimes sublime settings, such as that of the Samaritan. It is an honor and a mission to make the toy live as for decades, centuries... And besides, for having been there so often, you were really transported to the 19th century in the toy department of the Samaritan!

These women knew how much the traditional toy, so rooted, so "virtuous" and probably with a soul, could suffer from this new Japanese offensive. They certainly even experienced these torments in all their being and flesh! Little boys no longer wanted or wanted significantly less soldiers, knights in iron or wood, beautiful representations of pirate ships made by hand: they wanted a fight, car racing, Simulations, they wanted Mario or Sonic and these women were unable to get on this new train. They were even very certainly the last island of resistance of this war passed under silence, video game against the toy and lost before but not without a maximum of resistance with at least indifference when "Master Sega" will see them! At the initiative of the management of these large stores and that of Sega. They have always defended it, always cherished, yesterday as today, because they were born, they grew up with it! Because they passed them on to their children, and even their grandchildren. Because they are more synonymous with sweetness, awakening and especially sharing between parents and children! Friendliness that seems to be broken by video games, although in hindsight nothing of the kind, and even if the danger of a child's isolation is very real in some cases, when parents may not haveUnfortunately, there is nothing more exciting to propose and that they have a fortiori no time, or so little, to spend with them.

Sega and the management of the big Parisian stores had tried this very daring, completely crazy bet to "update" as we update the software of a PC!?! Their "toy" store managers! And we had met but it was a lost cause given the reactions, or rather the total absence of reactions from these women totally devoted to the traditional toy! If the video game won the war or rather the battle against the toy, that it has seriously shaken it, started at least a few years, it obviously did not disappear you know! Fnac, Virgin, Score Games and other Micromania have surfed the wave developing their business and their department! The big stores will not have benefited as much because the weight of the classic toy and their illustrious guardians will have weighed heavily. Video games will disappear very quickly from these large stores due to lack of motivated staff to make it live properly. They were indeed those fierce and indomitable Amazons who will not give anything to this other world that came trampling their without being invited.

They will therefore win this battle, at least on their own ground, definitively abandoning the video game to the specialized ultras "Micromania" or "Score Game", they will no longer have to manage these evil objects that were pushing them into what they had most dear: the beautiful toy, the traditional and for which, it seems quite obvious even to me, especially to me, you have to fight again and again, every day. Keep his magic, his aura, his divine essence. The video game is out of the universe of the Toy and it's so much better! The average age of gamers who have risen significantly year after year since the appearance of the Sega Mega Drive. These two divergent universes are never too far apart and they can even now coexist more than they ever will have faced each other. They even hold hands on some occasions as with the "Amiibos": both video game and toy!

I now have a little boy of five years old and he likes to play with dinosaurs like his Elasmosaurus and his Amargasaurus as much as with Playmobil pirates or knights, practice tree climbing or Judo, write and draw, listen to stories, Play Mario Kart, Sonic or Virtua Fighter Kids. It is the responsibility of each parent to offer his or her children education, enlightenment and entertainment that will make them grow up happily on the fringes of national education! Many years later, I have very mixed feelings towards these women who defended, deep down, a very beautiful and romantic model, because totally outdated! It is not at all a question of "good or bad" but it is nevertheless as that they will have received me, they will have perceived me: The destroyer! I saw it in their eyes and felt it in my flesh! As "Master Sega" I represented the video game but even more violent! Exit Mickey, Donald, Aladdin, the Lion King, Little Mermaid, Jungle Book, Flicky or Ecco the Dolphin...

I had not imagined for a single second what my mere presence could inspire them! Hatred for some of them seems obvious to me now, if not anxiety, fear and disgust. They had taken it upon themselves not to let anything appear because these scheduled meetings were supposed to change them, make them change their minds. They have never tried, never will be interested in it is to say how much they fought, certainly in silence, video game. An unexpected and very surprising episode of my experience of "Master Sega" that today, I recall as the amazing residue of a war more ideological than economic even if many "small" manufacturers, often French, have disappeared.

Chapter 23

Kalinske and the 32X, From Heaven to Hell
The twilight of Sega?

1994 was a very different year for two reasons. The first because I am called up and will therefore do my military service, for ten months, from August 1994 to May 1995. I will then be almost totally disconnected from the world of video games and therefore of Sega. However this new and very rich experience will be profitable to me as "Master Sega" and a fortiori as human being, on different levels. It will significantly amplify my sportsmanship, my combativity, my competitiveness, my cool and therefore "self-control", especially with shooting sessions and with real weapons! Léthales!!! All the more when I will sometimes be convinced, in service, that it will be necessary to make use of them!

After more than three years particularly intense in the heart of the hive of Sonic Team, and even if the passion, the love of Sega remains, I am mentally exhausted. My enthusiasm, however great it may be, has been eroded by thousands, tens of thousands of calls, shows, solutions, codes so often repeated. I gave everything or should I say "we gave everything"! Sega had been like a whirlwind of passion, a volcano of emotions, impossible not to love so much heat and fusion with all our young fans, but also impossible not to burn up from time to time. And even if it is necessary to drink his youth until the drunkenness and especially until the last drop. Maybe even, I am a little bit, but a little bit, worn! Still far from being disillusioned, and even though the backlash of the Mega Drive madness has clearly happened, that the party is really and definitely over for now, and we could probably start to have a hangover especially with the "32X". An accessory that will have nothing invigorating and exciting at all levels, for all the teams who work hard to keep Sega afloat, in any case in France and Europe.

The success of the Mega Drive day after day, week after week, month after month, year after year had been particularly euphoric and we were therefore condemned to one day or another, the bellows does not fall back... And pretty much violent. The Mega Drive had been such an extraordinary success, but it was now in the winter of its life. If the Mega CD had not been a great commercial success, it had at least kept the sales of the MD at a very good or even very high level! This is an important point that I will explain and develop, from my point of view and between two waters, two visions at the antipodes, one American and the other Japanese. The Mega CD and the 32X are often presented as very important failures in terms of "consoles" and therefore important failures for Sega. Do you have to know what we are talking about. First of all, the Mega CD and the 32X are not consoles in their own right but accessories! Even though there will also be the Multi Mega, the Wondermega... Luxurious accessories but accessories that can't work alone, not without the Mega Drive! It must be understood that the product which is, and remains, essential to the heart of the development Sega, these are not new and "wonderful" accessories but the console Mega Drive, which will follow in the West eight to nine very beautiful years of career including four or five (from 91 to 94) or she will hold her own and even be in front of her Nintendo competitor! YES Sega will be the surprising leader of 16-bit consoles for several years, before getting styled on the photo finish and while the Sega teams worked on the machines of the future.

Even if the sales of the Mega CD remained rather modest (six million units finally worldwide, a score of the most honest for an accessory) the price being for many prohibitive, they allowed to continue and even push up the wonderful dynamics and mechanics of sales of the 16-bit console. The Mega CD will not be directly and even far from being a financially profitable operation, but on the other hand it is a success for communication, awareness, research and development of the Brand. Sega remains at the forefront and never ceases to stir up its spur of new sensations with small successes more mediatic than economic, such as "Night Trap", "Silpheed" or "Tomcat Halley", it is at the heart of its strategy that sometimes works, but not all the time, as for all the other leading players in any sector. The Mega Drive continues to be a hit and it probably owes it, a little, to this accessory that will unfortunately be more of a dream than reality for a majority of players! If the Mega CD had not fulfilled these last objectives, certainly more qualitative than quantitative, becoming in this way a very effective technological showcase, there would never have been the "32X".

In the absence of a new true Gaming Champion, the "Mushroom" 32X will be dreamed and supported until the end by Sega of America and its illustrious boss: Tom Kalinske. But it was suggested and blown into the ears of the Americans by Hayao Nakayama himself, because if he is president of SoJ, he is also vice president of SoA. And nothing is done, nothing will be done in the USA without his approval and with the greatest faith. For Nakayama the 32X would be the answer to face the new potential threat embodied by the Jaguar 64bits of Atari! 32X as just before the Mega CD, a strategy much more defensive than offensive! Protect and make the huge success of the Genesis that is, after the machines of Arcades, a huge cash machine!

In retrospect it is easy to cast the disgrace on what remains, of course, as a very bad choice, the worst in the history of Sega, and which will cost economically, not so much, but especially not as much as in terms of trust and awareness among these partners, particularly the large distribution. And it is probably the Saturn who will pay more for this misstep. The 32X was, of course, such a disaster that many commentators like to make a fool of it as others like to shoot at ambulances every time they see one passing. And yet the 32X is not so much a symbol of historical failure as of Domination and its confirmation. Otherwise how to justify such a risk taking in such a narrow vice technologically and economically speaking? When the 32X comes out in 94, Sega is at its zenith in Europe but especially in the USA, where it dominates head and shoulders and largely the 16bits segment, with more than fifteen million consoles sold on the only North American continent! A real hen with golden eggs who is still far from having given everything.

For the time, we can even talk about dizzying success, but which was probably starting to last a little too long. Empires always end up collapsing, to make room for new builders. They will fall as much by excess of confidence, on their strengths, as the erosion, the slow but certain disappearance of the necessary caution, with the consequence of the formation of a kind of artificial bubble having only one fatal perspective:

explosion or implosion. Probably they had not managed the overwhelming victory of the Mega Drive over its rival!?! Sometimes, some successes are harder to digest than defeats.

The boss of Sega in the USA had become a real Roman Emperor. Tom Kalinske was going to sell, ten, fifteen, twenty million Mega Drive on American soil alone and in record time. That's ten times more than in Japan or the 16-bit has not been sold for a long time. It's almost three times more than in Europe! Old continent that will still sell, by the way, almost as much Master System as Mega Drive. The US subsidiary had become the group's cash cow and Kalinske would have probably gained a lot of power and influence in those hands!?! As long as the Mega Drive was running. He had become the main architect of Sega's success in the West but eventually also worldwide.

He will beat Nintendo and its Super Nes four years, four years in a row and in a brilliant way: 91/92/93/94! He is almost a god for the Japanese who will still remain very surprised by such success. The latter, almost exclusively Genesis/ Mega Drive (the Master is a flop unlike Europe and Game Gear sales are much lower) will register it totally, and alas, definitely in this race, in this historic 16-bit fight! Kalinske succeeded in everything, he imposed his style and vision (at least when he arrived). Sega Does What Nintendon't: he will confirm the ultra-effective slogan of his predecessor, Mickael Katz, and not let go: he will hammer it to the point of being thus, a little wrongly, credited. Sega of America's communication will be and will remain as aggressive as it is ambitious, and Sega France will most likely continue to draw inspiration from this at least during the Mega Drive/Kalinske years. It will also impose the "razor business strategy" to the maximum: we sell at the lowest possible price, and probably even sometimes at a loss, but we catch up on the blades. A decisive strategy that will prove to be tremendously profitable at first and deadly in a second time. So that no one will want to take the blame! Especially not the Americans, let alone Kalinske. We relaunch the Genesis with an iconic character, a "killer-Game", which will replace "Altered Beast" in each reference console pack! Altered Beast which has often been controversial in many central American states, very religious, as being diabolical, belonging to the "evil" and then possessing the spirits of their children! And finally we develop on the American soil games in priority for the Americans! It's time for many US sports licenses around the greatest champions of the time. In 1991 and 92 Kalinske will blow up all the counters and knock out Nintendo with his new console by taking no more nor less than 2/3 thirds of the market! So it sells up to two Genesis for a SNES. The Mega Drive madness had started with Sonic the hedgehog and it will last several years. Too good, too strong, too fast, too successful, never digested yet...

Probably because of his overconfidence and in search of eternal glory, he had ended up thinking, at least a little: Kalinske does what Nakayama don't?! Nakayama is the historical boss of Sega in the world and for more than fifteen years. Before coming to manage Sega, Kalinske had already wonderfully straightened the situation at the toy giant Mattel, boosting sales of "Barbie" and "Hot Weels" cars in pink, lots of pink, and "hot wheels"! It will be the birth of a formidable, incredible but damaging schism between Sega America and Sega Japan. Many observers now speak, after the fact of course because it is easier and more sensational, of a war, a confrontation, a showdown between "mother and daughter" with anecdotes that are real but with interpretations and consequences that are supposed to be farfetched. The two entities have never been at war or even in rivalry, as may be the case between European subsidiaries. Everything is opposed, more exactly everything separates Japan and the USA if we exclude David Rosen the American creator at the origin of Sega: an archipelago on one side, a continent on the other, separated by a huge ocean. Culture in general is very different on both sides of the Pacific and you can even see it in the video game market alone. Also, how could we be at war or even in rivalry when we do not really have the same interests? Two countries, two worlds that don't work the same and the Mega Drive is certainly the best proof of this! Failure in Japan, triumph in the USA!!! Nakayama understood it well even if it was not easy to accept! Maybe he would be a little jealous but he left carte blanche to Kalinske on marketing and communication because the latter had shown imperial and unyielding on the American continent and the results were finally falling! And anyway he would still be there to validate, or not and vice-admiral of the USA aircraft carrier! When it was not simply a matter of suggesting a little or even a little much! There was probably the evil, the "vice", the malice, which almost would blow everything up! How to walk straight when you have one leg that is dead and the other one gallops like in the 100 meters of the Olympics. Japan and the US were not moving in the same direction, nor at the same speed, yet they should continue to move together. A real team in the "Laurel and Hardy" style, very close to the buddy movie...

 The time for history, the time for those who comment and write it more or less skillfully, more or less accurately, is not the same as the time of action and inaction under tons of pressure! Many commentators laugh, mocking these supposed imbroglios and other evasions of the time rather than trying to decipher the situation as it really was. But it is perhaps totally natural to want to find and design a "guilty" dreamed!!! But too much fantasized! When you have loved so much, endured so much, and feel betrayed. A rivalry between the two American and Japanese directions of Sega and that would lead to a kind of mini collective suicide would be timely, because such a fiasco required one or more culprits to be identified! Question of honor and pride for those who did not feel the least "responsible": it was necessary to find the culprit.

While it is extremely easy to comment and make fun of the past, it is much more difficult to glimpse the future and propose the right solution. Criticism is easy, especially retrospectively, but Art is difficult". Rather among the "Latin commentators", it must also be specified, because in the Anglo-Saxon countries we never miss the opportunity to do, try, succeed and especially, most often, fail! The small failures of yesterday often lead to the great successes of tomorrow. Those who have tried are rarely mocked, quite the contrary.

At this time, there is Sega Japan on one side and Sega of America on the other, and they are two worlds both geographically different, culturally but maybe more "temporally"! In the first world, the Mega Drive is a total failure and it has disappeared. In the second, it is like an episode of "Slider, the parallel worlds", it is called "Genesis" and it is a historical card. Tom Kalinske will work like no other to reinforce the success of the 16bits and that he thinks is his success!!! Too much! Tomorrow is not, tomorrow is so uncertain... While the Mega Drive is there, and well there. The first accessory to boost the Mega Drive, failing to sell itself very well, will therefore support historical sales because record. Kalinske will get back on his feet! Who's gonna stop him? Especially not Nakayama who will always encourage him, at least until the release of the Saturn, then breaking too quickly and definitively this "schism" that seemed to be unable to last. Also breaking the contract that had united Sega and Nakayama to Kalinske. He was the Roman

Emperor of the console and "Genesis does what SNES don't", and will not want to be demoted into simple general, condemned to a weaker legion named Saturn.

Faster, smoother, more animation, more games, more sports, more licenses, more Disney, more Michael Jackson, more action, more war, more "strike", more speed and simulation, more uncensored "Mortal Kombat"!!! With a leader, as a flag bearer and ultimate hero: SONIC who becomes a world icon instantly! And in the very religious nation of the USA: "Genesis" had even found its prophet. Sonic was so fast that he could walk on water!!! Make it speed up and again and these waters might even separate and spread to let hordes of new heroes more sensational than each other. Tomorrow does not exist and Kalinske was convinced that the Genesis had not said its last word. In the United States, Kalinske would be an emperor but also a prophet. Tomorrow does not exist, 32-bit consoles are far away, they will probably be expensive and Sony it stabs less than Sonic! The Jaguar 64 bits is out and it offers games in cartridge!?! The door was wide open to try the 32X, both to counter the Jaguar, but also and above all to maintain the success of the Mega Drive. It's so easy to say that this accessory was too expensive, there weren't enough games, not enough good games but isn't it always a bit like that when new consoles are launched?

Kalinske would do the 32X, blown, validated and blessed by Nakayama, because the potential success of his Genesis forever scenario, held well, at least during its conception. It is necessary to be able to go back in time, in the American way, especially in the Kalinske way, in the "present" but that of yesterday's time, with all these components and to grasp the "reality" of the world at this moment, all these opportunities, these challenges and bets. All the planets were aligned at that moment, of their own initiative, and in this permanent tension of a totally improbable and terribly obscure future, hyper competitive, action always prevails over inaction. Ambition, from Sega to Kalinske's more personal one, has already paid off. It must go on and on but without overconfidence, without fatal hybris, risk, the main sin: believing that we can always win! You must sometimes know how to withdraw and even fade, a few moments, to better regenerate.

Kalinske had become the Roman Emperor of the "Holy Western Empire" of the very powerful Rome when Nakayama was rather the Roman Emperor of the "Holy Eastern Empire" of the incredible Byzantium (and future

Constantinople). The two superpowers will live together for several decades in full brotherhood before Rome finally explodes. Constantinople will try many times, but in vain, to restore the Imperial Rome. It will rise again but will never be more than the shadow of itself. The boss of Sega of America may be the Master of 16 bits in the USA as in the world, he is far from being the Master of clocks and he knows it! He would choose not to project himself in time, he would see only the present, comfortably bathed in success, his own success in which he was bathed from head to toe, how to add some more decorations! We would like to be able to control time when everything you, when everything succeeds us, sometimes we even believe to tame it, a formidable illusion that always turns into cruel and very bitter sensation, when in the hourglass of time, the slightest grain of sand that goes astray, Time seems to take back all these rights, all its freedom: and especially that of escaping from you. Definitely, reminding you that he is always the Master whatever you do.

Everything would go too fast, sooner or later, but who could really guess it, before and like everyone else, see it? Not even him! Especially not him! Tomorrow does not exist, fifteen million Mega Drive sold at the end of 94 to accommodate the 32X, they are there and there are at least as many players. Kalinske doesn't want to turn the page on Mega Drive, does he have a good reason to do so? Because it is the story of a triumphant, glorious and he would like to be even more in the Legend! "Eternity is a day" ! Tomorrow does not exist. Could the Queen of 16 bits become a Goddess, adorned, wearing this electronic diadem for mycophiles!?! Kalinske, after these successes at Mattel with "Barbie and the hot wheels", then with Sega and Sonic with fire legs, it was perhaps not as surprising as this, that the meeting "Barbie-Sonic" would generate the 32X!?! With this probably sexiest color code: the Violet, mix of Blue and Pink!!!

Kalinske wants to keep these fifteen million Genesis vibrating and enchanting and, as with the Mega-CD, stimulate new purchases. This is the new, but also the last, Poker hit of the Great Master Sega of America! He is so powerful and has been so visionary in his strategy up to now, that he will continue to promote it and extend it even further. A strategy yet limit Schizophrenic with the upcoming and even accelerated arrival of the Saturn because the release of the Playstation will change everything! SoJ was shaken, projected and transported to another path, another timeline. The

Mega Drive no longer exists in Japan, so you must devote yourself fully to the new generation and much less not be overtaken by Sony and its Playstation. Schism so totally inevitable and yet initiated and validated by Nakayama a few weeks before! Two different worlds, two different temporalities. The "cow boys" want to stay on their railroad crossing the continent, while the "samurai" prefer to go by boat. Can these two worlds coexist? The 32X is probably not more risky than the Mega CD!?!

Titanic fight against Sony that is announced but for the moment probably hidden! The War would be changed from two to three dimensions and Sega of America would remain in two-player mode. The 32X would make the Mega Drive the most powerful of the 16bits for sure, but also the worst of the 32bits, like a kind of schizophrenia of the most disturbing impossible to treat on all levels! The 32X was released or a two years too late, the 32bits one or two years too early?!? It is useless to try to rewrite history, time will have left no place for it, no chance. With three opponents, it is no longer the same, it is more compressed and it will be even more so with the arrival of Microsoft and its Xbox.

This accessory will be a huge failure all over the world but especially in the USA, market for which it was almost entirely intended. Failure so important that it will more or less interfere with the launch of the Saturn at the level of publishing and distribution, more than at the level of consumers, because ultimately very few people will buy this accessory, Japan where players will rush to the Saturn and its Virtua Fighter a few months later. Nevertheless, the new bet of Kalinske will not be totally lost because it will still sell nearly five million additional Genesis! With or without 32X in support? Indirect!!! Twenty million Genesis consoles sold, surely that the prospect of innovative accessories will have contributed to this success.

In the end if the 32X had been thought, had been dreamed as a kind of ultimate consecration of the Mega Drive with millions of additional sales, like the Mega CD, it would be well the Swan Song, announcing, a little ahead of time, the twilight of a machine now in history, the Legend of the video game, with these conquests, these victories and before its inevitable end. But it is so human to want to push the deadlines on Life, on Death, as late as possible, that we often come to this form of therapeutic and pathetic acharnement, often the most expensive. The 32X is not so much an economic failure of a manufacturer of consoles as the disastrous consequence of a sweet fantasy crossing humanity, history, civilizations, those of "masters" or powerful people taking for immortal Gods! Just as much as you are immensely great, extremely powerful, whether you are glorious and revered, modest or vain, sooner or later you will die! And/or you will be replaced! The Genesis in the USA had become so powerful, so iconic, that we did not see it die. Kalinske thought she could make her cross through time. While she was six feet under the ground and for a long time in Japan. A situation impossible to manage and that would inevitably create a commercial distortion and marketing before an economic chasm.

The higher you go, the harder it is to get back down on or even under the ground! Kalinske resigned from Sega of America in 1996 not wanting, in some way, to endorse the failure of the Saturn, especially since he had wanted to support the Genesis like no other until his last breath.

Chapter 24

Out Run and Virtua Cop Lives

1994, after a limited success of the Mega CD, it is the year of the Fiasco 32X. I need a regeneration and my call to the army is therefore timely. Military service was still compulsory at that time. Not being, no longer a student I was able to postpone the date of my departure until I turned 21. The 22 approaching I scheduled my incorporation during the summer, in August to be more precise. And why in the middle of summer when it would be just to rest and enjoy the summer sweetness? Because this is the period when there are least departures and incorporations, whether you are a student or in working life, the vast majority of young men want to enjoy this period of relaxation and recovery, and therefore begins his service rather from September, which therefore becomes the most requested and thus the busiest month. This is all the more true since national service has been reduced to ten months instead of twelve, which allows you to keep and enjoy the two summers that frame your mobilization.

For me, not a second, to "do the Army", I mean all in khaki, in the army more likely, and to simulate a "War"!?! What war?!? Conflicts that no longer exist at all or so little (compulsory military service will be abolished shortly after under the presidency of Jacques Chirac) and will not return for many years. My parents being in Auxerre, where I lived for many years, I know very well the "CIGA", the training center of auxiliary gendarmes! There are only three in France, and one of them is only a few miles from my family. I will therefore apply to the Gendarmerie d'Auxerre to apply for a place as Auxiliary Constable!

The places are very expensive, really expensive. They are most often obtained on file, with priority being given to the sons of Gendarme and military officers, the sons of the Pistonné, of course, and then to the graduates. I am neither the one, nor the other: being "bachelor" will be just the minimum union to present and hope. However, I ended up discovering the fault as I mentioned it earlier: the summer period! Applications for incorporation in July and August are extremely low while the needs of the

Force remain the same. That's why I asked for my incorporation in the Gendarmerie and in the month of August!

Bingo I will be taken! I will therefore do my classes at the Auxiliary Gendarmes Training Center between Auxerre and Monéteau! We will then be a "small" class of sixty auxiliary gendarmes! With many graduates and other engineers, some sons of Gendarme and a handful of pro and semi-pro football players from the AJA Auxerre! Once again I will be blue, completely blue from head to feet! And with a gun! No question of promoting weapons, but I will have one on me every day of my service and for almost nine months! " CIGA it's already stronger than me" !?! And it was probably written long ago.

I tell it through a fictional character in my first book "Thanatose", a very dark novel about dreams and our subconscious. Many years after my military service in the Gendarmerie, probably more than ten years, I will re-read all of the dreams that I had begun to tell, detail, list and archive, following my slightly traumatic but so exciting meeting with Freddy Kruger in the summer of 1985 at the fire cinema of Auxerre: the Alpha (when there were still three cinemas while now there is only one left). So I go to see, accompanied by my older brother: "The Night's Claws" and that I should not have seen at the time because it was forbidden at least 13 years old, but I was big enough for my age and the latter will therefore not be checked. I read back my first dream sessions, dozens and dozens all more or less delirious or just amazing. I dream of my military service, which I do not identify as such at this moment of course: no trivial things that would be statistically probable and could probably be experienced by hundreds, thousands of other people. Even "weakly probable" it would already be too much and could just be perceived as projection, then a coincidence! No I will dream of scenes, things totally and definitely improbable. Things that have absolutely no meaning, no explanation, and especially no interest in themselves except to compare them five, ten, twenty years later with the events you will live! All this to say that since this rereading of my first dreams archived and dated 1986 (a year which is increasingly presented as a mystical crossroads in my case) I am firmly convinced that everything is written in advance in our lives!

We all have a Destiny, and as on a Highway, we will only be able to "at best" change of lane but not direction. I read these dreams twenty years after having written them, my dream "Gendarmerie" is much too precise, hallucinating of details not translating any desire, no fear, no adolescent neurosis. No Freudian interpretation is possible either in substance or form. It was so disturbing that I threw away the entire archive immediately because some of these dreams were dramatic or even tragic and there was no question for a single second that they could affect me more than reason and interfere with my "instinctive" choices and all the more with my so-called Free Will. Even though I also know now that all our choices are very much influenced and oriented by the infinite treasures of our subconscious, that our dreams have fun to project while we sleep. How and for what reasons? The whole theme of my first two books Thanatose and La Cité des Scorpions. Smile...

Fate as a motorway? And as the A5 just opened in this back-year 1994 between Paris and Troyes and on which I will be assigned! After a few weeks of classes, I will be armed with a Pamas G1 9 mm semi-automatic, specific model of Beretta 92, I discovered this very amazing feeling to carry all day long a lethal weapon! I was not in a video game, and beyond the really exciting shooting practice sessions, it will happen to me at least twice to prepare myself to use my gun! Including once after a shooting, a settlement of accounts, which will make a death in the camp of the people of the traveller at the exit of Auxerre towards Augy. One dead!!! And therefore a criminal armed to arrest!?! The gendarmes of trade had even come out and equipped themselves with machine guns for the famous plan "hawk"! I played dozens of hours at arcade Shooting games, starting with the mythical "Operation Wolf", then the unforgettable Terminator 2 from Midway, Alien 3 and Jurassic Park from Sega, Lethal Enforcers from Konami. I have of course enjoyed, very strong sensations for excellent memories. However, nothing but strictly nothing to see in intensity, with this day to track down a criminal, even if in the end, my clone of Beretta will not come out of his sheath. In the "real mode" you have of course only one life and impossible to make "continue". A publisher, and even a manufacturer that I will not name for the moment, will try to make you believe that by being a great champion on a type of video games, you could also become one in reality: it is totally wrong. You can be the most incredible Gamer on shooting games for example, the most effective, the fastest but it will never teach you to manage the stress of reality, that of a possible and probable drama. This experience, and others in the Gendarmerie, will teach me to keep my cool in all circumstances, rather than actually know how to shoot.

In our brand new building near the A5, and this while I'm on call for our brigade or rather our highway platoon, it's a battle-off! The gendarmes of trade run in all directions, they were warned of a shooting that resulted in death in the camp of the people of the traveller near Auxerre. RED ALERT! Plan Epervier activated, all the forces of the department's gendarmerie immediately mobilize to intercept the criminal or criminals by placing on the most strategic axes around the crime scene! We would then go to the big roundabout that precedes the entrance of the A5 toll at Sens, the second largest city in the department of Yonne. Beforehand the two gendarmes that I will accompany go into the vault to equip with machine guns!!! The total HALLU! Big rush of adrenaline. It's the first time I see weapons of war, I had completely forgotten that we were equipped. A gun is already impressive but there frankly!!! In a fraction of a second a movie script, novel became reality! We leave to intercept, perhaps, a dangerous criminal, armed, on the run, by car and going up from Auxerre towards the North and therefore in our direction! We are still far from panic on board but we are at maximum tension and I feel it well through the two gendarmes of trade! They, at that moment, they "play" perhaps one of the moments, if not the most important moment in their career! What they have committed themselves to. They are at full speed while I am still bewildered, as much as incredulous!!! "Uh... We must go and arrest a criminal with a gun!?! Mazette it's crazy the life sometimes how it accelerates. But the craziest, the funniest, is that in this extreme tension or hovering the shadow of death, it's me who will take the wheel of the R21 Nevada break! Because in the Gendarmerie and all these units, it is the Auxiliary Gendarmes who drive! We are the very officially recognized "Drivers" for the entire duration of our service and any other potential future mobilization. In all circumstances and to free the career gendarmes from their hands and so that they can perform all the most decisive manipulations, radio contacts, decision-making, such as possibly shooting at criminals on the run.

Unlike the police, the gendarmes, the military can use their weapons without being in self-defense! And as one of the instructors, a captain of gendarmerie, will point out to us during our classes, "it is better to shoot than to be shot". Of course he was talking in the case of contacts with proven and armed criminals, and that it was therefore better to have a "little bit" than to find themselves with four irons in the air!

So the driver is me and I take the wheel, always equipped with my 9mms charged, while my two colleagues are upgraded and equipped with machine guns! No but seriously, I will not believe it, I will never believe it is not at all like on TV! One of them tells me to go faster, he puts the light accompanied by the super powerful "two tones"! Big pressure, the siren is screaming and it's like in action movies, in fact it's obviously much worse because here you are and it's for real... I start, I "rush" because the race against the clock has begun and my neighbor who holds his machine gun a few centimeters from me, keeps telling me to rush! To accelerate! "Go, go, run, run..." He is excited!!! And does not seem afraid that I can drive very, too fast! He's wrong, I'm almost terrified, not so much by posting us later to try and intercept the criminal, but because I'm driving a Nevada R21 with a Gendarme right next to me and armed with a machine gun that he says he doesn't even know if it works, and then he keeps looking at it, keeps fiddling with it, fiddling with it in one place or another and as if it were a toy! It was obvious that there was a lack of practice, but obviously he had not been able to check its proper functioning.

Fortunately we go through the highway, or only a few kilometers and rather straight line, without too many traffic, until the ramp exit of the highway! We'll get there fast, very fast... There is a 90% turn, but fortunately quite long, just before the exit and that must necessarily slow down the vehicles, and frankly, I do not know how we managed to pass. I think I slightly moved away from the central axis, until I tickled the concrete wall!

At 80 or 90kms/h when it is necessary to pass reasonably under 60. A very small even tiny steering wheel and it was probably the accident. My heart is close to exploding. I didn't think an R21 Nevada would hold up so well on the road, but I will never take a turn at this speed again, unless it was a competition car or a "super car". I don't know if we were lucky, I was under maximum tension with my colleague who always pushed me to go faster, with the howling siren. Totally unreal because never imagined, never thought, never prepared.

We finally arrive at the roundabout several hundred meters in front of the entrance of the Toll. R21 on the side of the road, one of the two gendarmes tells me to stay behind the car to protect me, use it as a shield while they both, will put themselves out along the two main roads coming from the south, coming from Auxerre, on the roundabout. We are ready to intercept the car reported on the run! We will stay an hour or two before you signal that our presence is no longer required. A time that seemed infinite and when I had unclipped the sheath of my gun without removing the safety catch. I pulled out my gun discreetly and quickly several times, without any vehicle around, before putting it away almost immediately.

If the criminal had to come through here, we would have seen it. An hour or two I was prepared to "draw" and maybe shoot! As we were taught to do but on paper targets!!! I was not disappointed that it did not happen. I love action but not with real guns. I will continue to make cartons on game consoles or arcade machines, or even in laser games; that would be more than enough for me. Not the least disappointed, and one or two hours finally sumptuous to challenge his composure, his self-control. And that while the shadow of Death hovered around us. I thought at the time that this would be the pompon for me but I was far from imagining that there would be much more emotionally strong.

A much quieter day. We are on patrol, in pairs, on a Sunday morning on the A5. I'm driving the R21 Nevada with a professional Gendarme by my side. I don't remember his name, but he was the youngest of a dozen career military men. Barely older than me, he still does not have the "boots"! Because beyond the hierarchy and ranks, it is necessary to know that in the Gendarmerie there are those who have boots and those who do not! The boots you have them when you passed the license Moto, allowing you, of course, to be able to drive the two-wheel cars, BMW. The "GA", of which I am, will patrol more often with the Gendarmes non bottés, in R21 or in the Traffic. The "booties" have for the most part very big motorcycles at home for their personal pleasure. For the anecdote, the gendarmes "bikers" were generally more friendly than the non-bikers even if we should not make generalities about them as much as the commander of the unit, a major far from retirement and "motard" was really the least friendly of all, but also the oldest. I didn't like him at all and he was fine with me, I will be the only GA out of five to patrol on New Year's Eve night between 2 and 4 in the morning on a totally deserted highway! A vision that I will see again much later with Covid.

But let's get back to my Sunday patrol. We drive quietly in the direction of Paris - Troyes when we see on the road like a huge braking trace for tens, hundreds of meters!?! A clean track; well straight which will however end up deviating slightly to the right, to finish on the side. This track was at least one kilometer and maybe even two, it was really curious and mysterious. At the end of the end and two or three hundred meters from the final goal we start to perceive something tidy on the sidewalk, but we have a lot of trouble to distinguish what it is because it is very "small"! Frankly we are both seriously confused: a mysterious track on almost two kilometers, a very strange and small thing all yellow at the end of this trace? A new top secret weapon? Pac Man? A joke? A third-rate encounter?

It's not something very common, on the contrary! We go all the way and we stick ourselves right behind this atypical object that must barely exceed the meter of height!?! What looks like a door, on the left of this object, opens and lifts up diagonally and high!?! We get out of our vehicle and approach this object from another world, we finally identify it: it is a brand new Lamborghini Diablo Yellow. The Mega Super car of the 90s, the fastest with these 325 km/ h in point, it supplanted all Ferrari including the last F40. But we can also immediately identify his driver, even though we ask for his papers to check especially the registration and insurance. Jean-Marie Bigard is driving. He greets us kindly and seems rather calm while he has just experienced a very big fright! Almost now!!! Probably one or two minutes before we enter the track ourselves and through our reserved access. He explains first that the right front tire exploded in the middle of driving, which explains the long trail on the road due to the spill of coolant, but not yet why it is so long.

My colleague will then carry out all the checks of use on the radio in contact with the PC and with all the documents of the vehicle, leaving me a good time alone with Jean-Marie. In 1994 he is already very well known but he is not yet the superstar of 2004 who will fill the Stade de France with 50000 spectators! It was closer to "La Classe" than the SDF and it is probably for this reason that he "played" rather modestly, but not at all levels. I tell him that my car is the same color! He asks me if I have a 4L from the Post Office? I answer him that no, it's just a 2 CV. He will explain to me that, contrary to appearances, he has been hard at work to pay for this car, which he worked a lot. That there have been highs, rather recently; but that there have also been lows and for a long time! It is a well-deserved reward for the amateur of beautiful mechanics and thrills that he is! I understand him willingly, I do not know his history perfectly but I know that it is someone, despite the success more and more certain, who knows how to remain humble, modest and generous. He tells me his story, his family, as well as him, who has settled in Troyes, we will sympathize quickly and even more when my colleague returns. Being a very "fan" of Bigard, he will offer to visit him at his home in the kingdom of andouillette. It will take more than an hour and a half before the repair truck comes to pick up the super car, because, time for him to do us live and exclusively the sketches of his new show which, and this was circumstances, his version of the "permit points" for the deputies...

In the very friendly and very relaxed conversation, which will remain so until the end when I expected eventually an offence, I asked him still, just out of curiosity, always thinking about the trail for almost two kilometers, and while it was my acolyte "Police Judicial" who should make a detailed report: "But then... How fast were you driving? Three seconds of reflection by Bigard but no more, before he lets go quite quietly, without trembling, without strangling: he is still surrounded by two gendarmes and here "the guardians of the road"!!! " Aaaaaah, I was in the end of fourth quiet and I was going to be more delayed to pass the five"! And I answer all softly but very surprised "Ah yeah anyway!!!" Without being able to calculate at that moment what it corresponded"...

The Diablo is 575 HP in its most powerful version and on 5 speeds and with a maximum speed of 325kms! So end of 4th is beyond 250!!! For a speed limited to 130. We can say that he had fun Jean-Marie with his XXL toy. He was quiet in the Out Run version but 100% Live. Because the 5th he had already passed it one or more times before, on this A5 often empty the first weeks of operation and well before the implementation and repression of excesses of "super-speed"! Besides, where the tire exploded is a long straight line of several kilometers... And it's true that we are bored at 130 on these portions!

Seeing me very curious around the beast, he was going to propose me to settle inside! And even without starting it is already an intense and unforgettable experience! The position at ground level, the front window picked up, crushed giving a kind of panoramic background in the distance: we already have the impression of going very fast while we are still stopped! Too bad the tire was blown, I'm sure he would have let us drive it a little: on this empty highway, there was no danger. I will have to wait a few years before being able to drive a car at least as powerful but on the circuit.

I've kept the best for last with an even greater sensation. One winter evening, ready to stay in the platoon for a night duty, we are contacted by the command of our Legion who reports many grivèleries: crimes that consist of consuming without paying, in a cafe, a restaurant, a hotel and therefore here in the service stations of the A5. A procession of travellers is reported, filling their vehicles leaving without paying and also committing thefts in the small self-service shelves. We are given the order to go immediately secure the nearest gas station of our unit and the side where these travelers are circulating: towards Paris. We can't do more because there are only three of us in the pack. We are leaving with two and I am with the smallest policeman, physically of course, of the band! He tells me in the car that we can do absolutely nothing at our level, we are not enough to stop them, control them and possibly stop them. They know it well and for this reason that they travel and commit their misdeeds at night, traveling very numerous and grouped, the night all cats are gray! We are going to simply secure the gas station and the policeman of trade give me some very valuable recommendations!

"Everything should be fine, they are thieves but not killers. We must remain calm, very calm and show them that we are law and order!" You must remain calm, with your head held high and you must dominate them with your eyes! Do not look down, you must dominate them and make them look down!" We are right in "Il était une fois dans l'Ouest" or "Le bon, le brute et le truand"! Atmosphere 100% Sergio Leone! I asked him how many were there? He replied that they were many, very many, but that it would be fine... What he said... And then maybe they would not stop at this station since they have already filled up before?

We arrive at the gas station very quickly and ask the employee to close everything! We are then locked in this tiny shop of less than 20 square meters! My chief also asks to block the gasoline pumps. And when they arrive he also asks him to cut all the lights on and around the station. We wait a few minutes, we are notified by phone that they arrive! My colleague told me to unfasten the sheath of my gun and keep my hand on it permanently: deterrence! They need to understand that we will use it if necessary.

The night has completely invaded the gas station outside the shop, and we can only see car headlights coming up and approaching us, from the window that separates us from the outside! Some cars, some vans, some caravans at first but the parking lot will be fully filled with various vehicles: twenty? Thirty? Forty? Impossible to count; to guess but it is a cloud that has arrived. An extraordinary, incredible, creepy and very cinematic vision! Mix of New York 1997 and Mad Max as the vehicles were different in size, decoration, sometimes unusual!

Some individuals have squeezed the first vehicles near the pumps and try to use them even though everything is off! Outside the lights, they are in the dark. Seeing that nothing works, some begin to get closer to the shop... Two men, then three, four, six, eight, ten, in the end a good fortnight will approach the entrance of the shop. And believe me, I'm probably living the most scary scene of my life! I don't know if it's the frame, if it's night, if it's stress, my imagination but I have before me caricatures of Western movies from the great era Sergio Leone! They are all more peckish than the others especially in these circumstances. And we will reenact anthology scenes! Fortunately I know that we are, a priori, protected by the glass, all the more locked! But there could very well be a moment of madness. My colleague seems to be handling the situation perfectly, even if he is not leading it very well! He tells me repeat me, as he says to our vis-à-vis who do not necessarily seem to understand perfectly French: "Everything will be fine". They ask to be able to fill up with gas: it's NO! They ask to enter the shop: it's NO. They will come in large numbers, clustered near the front door! They will look at us for a long time, very long time, they will look at each other and talk in an unknown language. I can't believe I'm in a situation like this! I feel like I'm shooting a new version of "Assault" or "Wasp's Nest", but I don't want to be on the front page with a news story.

On the outside, they all have the head of "fact" so when they look down at my gun, I start to squeeze it a little more as I start to take it out very gently by two or three centimeters! Ambiance Sergio Leone absolute, palpitating probably around 80/90 pulsations minutes but I do everything to give the change! I am the law, I am armed and I will not hesitate to shoot me then!!! Aaaaahhahaha the joke! Whatever I am just "Master Sega" me, I laugh inwardly but yellow. Time is stopped, it is suspended. We hear the flies flying, his breathing, his heart shaking.

I see above all in the eyes of these men, surprise, curiosity, perplexity and much annoyance before defiance and provocation appear in some! One of them will even pull out a bundle of big money saying they had enough to pay! He had just admitted what they could have been accused of. I cannot tell you how long they stayed. Time stopped at that moment for me, I feel like they stayed a long time! 10? 15? 20 minutes? The longest minutes of my life, playing it like Clint Eastwood ready to draw or hide in a split second!

They will eventually get back in their vehicles, undisturbed but calmly. Resuming the road to the next station surely.

The return is wonderfully well synchronized because I'm just back for a new epic! I came back to Sega in June 1995 almost as I arrived in September 1991! The Saturn even starts much better than the Mega Drive in Japan. A NEW HOPE! Yeeeeaaahhhhhhhhh!!!

Chapter 25

Sega UK vs Sega France

TESTING PROFESSION

The confrontation between Nintendo and Sega on the 16-bit segment resulted in a draw in both France and Europe. The Mega Drive had clearly dominated its rival at first, over three, four or even five years as in the UK, surfing on a very favorable dynamic initiated by an early launch, a catalog of games that will expand rapidly, a high-performance machine, especially in terms of speed and quality of animation, as well as a marketing positioning that had been successful over the fourteen years and more. Before the SNIN caught up and slightly exceeded it at the very end, and this when the Sega teams had already passed mostly and probably too early on the development of the games 32X and Saturn. Leaving the field free to SNIN who would remain the priority for Nintendo and then release very big games, more technically accomplished to finish at best and even fanfare, his career end with a huge and ultimate Donkey Kong.

At the time of the magnificent JO 2024 in Paris, I put you back in the race and as on a "3000 meters" between The Sega Mega Drive and the SNIN of Nintendo. Sonic started the race in a rush and in the lead, lack of plumber in the starting-block at the first shot. Sonic had already done more than 400 meters when Mario would return to the track! The plumber and the hedgehog were side by side but Sonic had a good turn ahead! Seeing his rival right next to him, Sonic turns into a ball and accelerates like never before, he will take another hundred and even two hundred meters ahead. Mario is struggling at first, but he also accelerates in his second lap. The gap then holds for two or three laps. Sonic is still well ahead and begins his sixth lap. As he passed near the finish line, he discovered two new Olympic athletes preparing to return to the track: one named 32X and the other Saturn. Passing for a seventh track length, and while Mario was still behind him and more than one lap, 32X called Sonic: "You've won, you're the fastest... You can go out, I'll replace you to finish the race, we have enough lead." Sonic a little disappointed that he couldn't finish himself, then left the track and 32X took his place. Saturn then saluted Sonic for his performance and then proposed to him to go immediately prepare the next race "32 bits" but on another track and against another opponent. On the 16-bit track it was now the Berezina for Sega, 32X did not move at all or very little, and Mario ended up overtaking him once and then twice! Mario had already taken the lead well before the 8th and last lap. 32X was almost at a standstill and Mario finished the 3000 meters with half a turn in advance!

The competition was very beautiful. But if Sega and Nintendo were officially rivals, they were also strongly antagonistic to each other. As opposites, more functional, who had, therefore, raked wide targets significantly different: older for Sega. The market had thus grown strongly under the impulse of two wonderful simultaneous energies and the Japanese manufacturers had benefited each on their side, almost equally, at least in the West and on the consoles of salons. The antagonism also worked quite well on laptops with on one side the monumental cardboard of the console Game Boy in black and white and at a very affordable price, this certainly explains it, and on the other hand a much lesser success but still a success of the Game Gear in color, significantly more expensive to buy and especially in energy consumption, but which will still find millions of players around the world and more than 800,000 in France!

It would be different in the next battle! The Sony Ogre finally landed on the field of Hardware with its Playstation, and it targeted exactly the same target as that of Sega. The impact between the two manufacturers would be only more violent, no question of pretending. The Playstation, first of its name, presented itself with superior 3D graphics qualities, opposite to the Saturn. So much so that the engineers of Sega will feel obliged to add a second graphics processor, in extremis, when finalizing the machine and to get back on track. If the Saturn had clearly returned to the game, or even was potentially superior in theory, it would be difficult to compete with the PlayStation without wasting a lot of time and energy. The Saturn would be much more, much too complex to program than its rival: eight processors, two Hitachi SH-2 microprocessors and two graphics processors. Finally, only Sega would really draw the quintessence with games such as Sega Rally, Panzer Dragoon and Virtua Fighter. A fortiori Virtua Fighter 2 a little later, which will certainly forget the 3D too polygonal of the first opus. 3D polygonal very spectacular in the first times but that will age much too quickly in front of the more "textured" 3D games immediately served by

Sony! Not only would the Saturn be unable to show all these qualities, but it was more expensive to manufacture, and therefore more expensive, too expensive, for sale!

But despite these important handicaps, the release of the Saturn in Japan will still be a success!?! It will even dominate the Playstation several months, several quarters especially thanks to its flagship game, the new master of the fight: "Virtua Fighter"! The first truly 3D fighting game, called "polygonal", it easily becomes the Champion of all category of fighting games in this new 3D category and it will remain for a long time with several variations. The game is extremely popular in Japan and will therefore ensure a very good sales volume to the console 32 bits despite its rather high price and above all significantly higher than its direct competitor! This favorable start seems to be a blessing for Sega, at least in Japan, and it is even a resurrection, after the very poor sales of the Mega Drive on the Japanese archipelago. But this very good start will most likely turn into an excess of confidence and therefore as a huge handicap for the other territories to conquer: those of the West. The Saturn won the first round. This clear and distinct domination of the Japanese territory would perhaps be too deep, too early in the heads of the Japanese leaders, that the Saturn could dominate the Sony Playstation everywhere around the world. Virtua Fighter is far, far from being as popular in the US and Europe as it is in Japan. Sega will learn it and even pay very dearly.

1994 Magical new year or tragic first year? Sega's Saturn dominates Sony's PlayStation in Japan while the Genesis continues to smash SNES in the USA. Nakayama has his head in the clouds and this is also perhaps one of the reasons why he will not pay much, not too much attention to these feet, then these knees slowly but surely sinking into a marsh as deep as inextricable.

In early June 1995, I rejoined the Sega Hotline after my ten months offered, although a little much forced, to serve the Nation. Back among the Sega Masters with batteries recharged to block, more competitive and competitive than ever, I will take the temperature right and left on all important topics of news that have rather escaped me, while I was essentially tracking speeding on the A5 with my colleagues in the Force. A job that Sonic would have probably done better than anyone else and without having to wear the uniform.

I followed a little, from afar and with a distracted eye, the world of video games. I completely skipped all the news of the 32X and it will not be a loss given its success. Nevertheless, this failure has weakened Sega, it has weakened us, but we are far from being on our knees. The proof is in Japan! I read the Japanese sales figures of the Saturn and those of the Playstation. The Sega console is ahead and will have a significant lead at the end of the first year of combat (1.5 million Saturn against 1.3 million Playstation). Some experts are already projecting global figures favorable to the creator of Sonic. But caution remains because the gap is far from being sufficiently important and it relies essentially on a single game, which could be described as almost "local"! Not to mention that if the Saturn is well ahead, the sales gap has narrowed and we are very close to 50/50. It would also be enough for the Playstation to release a game, essential, to turn everything in its favor. The beginnings are promising and also sound the renaissance of Sega in Japan on the console segment after very hard years of great upset over previous generations.

Personally, at that time, I had no doubt for a moment that the Sega Saturn was going to conquer the world. Sega the "Challenger" but who had already beaten Nintendo several years on 16 bits, is already ahead of the Sony Ogre in Japan!?! Too good, too strong, too fast, too early!! Bis repetita.

The 32X was already a bad memory. A fiasco in which I would not have participated. We were equipped at the Hotline with a Saturn but also a Playstation, two Japanese machines, with the most important games then available on the market for both consoles, as well as some Beta versions for the Saturn. We were going to be able to play, we'll take it out on Sega Rally, Panzer Dragoon, Clockwork Knight, Daytona USA, Virtua Cop, Virtua Fighter and confront them with Tekken, Toshinden, Destruction Derby, Wipeout. It is an important moment in our life and in our experience of Master Sega especially since I had just taken a healthy break of ten months to regenerate myself deeply! The magic period "16 bits" is over, the 32X had finished it rather miserably and so without transition, we could finally enter a new dimension, a new future, a new cycle of fights and struggles, probably even more heroic!?!

The Sonic Team offers us the opportunity to officially taste "Sony quality"! For better or worse. There will still not be, there will never be any "propaganda" instructions imposed, we will value our know-how, this should be enough. We see for ourselves and draw all the useful, necessary and optimal conclusions in order to make our new star shine. And as for me, I would soon see what it is, even if it is only a first batch for both. Sega has never needed us as "testers" so much, the most knowledgeable, experienced players, the most sensitized to take the temperature on both sides and exploit the strengths of one against the weaknesses of the other. This new war would be much more difficult to doubt. Sony is much bigger than Nintendo and, alas, the target identical to that of Sega.

But for me it's all seen and my job of super ambassador will be and will remain easy! As with the SNIN, the Playstation is generally more beautiful than on the Saturn. Not on all games, not tremendously more beautiful, just overall more pretty. On the other hand, in terms of gameplay, realism and sensations, Virtua Fighter and Sega Rally are far behind the competition. At Sega France, it will almost become a leitmotiv or even a slogan: "Play!!! Try!!! Compare!! You will see the difference right away, unless you are this miserable crustacean-affabulateur of handicapant Sega Gameplay. "Do not let yourself be fooled again by glitter and powder perlinpinpin..." It was almost "too easy" in fact, we were going to play the same competition as with the Mega Drive against the SNIN. It was certainly you know, a mistake, Sony is much bigger and more powerful than Nintendo and especially this time we are really playing on the same box and the same audience. Public who becomes a little older than for the Mega Drive, a "Sony" audience in fact means big teens, young men and young women.

Profession Tester and Evaluator. Quality Controller!

We, the Sega Masters, are no longer "technical advisors" within the organization of marketing and communication. Far fewer than before, more than five or six, against the backdrop of sales of consoles and games in net decline, and especially with the line of Master Sega which has significantly evolved because it is now overcharged (the "famous" and often hated 3668 at about 2frs per minute or 35 cts of euro) and presents tons of solutions and codes registered for a 24/7 service. The historical activity "Hotline" live has therefore considerably reduced and even become a minority in the time we devote to it. The Hotline's roaring years are definitely behind us. But the latest "Sega Masters" are more so than ever! Half of the team will have left us, some went to Cryo to perform quality checks and tests around console and PC games, others for activities no longer related to video games. Sandrine will notably retrain as "Hostess" in the society of "Wagons-lits" and for the SNCF: surely that these adventures the two years of the Sega Train had inspired him a lot!

We have therefore moved to the job of "Tester", which would be very officially recognized and registered on our payslips. One very important point about the modification and optimization of some of our prerogatives. We moved from a mission essentially oriented towards "consumer advice" to that of quality controller and advice both externally but especially internally. We the Sega Masters were the Masters of the game: the Experts as we could sign it sometimes and even often in different internal publications like those of the Sega Club. From Luc Bourcier to Bruno Charpentier but also the press associates like the director of communication Michel Bams will never hesitate to employ us, to use us in situations where "real experts" were requested and highly recommended! More and more interlocutors were gamers or were getting closer to them and we could not fool them for too long even with carefully prepared cards. Nothing more normal and natural and always for this incredible passion Sega. We would go as far to replace them sometimes even momentarily... Easily as far as I'm concerned.

In 1993 we started by filling out evaluation cards for all the games that were to be released on the different machines. Romuald had probably started even earlier in a first version, more "archaic", more confidential, more exclusive. But over time these assessments became more and more rich, detailed and therefore professional; because their interest and effectiveness was growing. If at the end of the 80s and until 1993 everything was sold almost easily with an exponential market that grew by the eye, it happened more and more often that we found ourselves with stocks of unsold games! Some mistakes were allowed, nothing is ever perfect, and it is also with these errors that we learned a lot, especially not to repeat them too much. These unsold will most often be at a discount allowing some players to treat themselves for less! The game cartridges were still quite expensive. From memory a game sold 400frs in store was charged by Sega Japan or Sega UK around 220frs. We had to learn how to stock up as accurately as possible: neither too much nor too little, because in both ways we would lose money. When we sell the games for lack of sufficient stocks, the games would be bought temporarily on nearby markets like Belgium, England or Germany. And in the second case we would sell at a loss. For the player, the consumer nothing visible, even anything that we can imagine, but for us a level, a threshold of profitability to hold, so that the level of the structure holds, is at least self-financed and therefore remains as sustainable as possible.

For us, no question of being nice, polite, measured, to be gentle with anyone! We could smash a game if it was really bad and there will be. Even though it would be more or less dedicated to us as with "Asterix" (Mega drive versions because on Master System the games were very good). Unlike Sega America, which could develop these own games in-house and control their quality, we could at best only issue opinions and sometimes reservations with more or less influences and therefore consequences! Fortunately we would have "David Perry" and these incredible action games like "Global Gladiators", "Cool Spot", "The Jungle Book" and "Earthworm Jim" and of course, the now eternal and elevated to divine rank: "Aladdin"! One of the best-selling games of all time on Mega Drive and that will completely crush the Nintendo version produced yet not the formidable teams of Capcom. The latter had the exclusive rights for Nintendo consoles and therefore the company Virgin Interactive could develop its version only for Sega consoles. An incredible boon for the Sonic Team allowing the Mega Drive, a third and even a fourth year after Domination, on its competitor, with first sales in "single" then quickly in pack game + console. A consecration, a mega carton for Sega in 93 and 94 with this Legend partnership again confirmed with those first and very powerful allies that were Virgin and Disney!

We would not do these tests nor to caress the publishers and other advertisers in the direction of the hair, especially since it was more and more often only us, as third-party publishers took their independence one after another, nor to make many readers dream and sell a maximum of papers, and even less to satisfy ourselves with our improbable literary talents! NO! We used our near-absolute knowledge of Sega games to separate the wheat from the chaff. This expertise, this finesse of judgment, became increasingly indispensable. It had even become vital, especially to face the constraints of an organization that was too vertical.

These 100% usage assessments, and even probably internal thoroughbred, were really milk for the big game lovers that we were and who wanted to have more and more challenges, more new experiences, and more simply better games! I let you imagine what a "real test" can be when you fear nothing neither in the background nor in the form and when you are The Master! We might not always be so soft on words when it comes to tracking down and reporting some evils. But these evaluations had to give all the necessary information, most valuable, to the "non-players" of Marketing to place their future pawns in the communication strategy of the weeks and months to come! Enlightened assessments, sometimes illuminated; to give a partial view to the disabled, the blind... Non-players!

We became a key player in intra-European negotiations and therefore with (or against) Sega UK or more exactly "Sega Europe"! A war or rather incessant brawls, a cold war, an exacerbated rivalry that can very often be engaged in brothers friends or enemies of the same siblings, when it comes to sharing cakes and other sweets. And when it comes to show Mom Japan and Dad USA who is the most beautiful, the strongest, the most intelligent for the more or less real place of the "darling" or the first in the class. Sega UK would be our "big brother" more than a father or mother! And the big brother, we always want to do better than him, because if he is definitely a brother, he is not as great as he likes to think.

A natural competition and a constant competition between two brothers not very far apart in size and age. The English and French markets are the two largest, the two main markets of Europe ahead of Germany, which is considerably more populated and far ahead of Spain, and Italy, which had little or no similar demographic. It was much easier for the Japanese to work primarily and directly with the English, but did they still have to keep the "lead" in sales, communication, marketing! They had to remain "number 1" on everything and for everything, show the way to other European subsidiaries. No question of being outvoted, their status as leaders, decision-makers and thus "served first and as they wanted", both as the head of the federation and as the most important nation, could then be questioned.

While it is common knowledge that the English were quite irritated, annoyed and especially jealous of our memorable advertising campaign around Punk and Maître Sega, advertisements that had dazzled far beyond our borders, all over the world and therefore from Japan to the USA, Luc Bourcier will also report that the treacherous Albion always had a little trouble explaining how and why we, the French, were sometimes able to pass them in one way or another and as indelible remains of old rivalries, of duplicity and betrayal, transformed into both defiance and suspicion. For example, selling more Game Gear in France than they did in the UK, they will ask Luc, with a little surprise, fake or sincere, but with just as much cynicism, how it was possible that we sold more than them! As if it was absolutely impossible that we were in front of them! They probably trembled as much with impotence as with misunderstanding as the Japanese did with the Americans.

By passing number one in a segment, we logically become priority, in theory and as during a cycling race or the team car would immediately support his teammate if he was lost. The Japanese of Sega, and like all efficient and successful companies, would accentuate their efforts in the most important and especially the most dynamic markets: you have to beat the iron when it is hot. Especially where it is hottest. Sega's organization in the world was, and probably remained for a long time, very vertical! In short, Sega Japan imposed and the subsidiaries arranged as they could. Sega of America will become so big and powerful with the Genesis (the Mega Drive in the USA) that it can sometimes propose and emancipate itself, on the surface because nothing would ever happen without the endorsement of Nakayama. Options, good and bad but as long as the Genesis continues to tear itself apart. As far as we are concerned, Sega Japan imposed on Sega Europe, which then imposed more or less on the various European subsidiaries. And that is why Sega UK/Europe was monitoring very closely the French performances and this "verticality" in the organization will generate some tensions. By the way, it was the same at Nintendo.

First example with the inevitable Patrick Lavanant which I will talk about extensively, who will be director at Nintendo, before going through Sega, and before returning to Nintendo over a decade! In the season 92/93 he goes to Japan at the headquarters of Nintendo to negotiate more Super Nintendo for the French market. He thinks, probably rightly, that it is poorly served to the detriment of the Germans (the European headquarters). Finally he will not have one more, many consoles will have been imported from "Germany" at the same time and will be even sold cheaper on the French market! (The euro does not exist and fluctuating exchange rates allow for great intra-community opportunities).

Patrick Lavanant will come back finally frustrated, the tail between his legs, with many more consoles to sell but not those he hoped: they will be 8 bits "NES"! For sale or rather to sell, because they are increasingly difficult to sell in Japan where the market is totally saturated, the Japanese then rely on Europe which seems to have still a little sales potential for this machine! This total failure in a negotiation with the Japanese will be reissued later with Nintendo as with Sega. Maybe it had absolutely nothing to do with the qualities of Lavanant, perhaps not? We'll see about that a little later. However, Bruno Charpentier points out in various interviews that the "Latins", and thus the French in the lead, were rather frowned upon by the Japanese: victims of clichés, which worked certainly in both directions, but not that...

A JAPANESE IN PARIS.

If I was pointing out that at the Hotline, and unlike Nintendo, our peers and superiors trusted us, I must nevertheless point out that Sega Japan had finally sent a Japanese to observe us, to watch us: us Frenchmen undisciplined, rebellious and unpredictable. Having no executive mandate, he would be the "eye of Tokyo" (or Haneda) and that is what everyone will have understood. His introduction to us was very funny. I don't know if his arrival was announced, and how long before it had been prepared, but when he arrived, the least we can say is that no one was waiting for him and nobody really knew what to do with him! He had been parachuted!!! Nobody knew very well, for what reasons, he was coming. He was standing in the hallway near the reception at the entrance of the premises, avenue du Colonel Avia, like a hair on the soup. It was there "The Japanese" who intrigued, who immediately intrigues all employees! There must have been someone who knew!?! DG Christian Brécheteau? His assistant? But probably that its exact function must have been the most intriguing and mysterious! How to qualify someone who, in the end, just comes to watch, see how the machine turns before referring these observations, these reports to Sega Japan.

It was beautifully mysterious, as in the best novels of John Le Carré, to see this Japanese from Sega almost incognito and see him standing in the corridor! I will see him several times standing, then sitting! He had gone to get a chair and was sitting quietly, well seated near the reception: I will have the impression that he has been there all day!?! I will see him again many times, and always at the reception, the following days! Will it be spent and stayed for many hours just to take the temperature!?! Very methodically, starting with observing and listening on the very first line of contact in society. Would he spend hours, days in all the rooms and offices, one after another?!? Will not be seen at the Hotline, or was he in shinobi mode and almost invisible? He will eventually disappear from the corridors of the seat and we will then see him only at the time of the lunch break outside.

Came to monitor us? Control us? Report for SoJ? He will nevertheless and very quickly be a victim of the Stockholm syndrome, with conditions of lives far superior to those he had in Japan, becoming by the way even one of our fiercest fighters for a certain "French exception"! And so in total contradiction with his mission and Sega Japan. He will even become a kind of double agent. What they will only know later. This situation will amuse the entire French staff. We loved our Japanese, he was like a child in a Disney park: all the time we took for lunch, every day and at the same times: he couldn't believe it and he was very happy to be with us, and to be able, sometimes, to breathe!

The battle of numbers.

This very friendly Japanese who will quickly take the case for us, was probably the consequence of the inevitable rivalry between Sega France and Sega UK. Probably that if it was sent from Japan, it was probably at the request of Sega UK. Indeed, to follow up the many, too many distortions of involuntary or voluntary deliveries? We therefore put in place various measures to mitigate this detrimental verticality for our operating accounts! To avoid being delivered sometimes too heavy we had set up and we used the expertise of Sega Masters, which would serve as much to be better served and/ or prioritized on certain titles. And conversely not to find yourself under tons of unsellable games. On these points, there was probably not much to say even if it could embarrass and embarrass the great Japanese and English strategists.

But what worked best, the most effectively, were of course the sales figures! And that's probably where we were getting a little bit out of the corner, giving inflated numbers especially at the approach of the Christmas season. The supply chain was not perfectly well oiled, and it always seemed to be to the advantage of the English and we could understand it as long as they have and they keep the lead: we could call it the prime to the first, a majority premium as it can be very often practiced. But I think that many people at Sega France were tired of being served according to the pleasure of the English, always priority and especially as it pleased them. The only way to shake the machine a little and drop a little more products than we could hope for, without stealing them of course, was to cheat, that is to force the numbers! Nintendo was caught in the act with SNES sales in the USA the first year of its release, announcing huge numbers that were just projections of orders to distributors! Far, far away from consumer sales, "real" sales! In the latter case it was more to not lose face before Sega but it is unfortunately a common practice to give figures, sales "distributor" and not sales "consumers".

In our case, the numbers were inflated on the same principle. And this allowed us to pre-empt more products for the weeks and months ahead! When the Japanese discover these "small arrangements", he will gladly understand them, totally close his eyes to this practice and even encourage them! Nobody at SoJ like SoUK will have none. He will cover this little make-up and even pay himself to rebalance in our favor some British privileges. Everyone sees noon at their door and our Japanese now saw the sun rising rather in Paris, than in London or Tokyo.

Sega Europe took the orders for all of Europe from Sega Japan, with the exception of the Electronic Arts games manufactured in the USA. That is to say, for such a console, such an accessory, such a game, the English asked for this or that quantity, not without reporting to the subsidiaries to more or less adjust the shot but the European headquarters also ordered stock for European sales outside the subsidiaries. It is extremely delicate, did the English have for this their "Masters Sega"? Masters "European" who can imagine sales in all countries with different cultures and influences? In addition to the difficulty of ordering the right quantities, it was also and above all to deal with this vertical Japanese! Most of the time it was Sega Japan that imposed a predetermined stock. Basically, and for example for

"Alisia Dragon" on Mega Drive, the Japanese had decided that this game would be a huge success worldwide and Sega Europe would receive 80,000 copies "in first batch", without ever having expressly requested them!?! The game developed by Game Arts, and published by Sega, is a good game or even a very good game in its category, however it presents a decisive originality at its time. The hero is actually a heroine, long before Lara Croft of Tomb Raider. "Identification" so quite limited for teenagers in need of projection and graphics are not yet fine enough to "fantasize" discreetly! I remember very well having discussed it with Romuald because it was actually a case of school as we had already and as we would have many more. We were perfectly in agreement that there was a problem of identification and therefore communication. We liked the game a lot, and we rated it "technically" very well. However, we had a very negative opinion about the potential sales of the game. Not so much because the hero is a woman in the game, but because the title of the game was that of a woman (Alisia) and that all the more the jacket presented her as a heroine. It was a bit like trying to sell a Mega Drive game called "Barbie". In some games, even sometimes very well known, the hero will be a woman, but nothing of her femininity will be highlighted, this is the case of the huge license "Metroid" at Nintendo. Few players will know that they will play a woman, a bounty hunter...

All this to say that this game will be a huge success, the Japanese have imposed tens of thousands too, that Sega Europe will more or less evenly distributed in one country or another! Sega France, but most likely the other German or Hispanic subsidiaries, could not tolerate being forced to make choices that had such a negative impact on the profitability of the subsidiary. It was enough to several failures of this level to plant definitively the results of a year! While Sega Japan, however, still collected the production of the print. It is almost certain that Sega, at a global level, would arrange for these subsidiaries never to make too many profits, in any case in all the countries which were more taxed than the others. This "verticality" allowed to distribute, optimize the profits where they were less eaten. Obviously this system of tax optimization quickly found these limits, it would be effective only with a system of vases still rather well filled. It is easier and more useful to spread profits than losses, except when the losses of one make disappear the profits of the other.

Counter-example, but no less interesting on the contrary, with the release of the game Flashback still on Mega Drive, a game developed by Delphine Software, French company therefore, and game entirely in French which is still rare at the time. Highly anticipated game because it is a Mega Bomb, it is even a "Game Killer" in power that will also allow the Mega Drive to stay ahead of its rival in the West. Absolutely sensational adventure game with a technical part in the "Prince of Persia", but even more realistic, a SF scenario close to that of Total Recall, and all the more translated into French! Although it is first released on the Amiga, Paul Cuisset will say that this game was designed and created for the Mega Drive! Flashback will become and remain the best-selling "French" game in the world for many years with more than one and a half million copies on the different media on which it will be released! A bomb, a tornado for which Sega France will have, from memory, only 20 or 30 000 copies? The game will almost immediately fall out of stock and it will take several weeks to be able to supply again to retailers! Sega Europe probably did not anticipate such a carton! Which was quite predictable, at least in France! How many copies of this game have they put aside for the UK? Mystery... The game that is out of stock quickly will be bought in large quantities in neighboring countries, most likely the UK.

We will never know exactly why this essential game, which will sell thousands of Mega Drive in addition, was so underestimated before its success, starting with France. What is certain is that if Sega France is still pleasantly surprised by the speed of these sales and outside of the "high season", we are also slightly irritated that we were not able to control our orders and deliveries on this "Game Killer" which can make all the difference had less than a few weeks.

It is probably from examples like Flashback or Alisia Dragon that the Sega Masters began to assert their expertise both as the shield and as the sharpest blade. We had the games well before everyone else, long before the press and even sometimes we received them when they were not completely finished! No presentation, no end, and sometimes some bugs. In "Eprom" version and physically at first, then directly downloaded via floppy disks or internet on blank Eproms. It was magical to put the right number of memories on the Eprom card before placing it in the cartridge port of the Mega Drive! Even better than the hot bread that just came out of the baker's oven. We were so privileged, so privileged. There really was no place better than this one, when you were a gamer... We could discover and play games just a few hours after they were closed in Beta by the Japanese teams! Remembering a little in this, that incredible moment or in 1991 we could even see day after day, Philippe Ulrich advance and evolve his Dune on PC and Mega CD.

If we were already "Sega masters" and ultra gamers, we had also become the recognized experts and essential deployment, qualitative and quantitative calibration of Sega video games in France! We were expected to know and evaluate the qualities of a game as first, incredibly lucky, perfectly happy, first "tester" but also and especially to determine all its commercial potential: in pure "Sega Master"! I can say it now, but I will not be less proud, to discover first, and before everyone else except maybe at Eidos the publisher the French subsidiary, the game Tomb Raider on Saturn! What a privilege and I will probably never have such great. The game would be released first on Sega's Saturn, because at that time, the "Sega Masters", were also going to become the most lucky adventurers in worlds by also becoming experts on Tomb Raider for several years! For Sega with the Saturn but also for other versions! An evolution that will be commented and detailed in the Volume 3 of the chronicles of Master Sega! So I'm going to play Tomb Raider and discover this amazing game for the time, both in the background and in form. I'm going to play it and finish it well within a month or two before it is available in stores. Probably one of my best memories as a player and one of my greatest pride. One of the biggest games of the Saturn, which will be the third best-selling of all time in the French market.

From our emotions, our assessments, our notes and our most insightful and experienced suggestions, very diverse and varied, there were still four or five of us to produce these increasingly existential assessments, we would then certainly initiate many negotiations with Sega UK, Sega Europe or even Sega Japan, when the positions of the subsidiaries converged or diverged, to have sometimes less or the minimum, or have more and the maximum! Sega France would no longer allow itself to be easily imposed choices and quantities that may seem as random as risky to remain polite! For Sega France there would be the choice of the Master, as a bonus, against choices sometimes more marketing and/ or commercial.

Sega Japan would eventually offer games, a priori, more suitable for the French market, the best example regarding may be the license "Asterix". 8-

bit versions will be a success when the 16-bit versions are closer to an "Infogrames" quality. It's more than a shame to waste such a nice license by games quite average technically and often not very playable. Sega Japan wanted to please us but without giving themselves the means. The Asterix Mega Drive versions will be rightly criticized and we will not order tons of them. Although the game is still a good sale, it will not win the super star stripes of the game, as other adaptations will be less powerful in theory. Like for example Aladdin by Virgin Interactive! More than four million copies sold worldwide! A record behind the various episodes of Sonic. And also far from the "Global Gladiators", Cool Spot and other Earthworm Jim of the illustrious David Perry.

Obviously, our assessments would not always weigh, even heavy in the face of leading global marketing strategies and plans, but at least we would have a clear conscience when our "international" superiors would impose their choices and as to the end we would do the accounts on what had worked... Or not. The management in Japan would always have the last word, but we had organized ourselves to make our difference, to show it and sometimes also to impose it.

Always listen to our players, our most deserving fans like those of the Sega Club or the Hotline, their tastes and desires, through the ear of the Sega Masters, their experience of consumer services and also as "first players". That's what Bruno Charpentier would do, I've already told you, especially by using and exceeding his experience with Nintendo, and Véronique Cosatti in the commercial management by listening as closely, as accurately, just listening to their business partners, who were most often echoing their own clients! Even if for a majority of them, we were aliens, Sega France had managed to be close enough and to value these Masters Sega, as the latter had managed to be and stay very close to the players. Passion could then circulate freely, quickly and smoothly, without anyone forgetting, with much more horizontality of the players, enthusiasts and the entire distribution chain. Who in some way took revenge on a rigid Nintendo, right in his boots seeming to be deaf, blind and dumb. Sega France ex Virgin Loisirs clearly understood how this "passion for video games" was stronger than anything and that it had to be adapted to the tastes and colours of the French, with more audacity, more realism, more transgressions, sometimes disruption.

And also sometimes just more simply with Sport and Disney, we can't be completely different.

Between Sega France and Sega UK it was a long time, if not a war, a direct confrontation, it was a permanent arm-wrestling, a competition of all moments. For the English not to be overtaken, not too often, whereas for the French, it was rather to be respected and to be honored as we had to be every time that it was justified! In this period of writing 100% JO de Paris, the one who has a gold medal draws much more glory and profit than the one who has a silver medal while sometimes only a hundredth of a second can separate them.

Being a leader for example on the sales of Game Gear, we claimed and demanded to be served at the height! Nothing more logical, be a little better served in games and first! Except for orders, stocks do not go through Sega UK first. The differences in sales could be sometimes small between the English, French and German subsidiaries, and the Japanese supply not always in phase. For this reason, it is installed in France, but also certainly in the other subsidiaries, a form of widespread doping! Internal doping, numbers always inflated, even oversized, and after all, we would always end up reaching these figures!?! Over time, months or even quarters later!

Sales figures, when they were good, were often a little bit arranged. The better they were, the more inflated they were. Not rigged, just inflated, unfortunately very common practice in the trade, we gave rather sales figures "resellers" than real figures "consumers". That's what Nintendo will do with its Super Nes completely overtaken by the sales of Mega Drive/Genesis, and not to make a pale figure, they will communicate the sales to distributors, it is always more spinning. This doping of numbers often served in terms of communication to play mechanics or appear a little less outdated to the general public, but it was most often used to inflate the order books and or not to be stolen all the merchandise by the other subsidiaries and also perhaps to anticipate a market acceleration! When you gave a "inflated figure" it was immediately an additional positive bargaining lever for everything that was affiliated with this "good figure".

This extra prerogatives, which had its importance in the commercial strategy and therefore the success of the subsidiary, involved me more than ever within Sega France. Very curious about all the official and unofficial figures around this business, I was going to take an initiative that would radically change everything! Now and for the twenty, thirty years to come! So convinced to be on the most powerful and deserving of the race horses, after years of dreaming with the Mega Drive and Sonic, with the first Japanese successes of the Saturn, with the reign without sharing in Arcade, I decided, I was about to buy shares in Sega! I was going to become a shareholder of Sega Japan, and I honestly believe that I must be the only one; outside may be executives in Japan, in the USA, and maybe the CEO of Sega Europe!? I was going to be the first and probably the only employee of Sega France to invest me both humanly, professionally and financially! Sega would no longer be simply my employer, my religion, my second family, my second home. A small part of Sega, very small part indeed, belonged to me. I linked my destiny still a little more to the Sonic Team and I congratulated myself! It was a very important step for me in my membership, my commitment, my loyalty to the Sonic Team. I did not yet know that this action was going to lead me into incredible adventures and not just, not only as a new "investor". Because by taking shares in Sega I saw myself as an investor, of course, except that the reality of Sega, its life and destiny, these unique, ambitious and risky choices, would push me even more, shake me up and ultimately shape my fate as "ultra gamer"!

With Sega, in Stock Exchange mode, I was going to discover the biggest, most incredible video game in the world! A game, a true one of truth, with the greatest, most powerful masters in the world. A game where you can become the king of oil in a few weeks, even days, or even hours when you know the right "cheat code", just as you can end up in your underwear in seconds. Nothing could be more exciting and like a final challenge!?!

"Bad luck" for me, I buy shares of Sega during the summer of 1995 and they take 50 or 100% increase in a few months with the new season Saturn end of year. Second in Japan, first in the USA and Europe. All dreams are allowed and speculation explodes! I earn 5000 frs in a few weeks (having invested 5 or 10000 frs I do not know anymore). I took this surplus because it was fast and easy and the success of the Saturn remained uncertain. I made a small bonus quietly with Sega, without the slightest doubt, without any drop of sweat, I saw myself keep them longer but I had already learned to "cash"! I was entering a new dimension but I was far from imagining all the consequences that this would entail for the 20/30 years to come. If I had become a "Sega Master" easily enough, without stress, I would discover how much I was possessed by the game's demon. But if there were only the Stock Exchange!

In this year of recovery 1995, we also became kind of actors by recording sometimes on site, sometimes in studio, all the codes, tricks and solutions houses on the games Sega and for the ligner of Master Sega now accessible 24h/24. A task that will be mainly taken over by Aude, Romuald and me, for our speech probably clearer, more adapted and therefore more effective. All of France could contact us day and night, and our voices were thus consecrated for many years.

In this period of return and then quickly fall, we are also under very high voltage with this new challenge named SONY. If we continue our standard professional activities of Master Sega, we will measure ourselves on the 32-bit consoles and without a priori. As much as we were, we find, and like a little everyone of course, that it is noticeably better on Playstation than on Saturn! In Toshinden but especially in Tekken, we opposed Virtua Fighter, and now it hurts! Obviously the first 3D Polygonal game in history has been faithfully reproduced! The "Arcade" purists will be happy but the others will discover a game, certainly interesting by its very realistic animation and more generally its incredible gameplay, but they will discover a game still quite even frankly ugly! We have more the impression of having a game "32X" than a console game Next Gen.

Tekken, on the other hand, offers beautiful textures and therefore flatters the pupil generously. Not being a big fan of fighting games, I play both without particular excitement and almost in neutrality. One can admire the beauty of the one and a greater realism of the other. I must admit that Tekken is much more "sexy" in the end, except to be a Hard Core Gamer, as I could be, but with the notable exception of fighting games. Impossible to draw a definitive conclusion on the state of the attractiveness of either one on the general public, especially since Sega already announces a Virtua Fighter 2 of beauty, and a Virtua Fighter Remix would soon come out with nice textured 3D.

Another comparison should however unfortunately cause much more damage to the Saturn: Ridge Racer on PS1 against Daytona USA Saturn.

The conversion of the arcade game from Sega is quite successful because very faithful, however impossible to miss the incessant "clipping" during the game and almost permanent! Flashing everywhere on the horizon and even if it does not take much fun in the game, this clipping is a big defect at least as a limit to the power of the machine and which certainly makes the Saturn as clearly less efficient than its competitor.

Ridge Racer is not free of this problem but it is much less common and therefore much more acceptable. The game is also a little nicer so, in one way, it's noticeably cleaner. And even if the driving sensations seem to be a little more pointed on the Saturn, it is far from obvious especially when discovering the game. It seems much more obvious this time that Ridge Racer wins the match on a single weak point. Sega Rally will soon be released on Saturn but it is not the launch of the console in Europe. The "Clipping" will still be present but much less than for Daytona. It does not appear as a deficiency. In terms of gameplay, Sega Rally is the champion of champions and will remain so for a long time! The qualities, the sensations of gliding, driving are absolutely exceptional and sensational! This game alone justifies the purchase of the machine if you like this kind of game of course! Sega Rally is clearly a "Killer Game". But talking, talking again about the quality of the games of one or the other is even more vain than at the time, because the difference will be made on other levels and on which there will not be much to say, and do.

SONY will smash Sega on the price! It is also necessary to (re)give this anecdote about the presentation of these new consoles by Sega and Sony at the huge video game show in Spring 95 in the USA. The Sega representative gives his detailed presentation: power, games, blablabla, AM2 teams, arcade games, know-how, Virtua Fighter, Blablabla, and console for 399 dollars. The audience applauds. The representative of Sega then leaves his place to that of Sony and he will say only one word: a single... 299 dollars! Before leaving immediately and under applause!

It was definitely folded at that moment in fact but we could not yet know, guess. By denial of reality certainly. But also and above all because Sega is eaten by an absolute evil, a real Cancer that devours him from the inside and since 1993! " Sorry, sorry did you say 1993?" Yes it is even rather at the beginning of year 93 that the more tragic fate of Sega will be sealed but everyone will close their eyes because sales are and become even more magical!?!

Chapter 26

Piaggio vs Peugeot : Story of O

Beyond video games, all games and in infinite mode, most often before everyone else, and sometimes exclusively for a while, we would also enjoy another fantastic privilege: meeting our audience, and maybe some of you who read me!?! We would go to bathe and communicate in the middle of hordes of children and teenagers, absolute fans, during video fun events always more sensational and warm one than the other and therefore very expected on both sides. These first appearances of playful video icons like Sonic, these first XXL shows are and will remain engraved in the hearts of so many players.

The fairs such as the Multimedia World Show Porte de Versailles, the ancestor of the Paris Games Week, events like the Train Sega in 92 and 93, and at many sporting events, at the highest level, where Sega had invited itself as a partner: Karting, F1, Football, the Olympics. I detail some of these events in Volume 1. There were also, from time to time but regularly, events, private parties, in which we were invited as Ambassador but all in Guest Star and of course, Of course, many consoles in demonstration. Because to be completely honest, it was more the consoles that were the Guest Stars, the VIPs of the evening! We would then be their voices.

The salons ended up being similar in the background, perhaps a little less in form and it is in this last that we would find the small difference that would bring its charm and excitement over time, as the seasons go by. A unique and exceptional setting: right next to a karting or F1 speed track for the world championships, a huge station, a football or athletics stadium would add an epic dimension to our performances "super Sonic. It was always great to be in the spotlight in magical places and to see all those eyes of children who were amazed. In all these remarkable and noticed events, which have been chained. One of them, had for me and much more than any other, a very special flavor. It's the World Two Wheels in the Autumn of 1995 and also in the must-see buildings Porte de Versailles!

The video game in general, Sega in particular with these arcade speed simulations and especially with its worldwide license Hang On, had become a powerful vector in terms of images, communication towards teenagers and other young men users of "Mega Drive". Sega was Cooool, it was stronger than you, it was super fast. Piaggio, one of the world leaders in scooters, had the excellent idea to associate Sega with its Stand this year 95. Piaggio was among the main exhibitors at the show and its very large stand stood back to back with that of Peugeot! The other leader of the scooter but especially in France. Did the two manufacturers choose to be back to back? Certainly, perhaps less antagonistic than could be Nintendo and Sega, the ranges still cultivated enough differences to compete but cordially even friendly! They had formed the heart of the scooter and all amateurs would enjoy it.

As a Sega master I had accepted very willingly, once again, more excited than ever, to play the ambassadors for Sonic and his band of ultra high sensations lovers. To find the world of two wheels, it was to return to the original source of Sega for me: The Speed incarnate and always celebrated by the inevitable HANG ON. I would come as an amateur of its sensations, these lightning accelerations, all types and all brands having already had three times, two motorized wheels (a Trail MTX Honda, a Suzuki RacinG Gamma, and a custom Red Rose Aprilia). I will be several days in a row on the Piaggio stand in super VRP happy very too happy! And guess what? Well he was still paying me for it and my salary would even be doubled!!! Are too crazy, too generous at Sega. There were about 10/12 stands of demonstrations and almost as many new products! It was always necessary to present new games, with the Best Sellers, on the fairs to trigger invariably the effect Whaooouhhh! And it will be there with the new and powerful 32bits Saturn consoles. Hang On GP and Sega Rally Saturn would amaze more than one and for the most courageous, daring ones of them, they will even challenge me to Sega Rally, the monitor screen then cut in half. Of course I will be intractable, but without any ostentation on my part, because it was mainly to hold my rank and embody the ultimate challenge "Sega" as much as this one I really knew by heart.

It was really great, I was even more than ever! Sega paid me to play video games, make them discover, make them love, show that the Masters Sega were really the strongest! I was once again in this moment of grace, The Game Master and in all humility! Segaaaaaaaaa! And as the dream in big, the dream in giant never stops, I was sent to immerse myself in another of my greatest passions! At the heart of the Sega Passion again and more, and now the Passion two wheels in one of these larger urban assemblies! Life in blue, life in pink, life in all those bright colors!!! " To be born and stay under a good star" !?! (Under Antares of Scorpio, one of the brightest and most massive stars in the sky and yet so "red"!?!)

Not too busy with the demands, I was doing the work of discovery and accompaniment at my own pace and getting intoxicated by this festive atmosphere sprinkled with competitions! The stands were beautiful and often very sexy, everything was done to attract the barge, to draw attention to the new two wheels more sparkling than each other. Piaggio had of course, very nice products and they breathed well on the Dolce Vita, with their scooters and especially their mythical Vespa! Italy has always been for me like a second homeland especially through the prism of antiquity, especially the Eternal Rome and its amazing timeless beauty. Rome, its Colosseum and these Vespas will always awaken in me the most acute form of my Stendhal syndrome, of Florence, of the traveller... Rome so beautiful, to weep. I could obviously admire all these two wheels as much as I wanted and I had a lot of time, but I will also go around all the stands during my breaks and I will enjoy! I will be on site several days and for several evenings, the lounge closing a little later the Week end to accommodate a maximum of enthusiasts and potential customers.

My little stand reserved for Sega demonstrations was on one end of the Piaggio stand. It was mostly wedged between Piaggio and its rival Peugeot! Perhaps to divert and attract the barge!? Meanwhile, a foot in one, a foot in the other, I was in the front seat on the part of the builder to the Lion and that offered, several times a day, on an elevated stage, superb and very spectacular animations, Dances for the least physical and even athletic of beautiful creatures, able to contortion the body in a very bluffing way! A true tribe of Pom Pom Girls, I took full eyes, ears three or four times a day for almost ten minutes or even a quarter of an hour and it was hard to get tired. An absolutely wonderful show, especially being as well placed, although a little off, as I could be. All these young women, even very young women, probably from 16 to 25 years old, left the show quickly and returned one or two hours later. They were really pleased to see as much by their beauty, their elasticity, that more generally by the show, the choreography they proposed. All went away... Or almost! A very beautiful young woman accompanied them, received them, assisted them. She did not participate in the show except to supervise it and certainly ensure all the organization, assistance and logistics.

At first sight, in the tumult and noise that engulfed the whole living room and disturbed all our senses, she had very clear blue eyes, beautiful long curly blond hair, a white and milky skin for a bright face of light and beauty, Highlighted by a full black suit, tight and therefore fitting, drawing generous and well rounded forms: the most charming hostess to doubt. But to look at it, that is to say much closer, and when we will approach by I do not know what combination of circumstances, while taking my breath back, it was above all a breathtaking vision! Those thick and silky hair cascaded on those frail shoulders, her hair glistening and floating freely around this face of perfect complexion, angelic, with eyes azurre and hypnotic. Her perfect silhouette, accentuated by her slim waist and curves as delicate as voluptuous, radiated a most sensual aura. No doubt, the Goddess Aphrodite herself had settled on the Peugeot stand, and while I had stranded, very close, at Piaggio.

I could not have seen it, not really see it, except as a wonderful, divine accessory of a perfectly organized staging of creatures more graceful than each other. It was a show for which I will certainly not be, and will remain only a spectator! Neither too far nor too close... But here, and this time for me, more than any other, the magic of Sega. My karma, clear, definite, and as I probably will not have another, not so powerful and shining in this life! What could we, what did we have to say about exhilarating things? Irresistible things? In such circumstances! It is mostly for me too full of emotions even if I do not remember having been short circuited! Perhaps sometimes everything would flow perfectly and naturally as our fate would inexorably flow, woven by Clotho one of the three overpowering Moires (or Parques in Latin) and unrolled by his sister Lachésis.

- And what are you doing here? Would she end up asking me to see me, still not very far from her!

- I'm in charge of an animation video games for Piaggio and I am Master Sega!!! And you?

She thought and then smiled "I am the head of the hostesses and facilitators of this stand, I am Maîtresse Peugeot!!!". Smiles.

I can tell you the rest but we would then very, too far away from video game, but I will not hesitate to choose "continue" whenever I can !

Chapter 27
Patrick Lavanant : the Black Cat of Sega

I remain very admiring of the greatest and sometimes huge characters, who have become essential figures in the history of video games and who actively worked on the birth and development of Sega and for being among the most fervent pioneers, the most ambitious creators and conquerors of their kind. Through commitments at various and varied levels, in the mechanics of building a group that will become global, and with a common passion always intensely raised, capital, vital, and which will be transmitted to many, all around them, at least in Japan. PASSION, we have found you a second name and we would write it, or we would say it thousands, millions of times: "SEGAAAAA". The "Sega Scream" as it is called in the Anglo-Saxons will cross time forever carried by a whole generation of lovers transis.

The company was originally founded about 60 years ago by an American named David Rosen (one of the first and most valiant pioneers and with exceptional longevity, who should not be too late to be centenary!!! We wish him), it developed especially and at an accelerated speed, under the presidency of Hayao Nakayama operational and executive side when the brilliant and unmissable creator Yu Suzuki along these sides, and in the mid-80s, fed by all his talent and work, the creative and even disruptive side of the company. Three names, three legends that should not be missed to include Isao Okawa, the main shareholder of the company of the blue hedgehog via its holding company CSK, who will also be chairman of the board, and who will save even Sega in the late 90's and early 2000, by lending initially no more than 500 million dollars taken from his personal fortune! Very beautiful and incredible sum on which he will eventually draw a line, certainly a little forced, in order to save and give oxygen to Sonic and these completely exsanggued teams and before allowing the salutary rapprochement with the company "Sammy". Finally a merger that will allow, once and for all, a sustainable and profitable activity, even if less glorious because seriously amputated the most prestigious branch but also the most uncertain level of profitability. Remove one or the other of these four musketeers and Sega could never have known its fate as fantastic as heroic of the 80s and 90s. Or Passion, Ambition, Stubbornness, Creativity and Generosity will make them grow wings as wide and powerful as those of the most incredible and powerful dragons. They will go much higher than the sky, even going to tutoyer the Sun itself! Losing, therefore, alas, all humility, and like so many other conquerors before, by hubris, it will be fatally replaced.

If Sega did not have the strong enough to establish itself definitively and everywhere in the world as the undisputed leader of video games beyond arcade halls, it has entered history forever by being the most daring Challenger, the most intrepid, the most flamboyant, until it is reborn many times from these ashes. Like the Phoenix, in a cycle of death and resurrection that my dear Hypnos and Thanatos would not deny and like the "Scorpion of Antares" I am, in this step of infinite dance well known to all players, the one of the "Game Over" immediately hooked and hooked by the "Continue" as epic as infinite, but also when passion comes to tutoyer addiction. The gamer will never count the number of times he has pressed! Or he has continued, as if nothing had happened! The "Continue" is louder. Sega is the embodiment of "continue". He is like Hades the god of hell, the absolute master of resilience, of rebirth, allowing you to rise from the dead. Sega will always be and remain "continuous" whatever the price to pay. It is stronger than you but it is also stronger than death. We lose, we get up, we die, we are reborn and we get up... Sega as all these real fans recruited from around the world never give up. Unlike some western leaders a little lost in the face of life and death instincts too far from purely economic considerations, Nakayama will never hesitate to take all risks to aim and try to catch the sacred seal of eternity. Nothing matters more than the desire to go always a little higher, a little further even when the difficulties will intensify and settle. She was there, and so the soul of Sega, until the end of Nakayama in 1999 after 15 years of fighting on the front: "Better to die, again and again... Better to die than disappear"! It will cost the society very expensive economically speaking, and even to the edge of the precipice, to flirt with the bottom of the abyss, but the Passion, the Force, the Generosity, the Honor and the Glory always exceed the questions of money, in particular on Nippon territory.

To a lesser extent, Tom Kalinske, the president of Sega of America from 91 to 96, will mark his time and his epoch for having beaten Nintendo several years in the USA on the 16-bit console segment with the Genesis. Other leaders have entered the history of Sega but certainly not as many as those I just mentioned. In this top five, we find three Japanese and two Americans certainly proving that the DNA of the Sonic Team was de facto binational and therefore much more "Pacific" than we let it assume, even if this does not exclude, on the contrary, a healthy competition coated with a pungent and sweet emulation as in all siblings, erasing some cliquetis as anecdotal as insignificant, so much success was prestigious at times.

Japan is obviously a huge market for video games. It is historically and for a long time, the country with the highest penetration rate by far. Next come the USA but Europe is not left behind (for Asia, outside of Korea, it will still have to wait a few years)! What is left of remarkable, unforgettable, thirty years later, of the European leaders? I have spoken to you about some of the French leaders. I also discussed the rivalry between the United Kingdom and France, which had nothing to envy that of the USA and Japan, even when one would play more in "Ligue des Champions" then the other would play more in Ligue 1. The entity "Sega Europe" probably never was more than a British, Anglo-Saxon entity, more or less under the influence of Sega of America but totally subordinate to it and increasingly so as the years passed, considerably reducing any truly original margin for manoeuvre! If Sega France allowed itself, with the success that we know, "The Campaign of Master Sega and Punk", while they were finally and viscerally still "Virgin Loisirs", these eccentricities will be quickly caught up and annihilated by a British centralization and standardization and by a European mutualisation of costs, with notably "Canal Sega" (or "Sega Pirates"!?!) Not always directly adapted to countries as different as Spain, France and Germany. The "Virgin Touch French" will disappear little by little and Master Sega with it, at least in cinema and television, slowly but surely with budgets communications and marketing increasingly reduced, targeted and screwed by the British authority. Ah if only France had been chosen as Leader and central point for Europe! Oh if only the British had never returned to the European Union, saving us their betrayal through Brexit, and thus offering Paris the center of gravity.

If we are an exception of "Jean Martial Lefranc" (who will never have been "Sega France" but only "Virgin"), and with all the friendship I can have for some of them, like Bruno Charpentier or Philippe Deleplace, the general managers of Sega France will have succeeded each other too softly, despite all their talent, to maintain the Olympic Flame of Sega! But did they have the power? If the great names of the history of Sega are mainly Japanese and Americans, we can also take a look at its history in Europe, and with the men who were able to write it, a little, a lot, crazy or not at all!

Starting with the first of them, both chronologically and concretely by his weight, his involvement in the organization: namely Nick Alexander. Patron of Virgin Mastertronic before being bought by Sega Japan, he is the main craftsman in the creation and implementation of Sega Europe. I had the chance and pleasure of meeting him at the first European seminar in Nice in September 1991, when he was accompanied by another historic artisan and principal of Virgin, the late Frank Herman. Nick is a very nice man, dynamic and above all competent and passionate! He knows the video game world very well, having founded Virgin Games in 1983, which became Virgin Mastertronic by buying the company Mastertronic. He will remain at the head of the European Directorate until 1994. A year of total reversal for Sega and which will precipitate him towards new adventures starting with the Press and the group Pearson then "Future Publishing" a name that should speak to many retro gamers!

Nick Alexander was certainly, with and even before Jean Martial Lefranc on the French side, one of the most insightful leaders regarding this reborn business, and even exploding, game console! And yet, he will also pay the price of disagreements, or rather misunderstandings, between the different objectives that the Japanese asked him to achieve. I admit, however, that there was plenty to become schizophrenic, and we can affirm it with a first example, the case of the Game Gear. This console must compete with the Game Boy from Nintendo, in black and white, which sells like hotcakes but the portable 8-bit color is therefore much more expensive, almost twice. This price difference will not find any solution because the console, like the vast majority of the others produced on both sides, is sold, at best, at a cost. Selling at a loss (dumping) is, in principle, prohibited. However, it is the production price that is used to set the red line not to be crossed, and not the price with all the distribution, management and marketing costs. Finally, in

1994, the Game Gear will be sold with a negative gross margin of 11%. That is to say that every time Sega Europe will sell a Game Gear for 1000frs to its partners, he will put about 110 frs of his own pocket, after all the fees paid. 110fs a priori quickly recovered by the sale of one or two games, on condition that these are "Sega" games and this while most third-party publishers have flown to a total freedom leaving the Sonic Team only a few euros (francs) of royalties (licence fees).

Second example of misunderstanding, more cultural at first sight or in first reading, during a meeting in London of Nick Alexander with The Big Boss Nakayama, between the "Japanese brain" but also and above all the great world leader and the "European brain" and this, while they both have their shop for almost 10 years! You can't find more "veterans". The owner of Sega Europe will report it himself and this is well to be specified, because in all these so-called "misunderstandings" we will never have, each time, only one point of view: his own and therefore the "western" one and especially that of the subordinate not having, In fact, all the cards are in hand. So it is at best 50% of the information to judge for yourself, but probably much less. Nick will therefore say that the Japanese seemed totally disconcerted by the huge success of the television commercials "Sega Pirate" (Best known in France and declined by the campaign "Canal Sega", Canal Pirata in Spain). Indeed, it is in the UK that Sega was the most successful in Europe, both in terms of market share and volume! Nintendo was completely fucked up and Sega sometimes had up to 70% of the market! Whereas Sega France was between 50 and 60% in volume (on salon consoles). The British were certainly not unproud of such performances and even if they were far from the absolute value of the American figures, They were nevertheless the most successful in terms of results, especially since they also sold tons of Master Systems that had been amortised for quite some time.

According to Nick, the Japanese did not understand these performances. And besides, in a counter-intuitive and counterproductive way, at first glance, Nakayama will even propose to use the Japanese ads to save money!?! What Nick will answer, to the botté, by the fact that having less than 15% of the market in Japan, it is rather they who should use the English advertisements! Remark that can not be more relevant in the background but which will surely have been well irreverent in form for a Nakayama who will always remain "straight in these boots", confident and determined in these ideas. In the US, Tom Kalinske will also report almost the same exchange, the same passing of arms with Nakayama, in a similar context, but with a much more piquant and offensive tone as to the response: "You have never exceeded 10% market share so why accept something from you that makes you fail on your ground"! At Sega we knew how to talk frankly!

These examples will be presented as so-called "evidence" of misunderstanding and tension between the different entities, mainly of a cultural nature or, in any case, they seemed to be. In reality, whether it was Spain, the USA, France, Japan or the United Kingdom, everyone saw noon at their window and ultimately, it would most often be Japan who would have the last word, but not this time. Because the entities remained sovereign for everything that touches local communication, the only square that will remain untouchable. These misunderstandings, as they might appear at first sight, are not really, not here anyway. Nick Alexander reports this disagreement with the Japanese, but it is most likely and even very certainly faked by the latter to achieve a purely and vulgarily financial objective: to make very banal savings. How it is certainly biased by the pride and the pride British around his "wonderful" campaign "Canal Sega" that he could have imposed to several European countries!?! Nakayama was motivated, at that time, only by a search for economies of scale and substantial because he tried this pressure or poker move, both on the European side as on the American side, and without success. If he had really thought that the advertising campaigns were bad or not effective enough, he would have removed them and imposed on Japanese ads.

Nevertheless, it is indisputable that there will be real misunderstandings between the Japanese and the Westerners! But it's breaking open doors! Cultural misunderstandings classical and traditional certainly but not necessarily more important and more numerous than those between a man and his wife in a couple and yet very much in love with each other! Love and passion does not exclude moments of tension and broken plates on the contrary. As if humans were able to agree on everything, all the time without two or three big disputes memorable! And before they meet again. Some swear by football when others swear by rugby! You don't have to go all the way to the USA and Japan to enjoy each other's tastes and colors. It is more often a wealth to exploit than a point on which you have to enjoy, laugh, try to make sensational with finally the extremely banal except to live all your life like a bear at the bottom of a cave.

Nevertheless, for the anecdote, it is still necessary to have a little bit, the Americans will issue, at first, very negative reviews on the draft of the future megastar game from Sega and its commercial potential: what was then the embryo of Sonic! A real crime of lèse-majesté retrospectively towards Sega Japan when we know the sequel but finally just a funny anecdote, fate playing very small things in appearance. The stakes were high and I find these initial disagreements as healthy and, again, as normal. A mistrust, a distrust that is difficult to remove afterwards but which really has nothing exceptional when we measure the cultural gap. The banal, nothing but the very ordinary but also, sometimes, the salt of life.

It is nevertheless very regrettable that for many observers, more or less informed (some probably seeking only to make a bit of sensational) these so-called cultural differences, these "misunderstandings", are made one of the main reasons for "The Fall of Sega". There were no less cultural differences at Nintendo, with the parent company and its subsidiaries, and "Patrick Lavanant" could confirm this after working for many years for the two Nippon giants. Many unjustified fantasies around Sega appeared, probably as cathartic, before so many disappointments, pains, sometimes suffering to see this video game champion collapse as violently as he had risen to the firmament. Myself, I will point easily, and like many others: SONY!!! As being the main cause of the end of Sega in the console market. Sony is certainly responsible but not guilty! Because the evil that has turned off Sega is of a very different nature. All this to say that, as much as we are, we have searched and found responsible, so-called "faults" (there were certainly some and as in all companies) because it was necessary to purify us of this pain, of this abominable loss of these "incredible Sega consoles" that had made us so much vibrate and would definitely be torn away, as if we ourselves lose a limb, an arm, a leg! Except maybe to gather them, collect them as authentic relics of a past era and glory, make them work again and again in this so cheerful, warm and increasingly popular "retrogaming"!?! Failing to find the true responsible, the fantasies had thus appeared and will be maintained for a mourning that seems, for some, never to end and that would seem to want to feed, perhaps, of our luminous nostalgia!

1994 is the year of the great reversal, the big upheaval, the party is definitely over, Nick Alexander will be the first and main victim and he will be for me the revelator of this nascent but invisible Apocalypse to the general public and probably even to the vast majority of western executives. He himself will throw in the towel out of boredom, out of spite, when he was probably one of the most passionate leaders for Sega and Sonic. Imagine! He is the most important, powerful leader in Europe of the Sonic Team. On the one hand, it is asked to sell a maximum of consoles for a maximum of games. He is asked to earn money, or at least not lose it. This is its main role as it is for all managers of commercial companies. And on the other hand, new conditions are imposed on both buying and selling prices that evolve unfavorably to meet all these objectives!?! The example of the Game Gear will not be, will not be an isolated case! And when he could be, at least a little, congratulated by Nakayama for the quality of his communications campaign and all the more so for the results obtained in the United Kingdom as in Europe, and finally all his work, They will be advised to adopt the Japanese communications campaigns! With probably the rocambolesque "Segata Sanshiro", kind of Master Sega as powerful and effective as comic, but without his full sandstone knowledge! There was really something to become crazy, frustrated and maybe even disgusted!

However, it is here that I could see the limit, unfortunately shared by the European and American leaders, in a form of self-importance and/ or blindness to the real situation of Sega around the world. But perhaps it was also, more probably a form of denial that tolerated only very little, an overview (each with its own scope, problems and troubles!?!) The case "Nick Alexander" is not an isolated case. In France, as in Spain, as in the USA, none of the main leaders will be spared by the disease invisible at first, insidious in a second and that will even end in generalized cancer! The evil we do not talk about, a real taboo that will put Sega on her knees. Of which we will not talk, or very little, outside of Japan!?! Nombrilism? Blindness? Incompetence? Denial of reality? They will all at one time or another wave the flag of misunderstanding and that of immense frustration, unfounded... Or simple smoke screens to create a diversion or even disassociate!?! Because "evil" was really of a completely different nature and nothing or nobody could take care of it.

MISSION IMPOSSIBLE.

The main task of a DG, and even more so of a CEO is to ensure the smooth running and sustainability of his company! But Sega Japan in 1994, and maybe already a little from 1993, imposes conditions that eventually dig the grave of European subsidiaries, and American! While in 90, 91 and 92 the results, a little everywhere in the world, are simply exceptional and fly from record to record, the trend will be reversed in 1993, quite violently, and especially against all expectations! The Mega Drive continues to sell like hotcakes and the meters explode, one after another, stronger and stronger. 10, 15, 20 million units is a real tornado that sweeps all American states. 1994 is still a record year in terms of volume, but not at all in terms of results and it's even the big gap!?! These exceptional sales hide a very sad reality that no one had seen coming or imagined, even in Japan. And that no one will want to assume, especially on the western side, even causing an allergic reaction and sometimes rejection. Sega insisting on selling consoles at a cost and often even at a loss after operating costs, significantly impacting the company's results, many executives will eventually throw in the towel just like the most important of them! When the results of Sega UK show more than 100 million pounds of losses in full year, Nick Alexander more frustrated than ever with his superior, will therefore decide to leave this ship, this liner, which is starting very seriously to take water. He did not go out of cowardice, but like many other European leaders, he could not understand the whole picture, he could not accept the strategy "to the end" of Sega Japan, which seemed doomed to failure.

Everyone will understand that selling at a loss on a good part of its activity (consoles) when the "game cartridges" no longer assumes its function as counterbalance and with huge margins (lack of volume reducing under the impetus of emancipation of third-party publishers) is just suicidal! But what could have changed and created a situation that became critical in just a few months? The Mega Drive is a hit, we're going to rip it off!!! The Playstation is still far away!?! 3DO and Jaguar consoles will not last long. The business model of Sega had done wonderfully well in 90, 91 and 92 and from 93 (really noticeable in 94 with consolidated figures) PATATRAS it is the beginning of the big, huge catastrophe!

THE BLACK CAT

Am I superstitious? Probably a little, and more and more with time, but thirty years ago frankly not at all as a rule and yet. Sega had become a second home, but it was probably almost like a religion. Religion rhymes with superstition, the irrational could then shake me up any Cartesian I could be, that I thought I was. During 1993, something really unexpected happened at Sega France! A major event in the small world of video games in France. The Japanese have "chased" the marketing director of Nintendo France to appoint him general manager of Sega France instead of the friendly Christian Brécheteau, who will continue his playful video path, called to build the French subsidiary of the publisher Acclaim (Mortal Kombat, NBA Jam) and that we "Masters Sega" would soon find again, me the first, me especially... I love Mortal Kombat, Sub Zero and Scorpion!!! The Japanese probably thought they had achieved a stroke of genius!?!

It was a real earthquake in this small, very closed world, especially for your narrator, who was, at that time, 100% Sega. I had read interviews of him, mostly in the economic press and frankly I did not like at all. Not so much by the fact that it is "Nintendo", but by that, as many at Sega of the rest, that he had little to do with this universe of pleasure, of Love and Passion except to grab the best "fruits", delicately plucked and placed instantly in the bottom of his pocket. Patrick Lavanant is nothing but a business man, sensitized and attracted by high tech products, which can generate strong margins and thus ensure comfortable incomes! In one of the few interviews he will give to the specialized press, he will simply affirm that he would probably be "billionaire" if he had all the answers to the questions asked, as to the evolution of the video game! As he will claim, in early 1994, that the success of virtual reality was imminent and would be monstrous! Thirty years later, we are still waiting and wish him not to have invested all these savings in this "Meta" Arlésienne. Maybe, as with video games, he had never tried because he didn't care, except to milk them to the last drop, and he would still prefer golf, tennis and young hostesses. Who would prevent him? Who would blame him, a little, except me? At that time anyway.

I saw its arrival with a bad eye, and even with a very very bad eye! Without questioning his real skills, he must have had a little of the rest, especially by having brought his most faithful and very effective lieutenant from Nintendo, Bruno Charpentier, and I will not be mistaken! But then really not!!! Patrick Lavanant was a real "Black Cat". Maybe, he was even our rider of the Apocalypse! Bringing with it many evils that we would have well passed. His arrival will clearly mark the darkest, most worrying, most painful period of my Sega years, except to put their head in the hole of course and as many employees will do, especially those at the top! The vast majority probably will not even suspect anything!?! And at worst, for the few and most conscious: "it will be better tomorrow", because you must always keep hope in what it looks like! This period of doubt will still be installed gradually, more seriously and more deeply, causing confusion and misunderstanding, not from the first day of his arrival, nor the first quarter, but (chance or coincidence) his entry into Sega in the current 93 and until his departure in 96 will absolutely perfectly coincide with the greatest challenge, the ultimate challenge of Sega facing the true evil that will be assimilated, in our situation, to the worst of Cancers! Patrick Lavanant is he himself the Evil? Without his knowledge? Black Cat or Horseman of the Apocalypse? If Sega sounded and vibrated with Passion, it would also sound to me now with superstition as I strongly think of a very probable imposture, to his last great proposal to the Japanese, like the final bouquet of a fireworks, who will take away my last doubts. At least at this time.

We could have guessed it, but the Japanese too happy with this "Nintendo" war take, probably did not know the file well enough, let alone the fact that the applicants to this position must not be very numerous. Yet as early as 1987, we can question the Karma of Lavanant! The clever one snatches the distribution of the NES at the American show with a false document, before suffering a delay of several months in the delivery of the first consoles, before being forced very quickly to bankruptcy because of financial crisis, liquidity crisis, while he and his ASD company bet on a bank that will be in the storm, one of the first to be taken away! We will have seen better as Karma but still credit him at this stage a simple misfortune all the more so that on the other side, Sega will have taken advantage of it, to launch without any accident of this nature. At Bandai then at Nintendo, it will be very far from sparks, with an irresistible and almost monopolistic material "NES" which has taken over 90% of the market in Japan as in the USA. It is therefore very much underperforming other markets and even the closer, more comparable German market.

No passion, no conviction, no energy in the narrative he chose around video games but if he was more visionary, he would certainly be a billionaire! Aahahah. Even Luc Bourcier could be considered a hard core gamer and an early enthusiast. But he will still eat enough, and he will do everything to eat the maximum, despite a very questionable quality of service, outside, perhaps, tennis. Totally disembodied, he could have asked his sister for some advice to pretend, Patrick Lavanant is a bit of the Droopy of the video game world and it may beFor this reason, it will be only read or heard in the media and outside of the economic press!?! And yet in the private, he is not without humor or even wit! And he has to hold of course, brother of "Dominique": "I do not drink, I do not smoke, but what can I suck... As suc des Vosges!!!". Patrick will be the only Sega boss I'll see shorting a meeting or assembly to go to the theatre!?! To see his sister play, of course. As a relief for him may be, not everyone is lucky to have a sister as popular as irresistible!

So I saw his arrival really with a very bad eye, I will never repeat it enough as my unease of pure gamer was deep and certainly justified. Because it was, or rather it would be (and remain?!?) "Nintendo"?!? I have to be honest, Lavanant was finally neither "Red", nor "Blue", nor "violet" or any other color whatsoever, but "Lavender color", pulling a little towards gold or at least silver!?! He was just ambitious, opportunistic and greedy. And that, of course, it displeased me deeply, and I really felt very strongly in myself that the wind would turn. Dogs don't make cats and I had been able to compare the treatment of Nintendo's technical advisors with that of the Sega Masters. Passion and generosity on one side, standardization and profitability on the other. I did not imagine for a second that it would be a storm that would strike us and for three long years he will be with us: Our Black Cat!

From my point of view, probably a little too literary obviously here, he was the Traitor (Nintendo) and a traitor would remain it all his life!?! He was most certainly coming to improve his treasury more than to take up a new and exciting challenge. He was, for me and only for me?!? The wolf who had entered the sheepfold. He was the mercenary who would eat at all the railing, never satisfied: if still he was passionate about the products that he marketed!?! Not once, not an exchange, not a word to try to let him think! Whether at Sega but also and especially at Nintendo! For me, it was an affront, a provocation, a wound, but above all a great lack of taste in relation to the image that Sega conveyed, especially since he was, before, this enemy, or more exactly this rival, This totally antagonistic competitor of Sega! It was like asking ice or cold to become all fire, all flame, or the opposite: stupid and unacceptable. Despite a bias on my part too charged because too passionate, too suspicious, too young, too inexperienced, I will not be wrong! Or so little. Superstition, imagination, certainly, but very embarrassing conclusions crowned with an incredible proposal worthy of Nicolas Machiavel and flirting with high Betrayal, and who will definitely sign "his sidelining" of the Sonic Team.

Yet, although the Evil, like a true Cancer, has arrived at Sega, we would not realize anything!?! This serious disease, in its onset, at first, is completely harmless and it is often very difficult to detect. 1993 will still be a wonderful year and we would celebrate it even in a great ceremony at Brazil Tropical. The party is over but we do not know yet because a last Bal is offered to us and the sales figures remain very good and often even "record". And this while France fell into recession this year, against the background of monetary crisis and a certain fragility as to the European construction! Almost 1% decline!!! Household consumption has fallen sharply!

Tic tac, Tic Tac... We are in 1994 and a new very nice year seems to present itself at least in the video game world. How could it be otherwise? The numbers are getting higher and higher, nothing seems to stop the rise of Sega!?! No one has any doubt about that. Nobody except maybe the Japanese because the Cancer De Sega has just been discovered, but any Cancer it can be, we must probably be able to cure it! It is not at all a question of talking about it, commenting on it. Worse we will do as if it did not exist and as if we were going to quickly cure it.

The evil has entered and it is growing, settling down, yet Sega will once again beat all these records in particular in the USA or the Mega Drive (Genesis) will once again dominate head and shoulders its competitor SNES. More than 7 million Genesis vs 6.2 million SNES!!! The 32X may be a flop, but it keeps the Genesis in the spotlight and eating more while 16-bit is still on the market. It's hardly believable and Tom Kalinske has become a demigod! With its second-best-selling arcade game of the year, Virtua Fighter, just behind SF2 (or update), SEGA will even have the luxury of winning the first round against Sony on the new 32-bit war front in Japan. Almost every Saturn buyer buys the game Virtua Fighter!!! Saturn far ahead of the Playstation with a lead of more than 250,000 consoles sold in favor of the

Sonic Team! It's too good! Really beautiful. This new super mega party will soon be ruined. These figures are particularly misleading for the most common quidams. Volumes are not very interesting if you do not put them in relation to the profits! And the time for accounts has indeed struck. Between bright sales and dark financial results, Cancer continues to grow. It happened as usual, insidiously and without our attention, and in a terrible snowball effect, he will bring to her knees Sega yet in the force of age and even thought to be indestructible, as Mega Drive sales accelerated and accelerated, except...

Except that in 1993 (bis repetita) France fell into recession and it is not seen and felt immediately and not for everyone! Especially when you are a young player immersed in the heart of your new passion!!! The European economy overall is not doing very well. Germany continues to pay for its reunification, and it is also necessary to tighten the belt in all the states wishing to enter the euro zone, to fit into the nails of the European agreements and the single currency! In the famous Maastricht criteria. While the Yen (Japanese currency) was very low in 90, 91 and 92 (the roaring years of Sega) it will slowly reappreciate until accelerating upwards and running very fast 93. In fact, of yen that would rise, to be really fair we should rather talk about the western currencies that stall or even collapse against the Japanese currency.

In an amazing and astonishing synchronicity, Patrick Lavanant arrived at Sega France just as the French franc was collapsing against the Yen! The yen will remain very high little or prou during these three years "Lavanant"! The franc will start to recover and return to historically "average" levels when Lavanant has left, or rather has been fired by the Japanese!?! Completely crazy, extremely disturbing when you compare the exchange rate charts to his time with us. We can never find such a bad Karma in Sega. And remember also that Lavanant will have also suffered a first financial storm by taking the fate of Nintendo, in a questionable way, a few years before! With bankruptcy on the line: Sega's Chat Noir? And Nintendo? It will bring bad luck wherever it goes...

Lavanant, but "without his full knowledge" probably, was definitely our Chat Noir or our Cavalier of the Apocalypse! Bringing with him, despite himself, three terrible years. The Yen which is at record levels, "very expensive" and especially too much, much too expensive. With particularly painful consequences for Sega as for all the Japanese export companies and even if there are some dampers to these flights (insurance/coverage of exchange rate, cheaper imported products thus generating a little deflation on production costs and especially relocation of production including the set of CDs of Mega CD then Saturn) but just bandages with very limited effectiveness in time and not covering, in any case, the phenomenal loss of money receipts with Western currencies having lost between a third and half of their values! The flows from abroad will be permanently amputated of a quarter, a third or even, at the peak of instability, almost half their values!

In summary and to make it as simple as possible: the rise, the increase of the Yen, will not leave any chance to Sega! THE YEN WILL FLY AND SIMPLY FLING SEGA!!! The results will automatically go from dark green to bright red while volumes are increased again!?! The Colossus, the new Titan had also feet of clay. Nothing, nor anyone else, will do her so much harm, everything else is derisory, as long as the Japanese currency is so strong. Sega is stronger than you" but not stronger than the Yen, on the contrary.

Patrick Lavanant, hunted by the Japanese, had probably agreed to sign with Sega for cash! Both in its fixed remuneration but also through premiums and other stock options, This is the simplest way to motivate executives and to avoid them becoming slippers and leaving or going back too easily to other horizons more remunerative at first sight. Sega had most certainly erected before him a golden bridge! Bridge which he will surely see, at best, only half. Because, and although it is certainly not at all responsible (except to be superstitious as I could be about it) the results of Sega France will collapse with its arrival, going from dark green to bright red, under the pressure of a Yen too high, Lavanant will see all these dreams of performance and enrichment fly away! The years will follow each other and be similar: operational losses, losses and more losses. Nothing will do (partial relocations of production especially) and as long as it is there! Nothing to put under the tooth financially speaking, when a few months before, it was paradise islands, Club Med, cabarets and big Parisian parties as with the Guetta, Trains Sega, bonuses, general increases for all brave soldiers Sega.

Our video game Droopy can always console himself by blowing on these legs our charming Press Attaché, or watching different sporting events on the big TV of his office, the door wide open so we can also enjoy his intense Rolland Garros matches!?! The heart was no longer there, but had he gone there at all? I saw again "my Traitor from Nintendo" from the first days of 1993, fulfilling his mission with all the ambition and speed of a gastropod. He could then go to see his sister at the theater every day if he wanted to! And why not go back to Nintendo? Not without trying to give him a little "Golden parachuté" gift back and (re)welcome!?! These little gifts that maintain the friendship!

If the heart was not there, if the passion had evaporated (smile), if all desire had disappeared, nevertheless remained his pride and his sense of sharpened and infinite paid service! Whatever its quality!!! When other leaders, who have proudly gone into the history of Sega, such as Kakinske in the USA or Alexander in the UK, will leave with the high heads of SoA and SoE with a sense of duty accomplished and thus finished, Patrick will prefer to do and propose anything, as a flight forward or a drink to Lavanant, just make foam, get foam, annoy as he could certainly be himself, and probably get sent with very substantial euros at the key! Magnificent dignity.

Patrick Lavanant will then hit hard, very hard and as no other would have dared before him! Maybe it was necessary to come from Nintendo or pretend to go to Sony? Crazier want to return haunting Nintendo? In what will also be its darkest, most troubled, most painful period (that of the Nintendo 64). Fortunately it was French and 20th century, because in Japan, and at another time, he would probably have lost his head. We must put ourselves in the context because today we know what will happen but at the time Sega and one of the two giants of video games and especially game consoles! It is his job, his talent, his honor, his greatness, his pride, his reason for being!

Lavanant will still propose purely and simply to the Japanese, it is Romuald who will come to announce me, to stop production, to totally drop the game consoles! ULTRA HIGH TREASON!!! The shock is sufficiently important that one cannot yet immediately think of its direct consequences... One can catch its breath after such an earthquake. Lavanant will therefore propose to dedicate exclusively to create games for Nintendo (Damned!!!) or for Sony, if Sega did not want to ally with its dearest enemy! What a visionary! He had solved this impossible equation of Sega, selling consoles AND games without losing money. It was enough to stop producing game consoles!!! Damn but of course!!! Eureka, Sega has found its new Master!!! Aahahaha (yellow).

TREASON! ABSOLUTE SCANDAL.

Inevitably when we know the history, twenty or thirty years later, one could think that this man was probably a great visionary! It should be noted that all the non-gamers, the "Never Gamer", did not understand why Sega was so stubborn to sell consoles at a loss when it would have been so easy and smart to make Sega games only for competitors! And therefore ex-competitors.

No, but seriously? They really believed it, all "pragmatic" that they were and pretended. Was it so simple? So much torment on both sides of the continents, selling machines with losses!!! But yes at first glance, they are right. When the yen is too strong they are probably right. But when the yen is weak, as it was during the first years of Mega Drive, you can conquer all markets! You can even become a leader and maybe stay that way, but you'll never know.

But to make this financial and monetary reasoning, certainly very important (the proof), is to deny totally the soul of Sega. And it was on this opinion that the gap between gamers and non-gamers widened and became even more distant. This is yet another demonstration that many executives did not understand anything in the mind of Sega. That they were focused, business school training requires, only on profits and profitability. Each one his job certainly. While Sega had surfed, many years, on this fabulous, irresistible emotional lift, which went as much on the development of machines always more and more "magical" as with increasingly fantastic games. Passion against Reason, the Sega of Nakayama and its main shareholder had fortunately leaned towards the "good" side until the disappearance of Isao Okawa in 2001. Abandoning his last console, as the last and greatest of these dreams. Dreamcast.

Chapter 28

The Berezina of Sega

The Yen has devoured Sega

The Hyenas will finish their meal

You can only truly understand the history of Sega, its philosophy, its strategy, its evolution over time, through the prism of Japan. Although, of course, the different Western views, especially those of the Americans, will constitute up to a small part of the DNA of the Sonic Team, and will never be to be discarded in a change of hand, especially under the impulse of David Rosen. But the DNA of Sega is and will remain mostly Japanese, the Americans are only relevant to epigenetics! We can change the color of the skin, that of the eyes but we do not change anything in the heart, lungs and all vital organs. The subsidiaries of international groups generating, by essence and it is still very happy, a bubbling, an effervescence, a mosaic of colors, tastes, sensations and perceptions equally rich, spectacular and varied as the cultures from which they come but on the surface!

The American and European subsidiaries as powerful as they may have been at one time or another were, remained and would remain subsidiaries, nothing but subsidiaries, with all that this imposes, starting therefore with a full and total subordination. Hayao Nakayama would still be Sega of America's Vice President (and therefore always at least in the shadow of Kalinske, as well as the very powerful board of directors of SoJ that is mentioned only too rarely or never, among non-Anglo-saxons very far from corporate governance). Sega France would have "his Japanese" behind the scenes to monitor us and better control us, in theory. Organization of the most banal and vertical certainly, but having proved itself through time, continents, civilizations, societies, as also showing all its limits.

The often legitimate desire for emancipation of the subsidiaries will always come to break, sooner or later, on the pride, the pride and the inflexibility of Hayao Nakayama, far superior to those of all these lieutenants together. The Boss is him and no one else and he will show it more than fifteen years. He alone, on the ground, but not without having all these decisions approved and validated by the board of directors and therefore in particular by the very influential Isao Okawa who will have been for a long time neither more nor less than the chairman of this council and whose we will never really know what he could have imposed himeven or not, in Nakayama, except to have also participated in the decisions of the many councils, or to have spies behind the scenes. Influences that will remain confidential or even top secret! I believe, but I can be mistaken, that Okawa had much more power than Nakayama because he will put all his heart, all his energy and all his fortune into it! He will donate $40 million to the development and commercialization of the Dreamcast! So it would never have been released without him! He will also lend more than 500 million dollars to Sega from 99, a debt that he will abandon a little later! And finally he will sell the entirety of his share of these Sega shares held by CSK, to Sammy, and still worth nearly 700 million dollars! The man who will offer almost all his fortune to Sega Enterprise to keep him out of trouble, from 95 to 2001 More than a billion dollars! If you were looking for a Sega Enthusiast, a real one, it's him and no one else. And without him, the Sega adventure would probably have ended with the launch and failure of the Saturn. MR OKAWA!

Although many commentators have been looking for a long (too long) who or what had shot Sega, we at least know who kept it alive for many years. What good or expensive decisions did he make or support before? Which is certain, that Nakayama will have kept all his confidence, until he failed one last time with the Dreamcast.

Tom Kalinske, very aware of this as vertical as brutal management of the Japanese companies on its subsidiaries, will obtain a formal agreement of "semi-freedom" to accept the position of management tendered by Nakayama. Conditional, conditional, contractual release on either side, negotiated by mutual agreement upon entry through an ambitious and wonderful four-point action plan that will make the Genesis a success but which will be reduced, a little later, to a skin of sorrow. as Sega's sales and profits in the US will decrease considerably! What some will then comment on "misunderstandings" against the background of cultural differences, material failures, but also by improbable rivalries and even croches! Never really looking further than the tip of their nose, or very little, and what could well hide these few gestures on a background of frustrations, these last one can be more real. How to create a smokescreen on a problem, a much more trivial equation but clearly less sensational and especially without solution. We then fall into this trap so common or when it works, everyone has been great and worked well and when it does not work, everyone points their finger looking for one or more responsible. It is a very human reflex of course, natural and salutary even if often it is biased by too many emotions. One of them, certainly Japanese, may have shown the moon but all the others will have finally looked only at the finger.

Kalinske will eventually, like Nick Alexander for Europe, resign, refusing to take responsibility for a failure that is not his own, the Saturn's, and all the more so as he surfs triumphantly, like a Kauli Vaaas, French and Polynesian Olympic champion at the fantastic JO 2024, on the impressive and irresistible wave that slides, this continental wave named Genesissss! Who seemed never to want to stop herself!

Sega Japan will keep full control over the design, development and production of these new arcade machines or Trade Shows consoles and therefore, ultimately, will keep the hand on the Global Strategy, as well as on the calendar! His, but unfortunately not the other. Sega Japan invents and manufactures and subsidiaries of the world market these products! With all the same specificities on local justified requests that will translate into necessary home adaptations but even closer. Let's give back to Caesar what belongs to Caesar, it is the predecessor of Kalinske, Michael Katz who will launch the first big wave of highly localized games made in and for "USA", especially with many sports games. Long before the Sonic carton on Mega Drive, there will be first ascents like Joe Montana for US football and James Buster Douglas for boxing. Sega Does what Nintendon't is also it! A tacky and very effective slogan that immediately hits all minds. It will therefore be necessary to deal with the different fortunes of certain products from one continent to another, and adapt without being afraid to take risks but always measured.

Total or almost total control, it's perfectly natural and no one will really find it to be wrong because these are the rules. Kalinske had fully understood and assimilated it as a veteran of high-level business management and a certain connoisseur of the Wasabi sauce business. These "Four legendary points" imposed in "all or nothing" on arrival, are the perfect illustration. He had the merit of giving the necessary impulse, the legendary boost that will make him go down in history, and probably he was very widely rewarded! Almighty and even half-god he would be, he would remain an employee, a subordinate. Even Ares the God of War is subordinate to Zeus. Each year is a new challenge and the cards are always replayed. Being a champion is good, confirm it once again better, stay is a colossal challenge. Kalinske was able to win over Nakayama at the entrance and hold out as long as Sega of America made money. Profitability is the only arbiter, the justice of peace or war, at this level of observation of course. This is true for Sega as for all other commercial companies it must be repeated.

As long as it is the parent company, and only the parent company, and for development purposes, to bear all the responsibilities and the heavy burden of financing, refinancing all the activities, and therefore subsidiaries, such as the even more stressful one, the maintenance of market confidence in general and those shareholders in particular! For behind Nakayama is far, very far from being a man alone, even if he seems to be. There are many shareholders, the largest of which are on the board, with many institutions or individuals who have invested and lent money to the company. And those who pay rule! The others execute.

Kalinske, like any other president before or after, will be only an employee, a subordinate almost like all the others. Certainly, he still takes a risk by engaging in one company rather than another, but much less than the vast majority of "shareholders" who are most often and very mostly retired Americans or Japanese, The pensions of these countries are almost exclusively provided by pension funds. If Nakayama has been able to put pressure on these employees and partners, a little, a lot, too much, it can never be as much as the pressure that weighs on him, directly through the shareholders, especially the board of directors. The most important, strategic organ of a company, but which is almost never talked about in the general public except that it is also, in part, a shareholder.

Many "commentators" have had fun, have mocked, and even still, the well-tempered character of Hayao Nakayama towards his relatives, these employees, these partners, without imagining for a second what weight he had to bear on those shoulders. Ignorance hélas traditional in many Latins a fortiori of origin or Catholic culture ("Money, capitalism is evil!") on companies, markets, competition and therefore ultimately inevitable misunderstanding. I do not blame anyone, one can be totally foreign to the world of business, especially in countries with a very strong public service and a pay-as-you-go pension, because even the highest positions within the company would not understand it, theyeven, not much. Not interested in it, of course, because no need to be enarch or scientific to understand the mechanics of markets and companies. And even if to take full measure of these responsibilities, you must become either an entrepreneur with development plans, investment, a business model... And know thus all forms of "stress" related to the management of business. What is far, very far from being within the reach of everyone contrary to criticism.

Sega Enterprises Ltd is a Japanese company. And therefore it must meet the requirements and all constraints of the Japanese market. It is financed mainly by Japanese capital and thus by the Yen. A very powerful currency, like the Japanese economy, but which has very strong fluctuations. Because if this economy, the third in the world still today after the USA and China, is very powerful, it is particularly dependent on external economies because Japan exports a lot, it sells a lot abroad and this is the case of Sega! Who will manufacture and produce mostly in "Yen" (things will change a little but not enough) and sell in dollars or euros, in pounds sterling or at the time in francs or marks.

Companies try to control everything in terms of costs, development and when they are well organized, they do it rather correctly as long as they have activity, but this is not counting a very important parameter but unpredictable. A parameter that will largely contribute to the success of Sega in the USA and Europe at first, as it will bring it closer to the Berezina in a second time and at the worst time. Something totally unpredictable and on which one cannot therefore bet, often deadly for the so-called "exporting" companies: it is the exchange rate! The latter allows some companies to penetrate and win markets and even sometimes explode everything! And conversely, many companies are shutting down because they are strangled by an unfavourable exchange rate, except for having a very large and sufficient domestic market waiting for better days on the exchange side.

It is therefore necessary to know the exchange rate Euro vs Yen, and a fortiori Dollar vs Yen to have a broader vision and a good appreciation of Sega's constraints, and their evolution, in the 90s. The foreign exchange market is the largest speculative market in the world. Hundreds of billions are exchanged every day in different currencies by financial institutions but especially the central and national banks. It is a monstrous market on which speculates the entire world of Finance because the exchange market is of an unprecedented depth, very fluctuating, allowing some to get rich quite easily and others to go bankrupt, often very quickly (with leverage) had the right visions, the flair before others or on the contrary a very bad tip. Monstrous because it will also destroy jobs in some parts of the world and promote them in others, even if it is a bit putting the cart before the horse as exchange rates are closer to the "thermometer" than to a hypothetical disease.

At the beginning of the 90s, the Yen is at very low levels! It takes 180 yen or 190 for a euro. It remains very low or quite low until the end of 92, but by 1993 it literally flies away to reach historically high levels with peaks at only 100 yen for one euro. It has become almost twice as strong, understand twice as expensive!!! Even if I force the line here by taking the extremes. To be as precise and accurate as possible, it is rather the western currencies that are falling against the yen and under the effect of a mini recession which has begun and is in progress, in most European economies, at least those preparing the future currency: the euro. The yen once again presented itself as a safe haven currency in the face of the economic and political uncertainties of the future euro area.

It only takes 120 yen for a euro! In a few months, a handful of quarters, to buy an item for 360 yen you need not 2 but 3 euros! Everything produced, sold and invoiced in Japan has taken a 50% increase! It is quite similar to the level of the exchange rate Dollar versus Yen and it is even slightly more accentuated! But let's stay on 50% deviations to visualize the problem in question quite easily. The Yen has become expensive, very expensive and like everything that Japan will export! These differences obviously make and break the smallest or most fragile companies and all those who have not taken precautions. They have a very serious impact on volumes and profitability. Exchange rate fluctuations are probably, in their excesses as at this time, real serial killers for export companies, growth and it is a major challenge. The "risk taken" is very substantial. The appreciation or depreciation of a currency, with manipulation of interest rates and money remuneration, is an extremely powerful economic weapon of sovereign states which can therefore destroy, or save, or create thousands, millions of jobs. Japan has been working for decades to keep interest rates extremely low in order to avoid a too strong currency! Generating a form of monetary doping that largely favors exports, or to be more fair, at least remain competitive with other countries and especially the "tigers of Asia" (like South Korea) who are cutting more and more dealers in Japan on everything that is technology. But this "zero rate" policy does not work at all in a period of recession as it will happen on 93/96 in Europe.

At this level of variation it is a poison or even a Cancer and Sega will become a perfect illustration and even a case study as far as we are concerned, because the video game industry is still very young. They built their business model with a very cheap Yen, a chance at first, but in reality a sword of Damocles that will sooner or later fall on them. Westerners could buy their products at reasonable prices, leaving a considerable margin to reward local employees with increases, tropical seminars and gifts, while generating many benefits for the Japanese. But the competition was such with Nintendo, that both manufacturers adopted a known and recognized policy of "cost" for consoles because "they would catch up widely with the cartridges"!?!

In 90, 91 and 92 this model works perfectly because Sega can sell these machines at affordable prices and without losing money on it, thus catching up on the very many cartridges, which they sell almost entirely, and with very nice profit margins (Electronic Arts, an exception, producing and distributing these cartridges itself in the USA). In 90/91 the Yen is at historically low levels, the cash machine is launched and it will spit tens, hundreds of millions of profits and it is also for this reason that Sega Enterprises is rushing to buy distribution subsidiaries in Europe. All planets are aligned. Sales of Master System and Mega Drive are booming and the margins are generous if not monstrous on cartridges! Although a little "artificial" because boosted by this exchange rate one could not be more advantageous: miraculous.

These are the years that will allow Sega France to pay for the most expensive advertising campaign in its history and even one of the most ambitious campaigns in the history of TV advertising! (Oh if only Sega had the same budget for the launch of the Saturn, and the Dreamcast, their futures would have been very different). In 1991, but especially in 1992, the Sega budget for communication was used to tickle the biggest mastodons of communication, until then untouchable, which were at the time Renault and Peugeot. Entered the top 5 advertisers in "high season" and touching the fabulous figure of 98% public awareness just behind Coca Cola, with also the Trains Sega in 92 then in 93... Tens and tens of millions of francs injected into the media and communications, the Sega turbine has never been and will never be as powerful. It's the breath of a new dragon who wants to burn everything, starting with the whiskers of the not Polish plumber. And patatras, almost nothing in 1994!?! While the sales volumes were still "record"!?!

In 1993, the yen began to rise seriously before literally flying above the clouds! Sega is now strangled! But as very often in this configuration, we will pretend to ignore the problem, holding our breath as much as possible and playing the clock because "it should not last"! And it's true that it never lasts. But how long?!? TOO!!! A little, a little more, a little more and finally totally, it squeezes very hard, too hard and Sega Enterprises will have no choice but to do the round back, to wait because he does not really have a choice. The Sonic Team will then lose a lot of money and get into debt (still no choice) by hundreds of millions of dollars to keep up this very difficult period of lean.

The purchase price of these consoles took 40/50% for its subsidiaries whose currency became very low. Or if we take the problem backwards, on the Japanese side, consoles yield 40/50% less than before with these currencies that have seriously shrunk! The competitive tension is such that it is not planned to raise the price of consoles, consumers would not understand it, the market could collapse. And if Mario doesn't raise his prices, if Sonic does, then Nintendo could easily take the lead on 16 bits! It's not a question for Nakayama, it's not a matter of money it's a matter of honor! Nintendo will also make the round back var they have something that Sega does not have: The Game Boy! It sells more than any other console, it is the cheapest to produce and it will generate so much money that Nintendo will accumulate a monstrous war chest allowing it to hold many years of lean cows and/ or strong yen, even to fail strategically (and like all companies sooner or later). We more or less willingly do the round back more than the exporting companies always hope that it is temporary and that it should not last too long! The coins regularly making the Yoyo, a few weeks, a few months, a few years...

Paradoxically, at first glance, Sega will sell many consoles, more than ever, but this time with losses outside of Japan! Volumes explode, the abyssal deficits begin to grow. Sega UK will announce in 1994 more than 100 million pounds of deficit while these sales volumes are at record levels! Sega Japan can't do anything, they have the knife to their throat. Not only do they sell their consoles at a loss, outside of Japan, but third-party publishers are increasingly selling directly their productions and so there is also less and less margin for "restoration" on this side. Fortunately the CD era has begun, they are much cheaper to make and will even be pressed most of the time locally, where they are sold: "made or assembled in UK" or "made in EU" appear for the Mega CD and Saturn games. Sega will even relocate some of its cartridge production and the latest Mega Drive games, Game Gear will be "assembled in UK or EU" when those of third-party publishers will often be Made in Mexico (for many American publishers like Acclaim) but we will stay far away from the majority. The purchase and production costs will therefore fall a little for soft-side subsidiaries but it remains that sales in dollars and European currencies are still very significantly amputated by an extremely unfavourable exchange rate. Sega Japan can no longer hope to recover by cartridges, what it loses by consoles! The business model has literally exploded. The sword of Damocles had fallen well and it was particularly sharp. While the planets were perfectly aligned from 89 to 92, from 93 to 96 it would be the opposite, with the plunge of 93/94 true black hole or vortex, for financing capabilities.

This Cancer of exchange rate fluctuation, failing to kill clearly and properly Sega, will put him on his knees and putting the rope around his neck. While all the operating accounts, throughout the world, were in a very dark green in 90, 91 and 92, they will go into red and bright red as of 1994 (with the retrospective accounting of 1993) allowing a much more enlightened reading, the whole history of Sega, in particular its plans and strategy from 1994 onwards. The overvalued Yen, it could not really be worse because Sega will launch its Mega CD (93) and its 32X (94) in the Western markets. These new assets, not yet amortised, were designed, projected and invested at a significantly lower level of yen. These two machines will therefore cost an arm, probably between 25 and 50% more than initially expected, and everyone will report this, for levels that are prohibitive for more than 95% of potential buyers. If the Yen had not gone so far, so quickly, the Mega CD would probably have been offered around 1400 frs (which is still a nice sum but 2000 it was obviously too expensive to make a machine for the general public) and the 32X at less than 1000 frs! A symbolic and psychological threshold where sales accelerate or even explode! Just look at the charts of sales evolution all over the world with the Mega Drive or the SNIN or even the Game Gear for consoles that will have been in great demand but launched well above the threshold of 1000frs. When we arrived at the "990 frs" we went directly into Super Hang On, Super Monaco GP or F-Zero mode for Nintendo.

In 90, 91 and 92 the Yen is exaggeratedly low and will allow Sega of the prosperous years, of the "Mega Drive" years! SEGA is doped! Completely doped by a dream exchange rate!!!

In 1993 everything is going to a reverse excess with a nightmare exchange rate! 94, 95 and 96 become years of depression, despite all the efforts, all the successes that the subsidiaries will have in terms of market share gains! But what's the point of making volume when every console is losing money, because Sega will never raise prices?!? In the "brown market" prices are very rarely shown again. If you don't integrate this parameter in your reading of Sega, then you will enter into all kinds of fantasies that I myself, partly, accompanied a good time. This overvaluation of the Yen has emptied the coffers of Sega, even though the volumes remained important or record! It would even be the double penalty because in addition to losing and losing a lot, the Sonic Team would get into debt via its main shareholder (CSK) on more than 500 million dollars! Then casting an even greater shadow on his future, compromising him with a more and more probable development inability that is emerging. The Yen was smashing Sega and Sonic was going to live for three years well above these means. No more exotic seminars, cabarets, princely events, gifts, prestigious partnerships! But we "Sega Masters" would still keep all our games, all our endowments! We do not tighten the belt of passion to their champions! OUF!

This allows a better understanding of the choices, orientations and certain renunciations of Nakayama. The Sega ship was sinking as fast as the Titanic and, ultimately, the fatal paradox, the more they sank. The more they sold, the more money they lost! And why would they insist on selling under these conditions? Simply because they continued to believe in their strengths, their abilities, they believed in a better future and quickly. Sega had become a leader in the USA and it was a position to keep at all costs. A prestigious position that allows, among other things, to maintain the confidence of the financial markets, which is essential for refinancing year after year. Being a leader, even in one segment, the most important, offers and allows to keep perspectives that you do not have, that you no longer have when you are only a challenger. This is the Champion's premium, second and third do not have the same attention.

Nakayama, his board of directors, some of these shareholders probably locked themselves in a denial of reality. Denying that the volatility of the Yen would affect them as much! Denying that such a black scenario could continue after experiencing a pink candy scenario. Japan is the civilization of shame! Not that they seek it, on the contrary, it is the absolute scarecrow. No other civilization will fear the Shame as much as that of Japan, if not, perhaps, in a time far distant, the Spartan civilization. In both, defeat is forbidden and it is better to die in battle than to give up and return after having given up! The Japanese never give up and as long as a breath of hope continues to caress them, they will try to get back on their feet again and again. A company is supposed to be able to weather financial and monetary storms, but it will last more than three years and dry out the accounts completely.

Three years of schizophrenia between SoJ and its subsidiaries, where you are asked to sell more consoles at a significant loss, to continue developing and marketing accessories to counter the competition, when we do not have any, when we really have more, the means. The main fault lies with this harmful exchange rate which seems to no longer want to vary in the right direction. If it is only adjusted "half" in the other direction, everything, absolutely everything would change again positively!

Nick Alexander will throw the towel first in 1994 not wanting to assume this suicidal strategy, Tom Kalinske in turn will leave in 1996 no longer collecting the exceptional manne of the Genesis and not for anything else to take the world the failure of the Saturn, and finally Patrick Lavanant was fired by the Japanese in 1996, selling his honour, dignity and pride for a big cheque, because nothing else seemed to matter anymore.

Sometimes some wins are much more dangerous than the losses and I am also very well placed to talk about it. There is nothing worse than conquests and "easy" victories because they take away the indispensable guard. Sega in 89/92 rose very fast, too fast, even allowing him to make fish tails at the Nintendo Giant (who of the two was the most surprised?!?) dominating undivided, until then, the video game market. In the favor of a weak Yen, Sega had become strong, very strong and when the Yen turned to become strong, Sega found himself completely naked! It's almost a fable of Lafontaine. Sega had not anticipated such a success with the Mega Drive and they never had time to digest this colossal success! Genesis would therefore also rhyme with hubris.

So can we say that it is the Yen and its fluctuations that have in part shot Sega? Yes and no, it is mostly a shortcut. The evolution of the Yen, if it seems to be directly the closest cause, the most direct is obviously the consequence of other very real events! And without going back to "Adam and Eve" as in a famous sketch raising all the responsibilities, a little much by the absurd, up to the original sin, If the yen rose so high it is mainly due to the European monetary crisis in 1993 linked to the vote and ratification more or less enthusiastic of the Maastricht Treaty by the EU member states. Exacerbating the fragility of the European construction. If the prospect of a stronger Europe with the signing of the Treaty had pushed up the European currencies at first, the "NO" vote of Denmark will scare all economic markets! The European construction did not seem as joyful as one could imagine! German reunification would cost very expensive and the Maastricht treaty, in the perspective of the single currency, imposed very strict economic conditions on the member states to reach the "qualification"!

So yes the Yen shot Sega! But it is the revealed fragility of the EU that made it rise to historical heights!?! The Maasstrich Treaty and its adoption (or not) gave much energy to speculation in one direction and then in the other. So Europe has become Sega? One could, like the sketch "by the absurd", but not so much, specify that in this weakened Europe, it is "the fall of the Berlin Wall" and its consequences on the biggest economy of the euro zone which will be the main vector... The fall of the Berlin Wall responsible for the fall of Sega? Yes in part! We continue? If the famous Berlin Wall fell it is mainly related to the decomposition of the USSR accelerated by the program "Star Wars" of Ronald Reagan! " The Star Wars "responsible for the fall of Sega"? And yes also by ricochet and one can have fun to trace each cause as the consequence of another cause itself the consequence... I let you have fun and go back to Adam and Eve or the dinosaurs or even the protozoa if you have less faith (Judeo-Christian)!

It is up to each of us to place the cursor where its logic seems to be strongest! As far as I am concerned, and although this is not entirely correct, I will merely say that it was the fluctuations of the Yen which both carried and crowned Sega and also undressed and crucified it, and although there are of course many other parameters, often very important, to explain these successes and failures.

Most of the Western leaders at the top seem to have understood little about Sega and its strategy by denying or simply not being aware of this scourge of exchange rates! With the weak yen Sega was like a mighty dragon and spinning in a clear sky, with the strong Yen a big slug in the sun trying to accelerate in the middle of the desert. Patrick Lavanant but also Bruno Charpentier in his succession, will propose to Sega Japan to stop the manufacture of consoles. Who seemed to be the author of all their misfortunes!?! It was not understanding much about strategy and especially the philosophy of Sega. Which had developed precisely through the development and innovation of materials as much in arcade as in adaptations, "mainstream" versions, that is to say consoles. The Motorola 68000 for the time 16 bits, then the Hitachi for the 32 bits and before the common processors of the Dreamcast and the "Naomi" in Arcade. Sega these are games certainly but it is above all the creation and innovation and they go through the total association of hard and software. Sega was, and still is, a manufacturer, a merchant of dreams, everything was good, everything was justified to produce the perfect emotional lift that would take us beyond the clouds.

Chapter 29

Parody and Nostalgia

30 years later, the mystery remained, at least in France, in the West and for the "general public". And we could then ask ourselves, the band of "a little less young", retro gamers nostalgic and passionate, why all these urban legends around the decline see the "end of Sega" (console side) had appeared and continued to spread over and over, and often more and more parodic reality. Disappointment, misunderstanding, lack, nostalgia, anger, betrayal, as many frustrations, ghosts, demons and other fantasmatic projections embodied in anecdotes more or less serious and boring, served with a mayonnaise increasingly pungent and indigestible, in a fillet but pierced everywhere, sometimes even with smiles and other Hyenas' laughter, and whose purpose would probably not be as cathartic as the search for an umth media buzz. Sega seemed to have passed away and everyone would go on "revelations" of dark secrets and other totally outdated anecdotes to tear off a last piece of putrefied flesh.

But let us not be more scavengers than the scavengers themselves because I must confess, once again, that I was myself in this total confusion concerning the subject, and if I laughed or smiled sometimes well yellow but as discreetly as possible. Having been dismissed from Sega France in the spring of 1996 (before continuing to be Master Sega for Cyber Press Publishing via the company Audiofil, a little pass to save some people in Marketing, and for no less than eight years) to follow up on the not really good results of Saturn, I could only be convinced by the prominent role of the Playstation in the fall of Sega. The 32-bit Sonic Team would not replace the cardboard of the Mega Drive and the Japanese were going to have to tighten their belts, sending more than half of the European employees to other horizons. The success of the Playstation was such that it would naturally impose itself in the collective unconscious, as the main cause, not the only one, of the decline of Sega. If Sony, like the Brutus of video games, had indeed dealt the fatal blow to César Sega, it would then very effectively and quite long hide the main cause, much earlier.

Whether Sony beats or crushes Sega, in the end, it would make everyone a little better. One could also say that Sony has cheated a little in the fight with its "Mega Sponsoring" of the specialized press, many "testers" accumulating gifts and endowments of the most flattering, and as so many "supporters" and generous partnerships with third-party publishers, who found in Sony a new Godfather much more reassuring and benevolent towards them and for some even more fragile, such as the Prophet. Sony among the world's largest companies and therefore capitalists had been tremendously generous and probably even a little communist as it will share its resources without counting, until it has definitively triumphed! Sega had been beaten, but by far stronger than he was, economically speaking of course, with also the most effective marketing and communication and walking on the Sega's lawn, reducing any chance of a recovery at some point. The disappearance of Sega Constructeur, and the suffering it engendered, would be great for some but the Honor was safe. And even if some Sega Fans would still not completely mourn, writing, rewriting history to infinity with more or less serious and impacting motives, but rarely documented certified. Nostalgia and a mourning not really finished, had therefore engendered, and still generates today, the most bizarre speculations. For a healing search, for the buzz and all its sensations!!! But not only. Two main reasons for this, the first feeding and especially never correcting the second!?!

On the one hand, the lack of love, passion and curiosity, during the life of Sega and at its peak, in the era of the "conquistadores"... Most often and only: Japanese. Most European, even American leaders will have just passed by. One year? Two? Three or four years for some of the most committed "veterans"? And that's it, more often than not. They will have been at Sega as others at Casio, Moulinex, Casino or Spontex. The History of Sega, in France, will then be told, at best, by Luc Bourcier or Bruno Charpentier and waiting for Pascal Rayer!?! (Too cool to talk about yourself like Alain Delon!!!). If I have a certain affection for the first two and in particular Bruno, if they did their job and often very well, they would not understand much about Sega in its deep soul, its authenticity, its sincerity, and I want as proof only a statement, anecdotal in the substance as to its content and thirty years later, but symptomatic of a thought, too widely shared, in the form with one word, only one! The devil is in the details and this interview sums up quite the spirit, let alone the curiosity, of a majority of executives towards Sega. In 1996, Bruno who then became CEO of Sega France and to the merit, then spoke of video games as "parodies of reality"! Obviously he is not completely wrong, but what is a parody and what is not? Literature? Television? Series? Theatre? Cinema? Politics? Even if we do a little metaphysics, just a little, we might even point out to each other, all of us as we are, like parody of the human race, some more than others, Copying us, imitating each other with more or less desire and talent. Disappearing one after another and leaving no trace beyond children and grandchildren, while we will still play Sonic or Mario in several centuries...

I know Bruno well enough not to suspect him of being contemptuous towards the world of Video Games and you can also see it in the chapter dedicated to him. But to speak of "Parodies" is not at all in the language of millions of players and for many it would even be an affront. If it is not contemptuous in his mouth, it is still a little bit devalued or condescending for the players but also and especially the programmers and all the artists invested to create all these new windows looking to improve, to dope, to illuminate our immediate reality. And rather than parody it!!! In first intentions.

Some video games may be deliberately parodic but they are and remain above all, and more simply, simulations. From my point of view, the smartest, most curious, most clairvoyant of the French leaders was largely, Past also, next to the deep Soul of Sega and his desire to discover and make live new sensations through a complete chain of creation and production. Simulations or parodies, the hundreds of engineers, creators and artists of Sega often working day and night for many years on the side of Haneda, always seek to get as close as possible to the "truth", and all the most passionate players will be greatly rewarded over time for these inventive and crazy creations.

Like Patrick Lavanant before him, and like many European leaders, he will side with those who will ask Sega of Japan to abandon the production of Hardware and therefore consoles! Can we ask someone to rip off their heart? Cut off both arms or legs? Mutilate themselves excessively? When was it even about saving his life? Nakayama, the Sega Shogun will tell all those, more and more with the failure of the Saturn, who dare to suggest him to give up, that he would rather cut off his right arm immediately, than make games for the competitor Nintendo. Bruno Charpentier will also throw the sponge in front of this Japanese "wall" but he won't return to Nintendo for that.

Stop the expenses, the bloody hemorrhage of the production of consoles most often at losses: the simplest and easy solution to financial problems... Certainly, but it is to be in a management of the present, the moment, and it is also finally what was asked of them, one thing before another, we stop at the most urgent. The longer time, the present and future is reserved for Sega Japan, Nakayama and its board of directors. Another source of misunderstanding between entities and which will further metastasize the "Cancer" of Sega. The essential parameter of the triumph and then fall of Sega: the exchange rate. The fall of western currencies and/ or the overvaluation of the yen. The rate, and these variations, are by far the most important parameters in the equation of success or decline for Sega Enterprises and its international expansion with its business model on a string. And when the vast majority of Western leaders will tirelessly ask the Japanese to lower the price of consoles, again and again, lower the price of consoles to gain market share! Giving them, then, increasingly and venerably, access to their necks, and a hypothetical but increasingly probable reversal of the exchange rate, in an infinite cycle of variations more or less sustained, in one direction and then in another. By lowering again and again to the last penny of margin, they were going to shoot themselves in the foot but especially to strangle themselves.

Hyper violent monetary crash that no one will talk about, or so little, when it finally arrives, in the West, outside of economic and financial newspapers who will more praise the export facilities of French companies to Japan rather than worry about the health of the Nipponnes companies established. Sega was well on the side in Europe and Paris, but with a fairly limited number of European or Western shareholders, publications and comments on financial publications will remain equally limited. The "retrogamers" of today reading more favorably "Consoles +", "Joypad" or "Megaforce" at the time and maybe even now!?!

I "married" to Sega in 1991 and on an indefinite contract, TOO HAPPY I was, you know! So much that I even married a second time just as officially and I was probably the only one in Sega France!?! Upon my return from the

Army in 1995, I became a shareholder of Sonic Team. And even if at that time I was unable to read the off-balance sheet, the goodwills and other depreciation, impairments of tangible assets, intangible, financial. A jargon that, at this time, escapes the vast majority of the public as much as an economic crisis has laminated the nations and that "La bourse" (at the bottom everywhere) does not make dream anyone but some retirees. Becoming a shareholder in the company that employed me allowed me to get even closer and therefore understand it better, through these legal publications, official and certified by independent accountants, of which at least we can say, It is that they are totally and definitively foreign to projections, speculations and other approximations. Only the figures and the profit and loss accounts can count, so they are fully detailed.

But although I am a shareholder of Sega, and have the possibility to access first-hand financial information, official financial reports and filed, I will still settle at this time for the scenario "Sony killed Sega", the most likely, at first sight, but especially the least painful. Until almost thirty years later, we discovered the real problem.

So on the one hand, leaders who will only pass through structures, too little involved beyond the strict framework of their work and commitments, in search of profitability on their playing fields, more or less aware of the sacred fire that runs through Sega's veins. What would be left ten, twenty, thirty years later? Well, you don't know much. Time erode, erases memories except that they were those of an immense passion: the "official" French documentation remains, therefore, extremely limited!

On one side a great void and on the other, on the contrary, this immense passion, sometimes a little too big, and who it, crosses time! Nature having horror of the void, this passion, this nostalgia will make to arise this thirst, this hunger never satisfied with "truth" and the youtubers will then propose better to who better their versions more and more anecdotal, with a number of accusations more or less founded and transformed into multiple blows of water, and this when it will have sufficed only one blow, out of the field, to put Sega on Knees.

When Julius Caesar is attacked and then murdered, many senators will stab him. We will never know who of Brutus or another has carried the fatal blow. And yet it was enough only one shot, well placed. But it was important that it be the "Republic", the Res publica or public thing that murders its tyrant, and not just one man. Our "Brutus/Sony" was not satisfactory enough in the explanation, justification of the "assassination" of Sega, also the "Public Thing" will create its own mortiferous mythology: 32X, Mega CD, Corruption, Nakayama, misunderstandings, tensions, rivalries and all the tralala... Sega had been crashed for X reasons all more or less elaborate but ultimately all, diversion.

The reasons that had brought Sega to the top of Olympus close to Zeus were the same as those that will take him into the underground worlds, those of Hades! The planets had all aligned perfectly at the same time and for two or three years before going in every direction, for as long, more distant from each other than ever. It is not easy, it is probably even impossible for one or more managers, and for a company to recognize that its success, at least its business model, is essentially due to a parameter as random and unpredictable as the exchange rate. Sega, in Challenger, to win market share, had played on the razor's edge, currency conversions. The luck had largely smiled at this level of 90 to 92 before turning completely. A true case study in reality even if, in other sectors than video games, other Japanese companies of "growth" must have experienced the same hazards. Sega had not had time to digest his huge victory Mega Drive and Genesis. The wind was too strong and it turned too fast. I personally can't blame the executives and shareholders. They surfed on a huge wave and as much as it could carry them, without knowing for one second that the next would be much smaller or non-existent! They took a lot of risks and eventually lost, but doing nothing or just doing less would probably have been much worse. We can always evaluate this fall of Sega according to these own instruments and more globally its own perception, but not taking into account the parameters of the globalized monetary system a fortiori financial it is formidably risky and in fact, not really serious.

In the next chronicles covering the period 1997 to 2004: The years Cyber Press Publishing with notably the well-known "JM Destroy" but also and above all the Pope of the specialized press of the time: Marc Andersen! Mega Force, the madness of the internet bubble, Eidos and Tomb Raider, Konami, Activision, Acclaim, Cryo, THQ and of course new years Master Sega! A series of episodes that will be very busy.

To discuss all these chronicles and the following, find me and subscribe to my YouTube channel: Pascal Rayer Maître Sega and on Facebook: "Les chroniques de Maître Sega".